LIGHTS, CAMERA, DYNAMITE

First published in 2008 by
Liberties Press
Guinness Enterprise Centre | Taylor's Lane | Dublin 8
Tel: +353 (1) 415 1224
www.LibertiesPress.com | info@libertiespress.com

Distributed in the United States by
Dufour Editions | PO Box 7 | Chester Springs | Pennsylvania | 19425

and in Australia by
James Bennett Pty Limited | InBooks | 3 Narabang Way
Belrose NSW 2085

Trade enquiries to CMD Distribution
55A Spruce Avenue | Stillorgan Industrial Park
Blackrock | County Dublin
Tel: +353 (1) 294 2560 | Fax: +353 (1) 294 2564

ISBN: 978–1–905483–38–9
2 4 6 8 10 9 7 5 3 1

A CIP record for this title is available from the British Library

Cover design by Siné Design
Internal design by Liberties Press
Printed by ScandBook, Sweden

LIGHTS, CAMERA, DYNAMITE

ADVENTURES OF A SPECIAL EFFECTS DIRECTOR

GERRY JOHNSTON

For my family –
Georgina, Derek, Audrey, Chloe,
Ciarán, Tara, Saoirse and Carraig – with love

Contents

FOREWORD

The first film Gerry worked on, *The Blue Max*, was filmed in Ireland in 1966, when Ireland was a popular location for filming but had no established film industry of its own. The following year, John Huston, while filming *Sinful Davey* in Glencree, County Wicklow, was visited on set by An Taoiseach and suggested to him that 'The time is ripe for the establishment of an Irish film industry'. This suggestion was taken up by the Irish government, and John Huston was appointed the chairman of the first 'Film Industry Committee', which published the first 'Report of the Film Industry Committee' in June 1968, exactly forty years ago. This report set out the basis for government support for the establishment of an Irish film industry, which was ultimately put into effect with the first Irish Film Board Act of 1980.

The vision of those early pioneers was to 'encourage the development and employment of Irish creative, artistic and technical skills' and to create 'the opportunity for Irish cinema audiences to see themselves and their way of life reflected on the screen, and the projection abroad of a true image of Ireland and the Irish way of life and traditions'. The clarity of this purpose remains at the centre of the Irish Film Board's efforts today.

So Gerry was in at the start of what, by European standards, is a very young film industry. Gerry was – and is – one of a group of highly skilled and expert film technicians and craftspeople who learnt their trade on some of the greatest films to be made in the last fifty years. It is certain that it was these technicians that John Huston had in mind when he first suggested the idea of government support for an Irish film industry. He knew first-hand the quality and character of film technicians in Ireland and saw the potential to harness these qualities on a larger scale. Gerry is of course by now a legend in the field of special effects. Interestingly, in this age of digital visual effects, the 'real thing' – special effects on set – are staging a comeback, with many directors in search of the more authentic film image. Gerry's career is almost a diary of the first forty years of the Irish film industry, and his book brings to life the real world of film-making. It is a must-read for anyone interested not only in the establishment of the Irish film industry but in the mysterious art of special effects.

JAMES MORRIS
Chairman, Bord Scannán na hÉireann/The Irish Film Board

PREFACE

'I think that the Internet is going to effect the most profound change on the entertainment industries combined. We'll be tuning into the most popular Internet show in the world, which will be coming from some place in Des Moines. We're all gonna lose our jobs and we're all gonna be on the Internet trying to find an audience.'

STEVEN SPIELBERG

The Digital Era has indeed dawned and the sands are shifting. Film-making as we have known it is becoming a thing of the past. People of all ages are launching their own 'movies' on YouTube and beyond. Ever-advancing technologies have ensured that, in one sense, the sky's the limit, but the film industry is affected, just like any other, by uncertainties in the marketplace as much as by changing technological trends. Although wholly computer-generated blockbusters have already arrived and aspects of conventional film-making now cost a lot less than before, Ireland is finding it difficult to compete – with or without tax breaks – due to cheaper labour costs in eastern Europe and elsewhere, advances in IT capabilities in other countries, and better access, in the form of low-cost travel, to cheaper locations across the globe.

Technical requirements on a film were, at one time, simple and straightforward. The story unfolded against a theatrical, unmoving background, shot indoors. By the 1970s, the industry was approaching a renaissance. Scripts became more elaborate and writers and directors wanted to venture into new territory. 'Location work' grew and became the norm, and with it a whole range of movies came into being, requiring lavish sets with effects depicting events that were as close to real life as possible.

When I started in the business, special effects were just coming into vogue. 'Effects' soon became big business and a whole industry grew up within the film industry itself, requiring more innovative technical skills, stretching the imagination and providing the 'thrills and spills' that spellbind cinema and TV audiences around the world. Until then, I wasn't aware that much of what I was interested in had anything to do with film-making! But as it happened, my childhood obsession with gadgets, gizmos and the outdoors led to a long and exciting career working on some of Ireland's most prestigious movie projects, beginning with *The Blue Max, Darling Lili, Ryan's Daughter, Barry Lyndon* and *Zardoz*.

In 1974, I set up a workshop in a ramshackle cowshed at Ardmore Studios, and in 1981 'Special Effects Ireland Limited' was born. It was the first special-effects company in Ireland. I had already notched up about twenty or so film credits and had risen through the ranks of the profession, training crew and obtaining a pyrotechnics supervisor's ticket. I was now one of an elite bunch of technical professionals in the UK and Europe. Pinewood, Shepperton and Elstree Studios were the hub of the UK's film and television industry, and English effects technicians were well established. Living outside the UK, I was at a disadvantage. However, right from the beginning of my life in film-making, Hollywood's crème de la crème had come to *me*. I began my training with American wizards of Effects, who came to work, for a time, in Ireland, and although still a trainee, I was offered work in California. I opted to stay at home: a mistake, perhaps, because the industry in this country has always operated in fits and starts.

After *Images*, directed by Robert Altman – my big break – I did work abroad, and by 1981 I had achieved three goals: I had travelled, I had become well established in the special-effects fraternity, and I was a company director. My father said: 'I never expected you to do so well!' It was an unexpected accolade and the recognition I had been waiting for all my life.

Looking back, the obstacles that faced me in my pursuit of a decent living seemed insurmountable: a dismal academic record, corporal punishment and paternal disapproval. Then the gods smiled on me and I joyfully embraced a way of life others could only dream about, working with movie stars such as Pierce Brosnan, Tom Hanks

Tools of the trade: With some of the equipment I use to create effects

and Mel Gibson, and directors who included John Huston, David Lean, Stanley Kubrick and Steven Spielberg.

The sound stages at Ardmore Studios – Ireland's first major film-making facility – lie idle for many months each year, and every year rumours abound as to whether Ardmore will be in business at all in the near future. The hope – generated in the 1980s by tax incentives, marketing abroad and the subsequent arrival of several major productions to our shores – seems to have faded. Film-making in Ireland is fraught with uncertainty, but despite this uncertainty, the industry has served me well, and I have given it my undivided commitment.

Maybe it's because of my forty-plus years in this itinerant profession that I have never taken the long view, nor taken root in one place – at least not yet! Having been constantly on the move, I have garnered only scant knowledge of family history – mere snippets of information, in the form of random freeze-frame shots that I have found among old photographs and old letters, or from hearsay. No one in my immediate family had any association with show-business, and I didn't 'marry into' the industry. My children weren't involved, apart from cameo parts in two features in the eighties: my son Derek appeared in *Excalibur* in 1981 and my daughter Audrey was in *Cal* in 1984.

In recording this account of my life and my association with film-making, perhaps I can give my children – and my grandchildren – a piece of living history! More than that, I want to encourage them, and all who read this book, to follow their dream and achieve their greatest potential. My parents thought their 'hopeless case' would never make it. But I had a dream – and I lived it. This is my story.

Gerry Johnston
May 2008

1

THE ROCKY ROAD TO ARDMORE

Had World War II not ended before I cut my second teeth, I might have joined an Irish contingent on some foreign battlefield and my career would have been mapped out.

In 1942, as war raged across Europe, *Casablanca*, now recognised as a classic, was released. Dame Vera Lynn's 'We'll Meet Again' consoled battle-fatigued soldiers 'at the front' and Bing Crosbie's 'White Christmas' joined Vera Lynn as one of the best-selling records of all time. Japan took Singapore and the first US troops landed in Europe – and on February 22, I was born at Number 21, Tivoli Terrace North, Dun Laoghaire, in south County Dublin. I was the second son born to Edward and Lillie Johnston. My brother, Edward (Cormac), was older than me by a year. My parents had two more children: Terence (Terry) in 1944, and my only sister, Barbara, was born in 1949. The family moved to Williamstown near Blackrock, where I spent the remainder of my youth.

The Johnston brothers: Cormac, myself and Terry, in Williamstown, Dublin

13

By the late 1940s, the war was long over, but oppression continued – through the schools system and censorship. Entertainment in any shape or form was questioned, many books were banned, and clergy and parents tried their best to protect the young from 'contamination'. But by the 1960s, a new age had dawned and people were flocking to the 'pictures', and by the end of the decade every Irish home had television. There was no going back.

As I grew up, the 'big action' lay in the slick imports: Westerns and war movies. These films undoubtedly fuelled my interest in all things military. There was also a military tradition in the family. My grandfather Edward Johnston was a British army cavalryman who had served in India. After the war, he was billeted at the Curragh Military Camp in County Kildare, and he later worked in the Pensions Office in Dublin. He married a Wexford woman, whom I remember only as 'Grandmother Johnston', in 1907 and they had three sons, Frank, Edward (my father) and Jack. Grandfather later went to work as a recruitment officer for the British forces and travelled back and forth to London. His eldest son, Frank, was a commander in the British navy: Frank, who often held me spellbound with stories of his travels and sea battles during World War II, was my hero.

My first visit to a cinema was at the age of six or seven, but by and large, it was my imagination and the world around me which provided the drama and entertainment in my life. Across the road from our house, the 'castle' – a part of Blackrock College where banquets and other such events were held – became a magical fortress, especially in winter, as I gazed across at it from my bedroom window, imagining dragons lurking and sword fights taking place behind the façade. We lived in one of a terrace of red-brick houses facing the college – beside the 'Rock Road' in Williamstown – in an era when street lights went off at midnight and the 'Rock Road' fell silent. By day, traffic consisted of just a few cars, rumbling trams and the occasional herd of cattle and sheep being driven from the livestock market in the city to the Dun Laoghaire 'cattle boat' – the B&I cattle carrier, which transported livestock to Britain. In the animals' wake, heaps of steaming dung lay splattered all over the road, and resourceful local women scraped up the dung to spread on their flower patches or in their window boxes!

Our kitchen, which was heated by a large black iron range, was my world of an evening, with my comics and the radio. It was a cosy place, and I was happy to sit by the glowing coal fire and dream. The phosphorescent green radio dial connected me with a world of adventure: 'Dan Dare, Pilot of the Future', which I listened to religiously. Even then, I worried about my own future, trying to decide whether to be 'Dan Dare', join the priesthood, get married or be like my uncle Frank, in command of a massive gunship! I prayed for someone to wave a magic wand and solve this riddle for me.

The closest I came to a 'command', however, was on the sand-banks beside Blackrock Park. My friends and I, in two 'platoons', would painstakingly build two gigantic battle cruisers. We carved, shaped and moulded until the sand-ships rose two or three feet high. We loaded the gunwales with cannonballs – sand held together with water, like snowballs – and the war began. Whole days passed in a frenzy of building and fighting until the tide crept in: our ships shifted and finally disappeared beneath the waves. Gazing into the fire on a winter's night, I would see those battles again – in the flames.

All grown up: Cormac (in uniform, standing) and me, with Terry and our sister Barbara

One evening, I was making my way, as usual, down to my haunt in the kitchen. I opened the door and was met by a blast of hot air. I could hear a loud rumbling in the chimney, the range was glowing, and lumps of molten soot were dropping down into the fire-box, sending sparks through the grating and on to the floor. Someone called the fire brigade, and a tender from Dun Laoghaire Fire Station arrived. Hoses were pulled out. There was a gush of water on molten metal, a hiss of steam, and the range exploded – sending soot, smoke and ash into every nook and cranny, out into the hallway and even up the stairs. We were left with smouldering cast iron, sodden carpets, peeling wallpaper, blackened paintwork and a burnt smell that would linger for months. After the fire, the range was replaced but the kitchen never had the same feel to it. Maybe it was time for me to move on – to engage with the world and stop dreaming. But it would be the dreaming – Dan Dare and the movies – that would sustain me, and my pals, as we recreated our heroes' adventures – and set out on our own.

And most of these adventures were outdoors. On the first day of the school holidays, it seemed as though a whole year of freedom stretched ahead of us: three months of climbing trees, swimming in the sea, building sand-ships and soaking up the sun. Sometimes we were sent to the country for a month, during the summer. During one of these annual 'farm holidays', in Roscommon, I had a terrifying, surreal experience. Terry and I were wandering through a field. Away in the distance cows were grazing, and we could hear a tractor coming and going, as the farmer went about his work. Suddenly, we heard snorting and tramping, and we turned around to see a large bull, at full charge, heading straight for us! Hearts pounding, we started to run. The field was bordered by a thick, thorny hedge. We kept on running – and had no choice but to dive into the thorns. We could still hear the rumbling hooves and the ground trembling beneath us – only now, it seemed to be a stampede! A horse whinnied, and I glanced back towards the field, to see two large shire horses galloping, one on either side of the bull, heads thrown in the air, manes and tails flying as they 'steered' the bull, like dogs rounding up a flock of sheep. The bull skidded into a U-turn inches from where we squatted, and galloped back the way he had come, the two horses still 'escorting' him. Though scratched and bleeding, we were safe. We tumbled out through the hedge, gasping for breath. Just then, the farmer arrived. As we blurted out the story, his face took on a quizzical look.

'What horses are yiz talkin' about? Sure there's no horses around here!' he laughed.

To this day, I have no idea where they came from.

In the autumn, we robbed orchards. On one of these 'missions' there was another chase – in the prize orchard at Willow Park, the 'junior' end of Blackrock College. This time, it was a couple of Alsatian dogs. But we made it to our rope ladder and over the wall, the baying dogs inches from our heels! The railway line provided another diversion: we placed ha'pennies or farthings on the tracks and waited for the 'Six-

Five Special' to flatten them. With a bit of luck, the coins could be passed off in the shops as whole pennies, buying a 'penny toffee' or a fistful of sweets. The railway was always a good place to 'hang out', as they say nowadays, and we hung out – literally – from the railway bridge, for hours, watching the trains, the tides and the world go by, in Blackrock Park. The whole world came to the park, especially in summer, and our mothers sat talking and knitting, while children of all ages played, and people walked their dogs. The onset of puberty and growing curiosity found us hanging out *in* the park – hiding ourselves in the long grass, spying on 'courting couples'!

Commander Frank Johnston, his wife Etta, my mother Lillie
and my father Edward

My father often took us down to the harbour in Dun Laoghaire to look at the boats. He talked a lot about boats and about getting one of his own. Although he was a 'pen-pusher', and worked in an office, he was an adventurer at heart, and I have inherited his love of the sea. He took us fishing at weekends, and later on we went night fishing, setting yards of ground lines, which were secured by hooks to old bucket handles, about twelve feet apart. I was good with a hand-line too, swinging left, right and back again, feeding out more line, feeling it gather momentum, and knowing just when to let go.

My friends and I also went spear-fishing in the large body of water between Booterstown and the Pigeon House in Ringsend, known as 'the Cockle Lake'. We waded into this treacherous bed of quicksand, brandishing home-made spears, which were about three feet long, with steel handles, being careful to stay around the edges. We were looking for a trail left by flat fish, tapping our feet to lure them in. We had to be fast: the fish could smack into our feet and upend us! I became an expert at spearing razor clams too – ideal bait for catching sea bass.

On land, we made bows and arrows from sally branches and reeds. I became adept at fashioning arrows and arrowheads – and even more adept at firing them. At home, I melted lead on the gas stove to make the arrowheads, and deftly carved a groove in the shaft of the bow, into which the arrow neatly sat. Pouches, to carry our arrows, were made from old leather or canvass and attached to our trouser belts. In the hollow of an old oak tree in the green behind the houses, I also manufactured 'bombs', setting them in the tree, priming them and then withdrawing to a safe distance, seconds before they exploded.

Some time in my teens I took up the guitar, learning from my friend Louis O'Connor. Louis's house overlooked our back garden, and Louis would whistle from his bedroom window – the signal for me to come over. We played records – Elvis, Fats Domino and Buddy Holly – and strummed or sang along, using wooden spoons as microphones!

I played Gaelic football – even making it to Croke Park, as a sub – and hurling, but soccer became *the* game for me. A man called Reggie Johnson happened to be watching us one day. He picked a team, and Burrough United, our first local soccer team, was born! My friend Sean Corcoran recently reminded me of the day we travelled to Drogheda to play the home team. I was on one of several buses that carried our team and our supporters from Dublin, but Sean and a couple of our ace players travelled in Sean's Austin 1100. Somewhere on the outskirts of Drogheda, the car overheated. Steam hissed from the radiator, and as Sean and the lads explored the car's innards, the buses passed, with flags waving and occupants cheering! Finally, a motorcycle policeman came on the scene. On hearing that our fate hung on the lads in the car, he escorted the limping Austin and its occupants to the stadium. Drogheda had a good team – well trained, determined and full of spirit – but we won the game.

I loved sport – the tactics and manoeuvres came easily to me – but school, on the other hand, was a nightmare. The years with the nuns in Booterstown, between the ages of four and seven, are a blur. From the outset, it seemed that my academic abilities would not be up to scratch. My first day at the Christian Brothers primary school in Dun Laoghaire began with a half-hour journey by tram from Williamstown. The only available seating was upstairs, in the open section to the front. The heavens opened and my mother and I arrived at the school, drenched. I was wearing short pants and grey woollen socks to the knees, my skinny legs purple with the cold. I shivered for the day, watching the ghostly shapes of passing traffic through thick, wire-meshed glass, wishing I was anywhere but where I was. Throughout my time at this forbidding place, I was caned for not knowing Irish, catechism and spelling. My hand was squeezed until my fingers were blue, then whacked across the tips with a bamboo. All thought, all reason evaporated in a sea of pain. I was even taunted by one teacher for having 'an English name'! I usually sat halfway back in the classroom, between the 'scholars' at the front and the 'hard chaws', who filled the back of the room with a heavy, unwashed smell and picked wings off flies and raced spiders. They sold comics at break-time and, in the evening, hung around the betting shops in Dun Laoghaire, marking time until they reached fourteen and could legally leave school.

It was a catechism question that led to my escape. When his question was met with deafening silence, the examining Brother lashed out and slapped me, this time across the face. My reaction was swift: my fist connected with his jaw. In the principal's office, I was ordered to take down my trousers, for a caning. I refused, and ran.

I was then enrolled in Blackrock Technical School. My father took me to meet the headmaster, who asked me my name, in Irish. I didn't know how to answer him! Undeterred by my lack of ability in this regard, he took me in and I learned metalwork and carpentry, as well as the regular subjects. I settled in and was beginning to catch up. I was especially drawn to physics and chemistry, and I was fascinated by Bunsen burners and the effects of chemical mixtures: the 'science' behind my 'oak tree pyrotechnics'!

Although we lived within shouting distance of the prestigious Blackrock College, none of us crossed the threshold. A former resident of Dun Laoghaire, Sir Bob Geldof, who hung about on the beach – 'eating sugar sandwiches and fantasising about his imminent departure', as he put it – spent a few years at Blackrock College, where, he says, he 'idled, dodged exams and dreamt of escape'. From his account of his experiences, it would seem that 'dreamers' were treated no better at this august establishment than at the Christian Brothers in Dun Laoghaire.

Cormac, Terry and Barbara were destined to graduate from school with flying colours, but I'd had my fill. As I approached my seventeenth birthday, still mesmerised by the adventures of 'Dan Dare', still high on the thrill of rocking the neighbourhood with my daring pyrotechnics, still heavily into all things military, and, like Bob Geldof, dreaming of my imminent escape, I applied to join the American armed forces. My friend Louis had applied at the same time, and together we fantasised about a future travelling the world in great ships. We were both accepted. As we prepared to travel to Fort Worth in Texas, my mother, who was dead set against the idea from the outset, fell ill and asked me to stay at home. While Louis was serving in Germany, where he met our idol, Elvis, I pressed ahead with finding work in Dublin. My father kept his ear to the ground and scoured the newspapers for factory jobs. My mother had always encouraged me to read, from about the age of six or seven, getting me to read notices on buses and billboard advertisements. Terms such as 'intellectual disability', 'dyslexia' and 'attention deficit disorder' hadn't been invented. 'Slow learners' were either harassed and beaten or left to fend for themselves.

It was Uncle Frank who came to my rescue. After a short stint fetching and carrying with an engineering company in Blackrock, I overheard discussions between my father and Uncle Frank regarding my 'career'. A new placement was negotiated, and my next job took me to Whitegate Oil Refinery in Cork, over a hundred and sixty miles from home. I was assigned to the apprenticeship of a Texan engineer who put me to work X-raying pipelines and checking valves and insulation in the crude-oil towers: dark, grimy, forbidding structures that rose more than a hundred feet from ground level. Around the outside,

Borough United: Terry is the third player from the left in the back row, and my friend Louis O'Connor is on the extreme right of the back row. I'm second from left in the front row.

scaffolding-type platforms rocked and swayed in the wind. But being athletic and agile, I soon became accustomed to manoeuvring about high above ground, imagining that I was aboard a ship!

Within a year, I was moved to Haulbowline, an island about a half-hour ferry ride off the Cork coast, to a team that worked on refurbishing retired Navy corvettes. One day, a stiff winter wind increased to storm force, and the ferry service was suspended, leaving the day shift stranded on the island. A flag with the 'skull and crossbones' was hoisted, to indicate the suspension of sailings. Two ferry boats now remained moored in the little harbour, as the storm howled. Then, just before 10 PM, the wind eased and one of the captains decided to sail. Cold, tired and hungry, we finally shuffled on board a second vessel and headed for Cobh. But at the quay, our boat couldn't pull alongside, and a few of the crew had to jump ashore and help passengers disembark. It was then that we heard that a man, trying to jump from the earlier ferry, had slipped and been crushed against the wall! In the aftermath of the accident, the corvettes were brought to the mainland, and we moved to Verolme Dockyard to continue the refurbishment.

I stayed at Uncle Frank's house in Rushbrooke, where I was spoiled by my aunt Etta and the girls, who also taught me to cook – a skill for which I am grateful to them to this day. I had been travelling by train or hitching lifts up and down from Cork at weekends for football games – and to see my girlfriend, Georgina. I met Georgina Ladley, a pretty brunette from Dun Laoghaire, at a 'hop' in the local Martello Tower, and we started 'going steady'. I wanted to be back in Dublin. In just over a year, I *was* back there, following a fall, in a ship's boiler room, that resulted in my cracking a rib. When I recovered, my company sent me, on a temporary contract, to work with Shell Oil in the North Wall, a mini-refinery. I worked on the laying of a pipeline and the installation of tanks, and was then sent to the midlands to work at a peat-fired power station, and from there to Mayo, to another power station. From my bedroom, in a cluster of pre-fabricated, flat-roofed buildings, I looked across an endless bleak bog and counted the hours till Friday, when I would board the train at 6 PM at Ballina and travel home to Dublin. It was a seven-hour journey, stopping at every town to drop off or collect mail and pick up passengers, many of them emigrating to England via the Dun Laoghaire mailboat. I was relieved when my contract ended and I was back in Dublin. My boss took me to various industrial sites that required maintenance and repairs, to make lists of materials, but by and large I was either looking down on the world from a roof or a tower, or stuck in subterranean blackness, suffocating. I had suffered broken bones, cuts and bruises. I had swallowed fumes and dust, and been blasted with so much machinery noise that I couldn't hear myself think. Then I was electrocuted!

It happened as I was crawling on my back along an underground passageway (ironically, in a hospice!) inspecting water pipes, with the aid of an 'inspection light' – a glimmer of a bulb, in a wire cage attached to a long extension cable. I felt water oozing from a pipe above my head, and as I lifted the light to get a closer look, I dropped it. The bulb smashed and I was plunged into darkness. I felt the pipe shudder and a shock running through me. I groped about for the cable and, once I'd found it, I followed it back along the passageway to the trapdoor and hauled myself up. In the corridor, I bumped into a foreman.

'Good God, you look like a ghost!' he said. 'Where've you been?'

When I told him what had happened, he advised me to go home and rest. But first, I had to fill in a report on the leak in the pipe-work and then write up an accident report!

My next assignment was at the Irish Sugar Company in Carlow, insulating tanks, X-raying silos and stud-welding. This assignment ended abruptly when I was electrocuted – again! The culprit this time was an electric drill. I almost tripped over it as I walked along a scaffolding platform, about sixty feet off the ground. I picked up the drill, and when I pulled the trigger there was a flash and a loud bang and the drill stuck to my hand. I grabbed the handrail, my body began to shudder, pain coursing through me, and I tried to call out. There were men working on another platform above me, but they couldn't hear me. Then, the world went black. When I woke up, three figures dressed in white were standing over me. But I wasn't in heaven: the figures in white were nuns – nursing sisters at Carlow General Hospital! For almost a year following the incident, I jumped at the slightest noise. I had taken to tying a shoelace around the flex of my electric shaver so that, if I got a shock, I could quickly pull the plug from the socket!

Following a course of evening classes at Blackrock Technical School – to learn more about mechanics and engineering – I joined a company in Hatch Street in the centre of Dublin. After a few weeks in run-down premises, with deafening noise coming from outdated machinery, the company moved to a state-of-the-art facility with welding bays, component bays and modern machinery and equipment, near the Guinness brewery. Then the bombshell came: the company had secured a big contract at the Ford car assembly plant in Cork – and I was on the team of four engineers and two apprentices. I set off, with my heart in my boots, sad to be leaving Dublin again. Up on the roof at the Ford plant, I witnessed another accident. This time it was my co-apprentice, who fell into a labyrinth of criss-crossed pipe-work, and tumbled, like a rag doll, to the ground. Unbelievably, he survived. And I had to fill in another accident report! I missed Dublin: my friends, the hops, football – and Georgina. Fortunately, when my contract ended in Cork, I found work with an engineering company in Blackrock, just minutes from home.

My parents adored Georgina, but I was not exactly 'flavour of the month' with her mother. Rosaleen Ladley was a chain-smoker whose only other addiction was church-going. Married twice, she ran three public houses, two in the midlands and one in Dublin. Georgina was the only child from Rosaleen's second marriage and never really knew her father. George Ladley died from TB about six months after she was born, leaving Rosaleen a widow for a second time. When Georgina was ten years old, her mother sent her to school in Dublin, where she lived in the care of an old housekeeper, above one of the family pubs, the Village Inn in Capel Street. After finishing school, Georgina worked for Arnott's department store in Dublin's Henry Street, where she had a promising future as an interior designer. Her

Our wedding day, 1965: (from left) my father, Georgina's mother Rosaleen Ladley, myself and Georgina, Georgina's half-brother Jimmy Gogarty, and my mother

half-brother took over the management of the Village Inn and Georgina gave up her job, because her mother had moved up from the midlands, and she and Georgina were reunited in a new business venture – a grocery shop – and moved to Dun Laoghaire. Georgina was twenty-one and I was twenty-three when we married on 24 February 1965. A short honeymoon began with our first plane journey aboard an Aer Lingus Viscount to London. In Heathrow's vast terminal building, a team of cleaners – all black – were polishing the floor in absolute silence, darting the odd look in our direction. They were the first real live black people I had ever seen: I thought I had landed in Alabama!

Our first house was in 'Beechwood', a new estate just off Rochestown Avenue, between Dun Laoghaire and Killiney. My childhood friend Sean Corcoran and his wife, Catherine, shared the house with us. Sean worked with his uncle, Vincent, a film cameraman, and they talked about 'the studios' and something big happening in the film world. It didn't mean much to me. However, my father, who was the first ground-control officer at Dublin Airport, had a colleague in Aer Lingus, who subsequently worked for Boeing in the States. This man now had connections with the film that I had been hearing about, and I was invited to Ardmore Studios in Bray to meet a friend of his, an American engineer.

I presented myself at a security hut and was told to continue up the avenue to the big house. To my left were large buildings that looked like factories. Up ahead stood a big house with stone steps leading up to the open hall door. I stepped into a large entrance hall with a beautiful carved wooden staircase, and in an office to my left a girl at the desk directed me to another room down the hall, where three men were sitting around a table, chatting. They introduced themselves as 'supervisors': one was German, one was English and the third was American. The Englishman's name was the only one I remembered. 'Call me Ronnie,' he said. Following an informal half-hour chat about my background and where I had worked up to then, 'Ronnie' said they would be in touch. I left, never expecting to see them – or Ardmore – again. A week later, I got a call asking me to start work, as a trainee technician. Just before 9 AM the following Monday morning, I answered a ring on the doorbell. A stocky, uniformed chauffeur stood there, beaming.

'Mr Johnston?' he asked. Behind him, a gleaming black stretch limousine took up half the road.

2

THE BLUE MAX

Eddie Dunne, my chauffeur, parked the limo in front of the big house, stepped out and opened the door for me. In the office, I was met by Ronnie, the Englishman I had met on my first visit. He took me around to the other offices and then down to the 'factory buildings', where he introduced me to the special-effects people. I was struck by the absence of titles: there was no 'Mister', 'Sir' or 'Miss', as I was used to. This business had a whole different feel to it: it was relaxed and informal.

The factory buildings were sound-stages and workshops, each workshop housing a different 'trade': carpentry in one, painting in another, and a combination of engineering and some sort of manufacturing in the 'effects shop'. Even some trucks had been fitted out as mobile workshops, with workbenches, storage compartments and shelving.

There was a great sense of ease among the workforce. Everyone said 'Well done' and offered help and encouragement. All I had to do was learn and carry out my tasks. I knew within the first week that this was where I wanted to be. In this strange new world within a world, with so many different trades, my head was buzzing with information. Keen to remember as much as possible, I got a diary and took copious notes as best as I could – reading over them during breaks and in the evenings after work. We were building vintage cars, model aircraft and weaponry, including guns that operated on gas. We were also modifying life-size aircraft that had been brought in from the UK. My job included building model aircraft for testing in a wind tunnel. It took a while for me to work out that we were doing all this for something called *The Blue Max*, that cameras would actually film our work, and that people all over the world would see what we had done!

The Big House: Ardmore House, still impressive today

Sometimes the supervisors took themselves off on something called a 'recce' to the 'location'. One day Peter Dawson, an English technician, asked me to accompany him to one of the locations, which was just up the road in the grounds of the Powerscourt Demesne. A massive pylon had been built, and I helped Peter attach cables to this pylon to suspend a full-sized model airplane from it! Peter explained that this would make the plane look like it was flying. Later it would 'crash', with smoke billowing out of it, with dummy pilots inside! Over the next week, as the work became even more challenging and exciting, caterers came to the location with hot meals, cakes and tea: a veritable treat. I was in heaven!

The following week, one of the English supervisors took me to Weston Aerodrome in Lucan, west Dublin, where we put steel pots into the ground alongside the landing strip. The pots would hold explosives! Days flew by, and weeks passed, working hours lengthened, and the pace quickened. The 'big day' was fast approaching, and money was rolling in! I was earning at least three times as much as I had been in my previous job. But I was away from home from early in the morning until after 8 PM, and people were telling Georgina that this type of work schedule wasn't 'normal'! The gardener added fuel to the fire. 'Who works till eight o'clock at night, Missus? C'mon, he's havin' ye on!' he jibed.

Georgina's mother advised her leave me and go back to live with her! No amount of explanation on my part made any difference. We argued, and Georgina packed her bags. By morning, nothing seemed to have changed, and I left for work. But when I returned home, Georgina had calmed down and unpacked her bags, and life returned to normal.

In the studios, trucks were loaded, and teams of people rushed about preparing for something called 'the first day of principal photography'. One morning, at the crack of dawn, in the spring of 1966, the 'circus' pulled out – and I was on board! Out on the location, at Kilpedder in County Wicklow and Weston Airfield in Dublin, massive tents had been erected, and all around them, the trucks and trailers parked up. The Irish army was now involved, and two dining tents – one for the crew and one for the army officers and men – had been erected side by side. Some of the officers and men played the part of extras. The rest were at the disposal of the special-effects department, overseeing the handling and transportation of explosives. I discovered that although these men were skilled engineers and mechanics, they were paid the same money as their colleagues who were extras, who just had to be on standby most of the time. (I understand that the effects supervisors later negotiated some sort of deal with the production office, to get a few extra pounds for the army guys who were helping us.)

At Kilpedder, a concrete bunker, half sunk in the ground, had been provided by the army to store our explosives. Each time it was opened, a dreadful smell met us, and whenever I went to collect an assignment I got a searing headache! I learned that the smell came from the nitro-glycerine in the sticks of dynamite.

Although the glamour began to wear off after a week of nights spent in the foothills of the Wicklow Mountains, I soon got used to the strange schedule: nights, days, and 'split days', when we started work in the afternoon and shot until 11 PM or maybe midnight. After all, this was show business, and being involved at the hub of things compensated for the long hours.

The Blue Max tells the story of Bruno Stachel, a German infantry soldier who has been trained as a fighter pilot. Because he is not an aristocrat, like his comrades, he is shunned by his fellow pilots. On the other hand, his fellow German countrymen regard him as a hero because he is extremely ambitious, daring and willing to do anything to win the ultimate glory: a tin cross, called 'The Blue Max'. But to win it he must shoot down twenty enemy aircraft – and survive. The film recreates the famous dogfights in the skies over Europe in the Great War. George Peppard, as Stachel, headed the cast, with Ursula Andress, who had starred in the early Bond movies, as the boss's wife – and also the object of Stachel's lust! The boss, Stachel's General, was played by James Mason.

I was a '007' fan and had seen Ms Andress as the 'Bond girl', but the other actors hadn't appeared in any of the Westerns that I was familiar with! Peppard, of course, featured in many of the action scenes but James Mason, Jeremy Kemp and Ursula Andress appeared chiefly in indoor scenes. One of these was a bedroom built on a sound-stage at the studios. It had a working fire – known in film terminology as a 'practical' fire – with a log fire roaring in the grate. Although I had come to love the action outdoors, I was curious about what went on inside, and so I was delighted to get the job of tending the fire in the bedroom! Just before shooting began, the director declared that it was to be a 'closed set'.

'That means everyone, except those who absolutely must be there, has to leave the set,' the First Assistant Director explained. 'Just the director, the camera crew, Hair, Make-up and Wardrobe are allowed.'

'But I must be on the set in case something goes wrong with the fire!' I protested.

'Sorry,' he replied.

I duly set up my gas bottle, checked the fittings, lit the gas and left. Outside, I hung about drinking coffee and chatting with the rest of the crew. Suddenly, I heard: 'Johnston! The set's burning!' I charged inside. The set was filling up with smoke. I turned off the gas and dowsed the back of the fireplace with a fire extinguisher. Apart from a scorch-mark behind the fire surround, there was no damage. When the smoke cleared and the panic subsided, the First AD asked me to stay, and filming resumed. The scene was a 'love scene' between Ursula Andress and Jeremy Kemp. They came in and took up their positions on the bed. The First AD called 'Action', and the two started talking – and smoking cigarettes!

Another scene involved Ms Andress smoking a cigarette and stroking a cat in bed. Ms Andress took up her position – to find that the cat had been there for a while, and had shat on the bed! A string of expletives brought people running from Wardrobe, Make-up and

Props. Her 'language' and her tousled appearance off-screen didn't seem to tally – in my mind – with her screen persona. My fantasy was shattered! I wondered if all my screen idols – Billy the Kid, Wyatt Earp and even James Bond – were just as ordinary in reality. Right now, it was better not to think about people too much. Action was simpler, and I was glad to get back out to the location – and the real action!

At Kilpedder, the 'battlefield' stretched for miles into the distance. A village was under construction, built to look like a place in Germany or France, so people watching the film would think that that was where it was all taking place! At Weston Aerodrome, nine World War I fighter planes were re-painted to look like German and Allied planes. The aerial sequences, including much of the bombing and anti-aircraft artillery scenes, were filmed in Weston. Every day, tons of cement, peat, paint powder and explosives were used by the special-effects department, and between various locations, miles of cable ran between firing mechanisms. Materials for the effects department also included oxyacetylene, gas, gunpowder, peat moss and cork. Based on blueprints provided by the art department, we made everything from scratch, including the guns, some with chambers for mixing gases. These would be mounted on the planes, which also had to be loaded with 'bombs'. Everything had to be weighed and checked, and the pilots had to be briefed in the use of the firing mechanisms that had been provided at the controls. Those planes were like tinder boxes, and we had to ensure they were blown up safely! The wings were made from a canvas-type material, which was stretched across the wooden frames. A preparation called 'dope' was painted on to the fabric so that it was firm and could be stretched. Sammy Bruton was the man in charge of the aircraft assembly. He went on to establish a biplane workshop and facility at Abbeyshrule in Limerick. After he died, his son took over the business. Sammy was a genius and knew everything there was to know about light aircraft; a veteran in his field.

In my field, I was still an apprentice with a lot to learn. I had been making up small, oval aluminium plates, and wondered what they would be used for. 'Bullet hits,' Peter Dawson said.

Each bullet hit had a small aluminium plate with a circle of black paint sprayed in the centre. A small charge was fitted, and a sheet of paper, matching the colour of the wing, was stuck across the top. When the charge exploded, it left a jagged hole in the paper, and the black spot underneath would camouflage the plate, creating the illusion of a bullet hole in the wing. Literally hundreds of hits had to be made up and glued to the wings, with yards of wiring connecting each one to the next, all fed to the firing mechanism in the cockpit.

Planes that would 'crash' had about fifteen feet of wire rope trailing from underneath the tail. Attached to the rope, a ball, about the size of a football, contained a 'burster'. When the pilot was given the command, he pushed a button and went into a dive. The burster exploded, and from the camera's position, in a helicopter above, the plane looked like it had exploded in a fireball. But of course the planes survived intact, landing safely. They were then often reloaded with explosives, and off we'd go again! On the ground, bombs were laid, anti-aircraft guns were loaded, and tons of equipment was maintained and hauled from one place to the next. If the director wanted a re-take, we had to rush to clean up, undo and re-do wiring, check firing mechanisms and load the explosives, and the cameras rolled once more.

During a 'bombing raid', we waited, fingers on buttons, as the planes drew nearer and nearer, until they were directly above us, no more than a couple of hundred feet away. With the order to 'fire', all hell broke loose – explosions, bullet hits, stuntmen and dummies flying through the air, debris falling, smoke and fire – and for the aftermath of the raid, we 'dressed' the bombed-out villages, or air-force bases, with fires, smouldering debris, smoke and 'blood' for the 'casualties'. There were several real casualties – and near-casualties – on the ground among crew, stunt people and army and FCA personnel, including a young army corporal who was bayoneted! His wound, though serious, was not fatal: after a spell in hospital, he returned to duty. There were also accidents among technicians; I came very close to extinction on a couple of occasions.

The first was at Kilpedder, during a bombing scene. One of our bombs, buried in the ground, had failed to go off. My supervisor asked me to check the wiring on the bombs. I dusted off layers of vermiculite, cork and other debris to check the cables on the first one, and found everything to be in order. As I approached the second, I looked back towards my supervisor. He was talking with a group of army personnel in the distance. Suddenly, I felt a blow, with the force of a sledgehammer, in my back, and a deafening explosion blew me off my feet! Apart from a loud ringing in my ears, I could hear nothing, as people flocked around me, to help me up. In a daze, I limped back to the supervisor, who stood with his mouth open. He had been demonstrating the firing box for the soldiers and had inadvertently hit the firing button! When he recovered himself, he apologised and we got back to work.

The next incident was at Baldonnel. The scene was the 'crash' of Stachel's plane. It called for a massive explosion. My German supervisor, Karl Baumkartner, took me with him to set it up. While the cameras filmed actors and extras, in all their finery, strolling around the airfield, awaiting the return of the famous airman's 'victory flight', we positioned oil barrels filled with petrol, diesel and paraffin over 'lifters' on steel plates, on a strip of ground about four hundred yards away. The crowd scene wrapped, and the cameras were set up to film the explosion. The First AD called 'Quiet, please', and the crowd settled. Suddenly, a ball of fire burst forth, into the air, followed by a deafening explosion. Cameras shuddered as barrels shot into the air, several of them crashing down into the hangars. Everyone ran for cover. I had no idea what had happened: it may have been a premature detonation. These were the rare, fleeting moments when I questioned the wisdom of having chosen to work in this profession! Karl acquired the nickname 'Boom-boom'!

The film had its share of daring stunts. An English test pilot flew underneath a bridge in Drogheda and caused quite a scare among the townspeople, and at Weston, as a squadron of four planes came in to land, in formation, a German plane went into a wobble and landed, on its nose, on the grass. It suffered fairly extensive damage but the pilot was uninjured. Thereafter, the plane was called 'Rubber Wings' – on account of the wobble. As the heat of the 'battles' increased, it seemed that the pilots were becoming like the World War I aces, rivalling each other in posturing and daring. It appeared that some of the Irish felt that they had to prove themselves in the eyes of the English, German and French visitors. During a break in filming, one flamboyant Irishman took off one day from Baldonnel in a Vampire jet, performed some stunning manoeuvres in the air, and spun into a victory roll over the runway, before landing, as gracefully as a bird!

Johnny Marr was the chief engineer in charge of aircraft maintenance. He was very professional and extremely skilled, and was someone I greatly admired. He was also amiable, easy to work with, and extremely helpful. Our department, in conjunction with specialists such as Johnny, was responsible for every piece of moving – and stationary – equipment on the ground: anything that would be involved in action of some sort, whether out in the open or indoors on a sound-stage against a blue screen. Aircraft were made from scratch to replicate, to the last detail, the authentic aircraft that had been shipped in from the UK and mainland Europe. While the real planes did their stuff in the air, our replicas took a hammering on the ground: crashing into trees, belching smoke and blowing up.

Vintage cars had been gathered from various collections in Ireland and abroad, but we built the others – cars that would suffer some sort of damage. We also rigged a train with hundreds of bullet hits, both for the scenes shot inside the train and for those shot from helicopters that hovered overhead. We removed some of the carriage windows and replaced them with 'breakaway glass', a resin glass that would shatter without causing injury to the actors or crew, or damage to the train's interior. These mock windows would then be rigged with charges. Most of the preparation took place back at the studio workshops, but as the weather improved we worked from sheds on location or from our fitted-out trucks.

The effects department was made up of many specialists: engineers, mechanics, and people like Sid, a biochemist, another of my floor supervisors. Sid was particularly averse to hanging around the set, and once everything was made up and ready, he would frequently disappear. There were a number of days when we did a lot of hanging about, waiting – for the camera set-ups to be finalised, for the lighting to be rigged, for the actors to finish rehearsing, or for the director to make his or her mind up! On one of those days, the director John Guillermin was smoking his pipe contentedly and 'lining up a shot'

The Blue Max: One of the real World War I aircraft takes to the air.

with the director of photography (the DOP). I was helping Sid while we were shooting on one of the sound-stages at Ardmore.

'I'm just off to the boardroom,' Sid told me. 'I'm leaving you in charge.'

I hung about the periphery of the set, 'keeping an eye out' and waiting for Sid to return. Guillermin called: 'Special effects!' It took about twenty seconds to register that he meant me! I ran up to the camera.

'Yes, that's me,' I muttered.

'What's your name?' Guillermin asked.

'Gerry.'

'OK, Gerry, here's what I want. Can you come up here and have a look?'

Knees wobbling, I climbed on to the swivel chair, still warm from the director's bottom, and squinted through the camera lens. I could see nothing!

'What am I supposed to be looking at?' I asked.

'OK, line up that shot for Gerry!' Guillermin called to the focus puller. 'Now, those pipes up there . . . I want steam coming out of those pipes.'

The set was a hospital interior with large heating pipes running around the walls, but even after the focus had been pulled, I still couldn't make out the shot!

'OK,' I said, and jumped down. I had to find Sid – and fast!

Outside, I asked someone where the boardroom was.

'Probably up in the house,' they said.

I ran across to the big house and into the production office.

'Where's the boardroom?' I asked, out of breath.

The girls in the office looked at each other. 'We don't have a boardroom,' one of them said.

'But I was told I'd find Sid, the special-effects supervisor, in the boardroom!'

Then one of the girls had a thought. 'Try the bar.'

I tore downstairs – and sure enough, there was Sid, sitting at the counter with a large whiskey to his lips.

'Sid, Sid, the director wants steam – NOW!' I said.

Sid drained the glass and left it on the counter, winked at the barman, and said 'I'll be back.'

Sid's forte was explosive composition and manufacturing. Firing mechanisms were another matter! We were at Weston again. The shot was of a pilot parachuting to the ground after his plane had blown up. We were preparing to drop a dummy pilot from a helicopter. The miniature dummy was in a small mortar pot aboard the chopper and was fitted with a tiny charge (a squib) and a length of twin-flex cable. The chopper took off and the cable dangled from the dummy on board, to the ground. Sid gathered up the cable and held the section of pre-stripped copper over a small battery, waiting for the order.

'OK, camera rolling! Stand by!' the First AD called.

'Ready, Sid?' the director asked.

'Ready, guv,' Sid replied.

'OK, fire!'

Sid struck the battery. Nothing!

'What's up, Sid?' the director asked.

'Uhm, don't know, guv,' Sid mumbled as he wiggled the chopper about.

The camera was still rolling. I looked at the chopper – and the cable – and I wondered . . . .

'Sid,' I whispered. 'Maybe the battery isn't powerful enough to fire that distance?'

Tests carried out earlier had been on the ground. This time the charge was about a couple of hundred feet in the air.

'Mmm . . . could be right, mate. This bloody thing ain't working anyway!'

'OK, I'll get another battery,' I said.

The director ambled across to Sid, who dropped the little battery into his pocket – out of sight! The camera was 'locked off' and still rolling! I arrived back with a twelve-volt car battery and left it on the ground at Sid's feet.

'Could be a problem with the battery,' Sid was saying.

'OK, Sid, just let us know when you're ready,' the director said, and strolled back to the camera.

Sid squatted by the car battery. 'This bloody thing had better work!' he whispered, through gritted teeth.

'Ready, Sid?' the director called.

Sid gave the thumbs-up sign.

'Fire!'

Our little 'pilot' shot out of the chopper, and drifted for about a hundred feet, then his tiny parachute burst open. The crew and army personnel on the ground looked on in silence as if some celestial being was dropping from the clouds! The dummy bounced off the grass, his parachute billowing around him. Applause broke out. The camera recorded the pilot parachuting to the ground – after hundreds of feet of film had recorded a length of twin-flex waving about in the breeze!

'I need to find a boardroom!' Sid said.

While pyrotechnics, World War I planes and vintage cars were fascinating, what I found most intriguing was the making of rain. Gun-barrel piping was delivered, out came the drills and the cutting and welding gear, and for days I watched the technicians making 'rain stands'. I asked Peter Dawson what rain stands were for.

'For making rain, mate. Ya know . . . ?'

I didn't know! But I learned that 'normal' rain may not register on camera and that it can't be turned on and off at the command of the director! On location, the stands were fitted with 'rain heads', which were like shower heads on folding tripod bases. The rain stands were attached to yards of hosing, which was connected to fire engines or water tankers with pumps, or to hydrants on the street. And then there was indoor rain! Interior shots on a sound-stage could require rain to be falling against a window pane, or in a doorway. This operation would require yards of plastic or rubber lining to protect the floor and pumps, hoses, valves and collection troughs. The rain would be turned on and off as the action required.

We also manufactured equipment: dry ice and smoke machines – even the 'gimbals', or rocking mechanisms, used for simulating a plane in flight, shot against blue screen. The Americans were experts in inventing and building such equipment. Their kits, shipped in from their own workshops in the States – toolboxes that were more like mobile cabinets, state-of-the-art stuff, even down to the drills and screwdrivers they used – looked like something from a science-fiction movie! The Americans were also proficient in 'workshop ethics', careful to tidy up the workshop each evening, clean the equipment and pack everything away. Following pictures like *The Blue Max*, days and possibly a couple of weeks were devoted to cleaning up, accounting for every spanner and screwdriver, and disposing of unused materials, packing and labelling. But for me, even this was fun!

My enthusiasm must have impressed Ronnie Ballanger, the English supervisor who had taken me under his wing, for he asked me if I would consider going to work in England. The Americans too invited me to work in Los Angeles. I was tempted, but the upheaval involved in moving from a new home, and Georgina's commitment to her mother and the relatively new business in Dun Laoghaire, took precedence over emigration.

It was autumn by the time the picture wrapped. The production company held a banquet in Dublin Castle. The entire Irish Cabinet was present – as well as members of the Opposition! The army brass was in attendance, as of course were the producers, the director and the actors. The place was crawling with reporters and photographers who had been following the progress of the picture. Meanwhile, we had our own party at Ardmore: my first 'wrap party'. Helicopters landed on the studio lawn, and stretch limousines delivered actors and dignitaries – just like in Hollywood! A feast was laid out – pig's heads, seafood, cold meats and champagne – with silverware and white linen. Men were in smart suits and women were dressed lavishly in chic gowns and jewellery. Everyone congratulated each other on a job well done. I felt important, as if I were in 'high society' mixing with the crème de la crème. But I was also wondering, yet again, about my future.

3

DEREK AND *DARLING LILI* – TWO NEW ARRIVALS

Halfway through filming of *The Blue Max*, I hired a car, and on a rare sunny Sunday in March 1966, I took Georgina for a spin to Wicklow. The mortgage payments for the remainder of the year were covered, and Georgina had been buying new furniture. I was happy, despite my heavy workload, and all was well with the world. We had lunch at a hotel in Wicklow and, after a stroll on the beach at Brittas Bay, we drove home to Beechwood. Nine months later, I drove Georgina, whimpering in pain, to the Rotunda Hospital and was told to leave. This was before the liberalisation of maternity-hospital rules, and fathers were not allowed into labour wards. The Rotunda was old and dreary but was said to be the best maternity hospital in the country. Behind the dim lighting, the drab décor and the smells of ether and disinfectant, there was a sense of mystery: this is where babies came into the world. For me, being in such a place – even for a short time – was a new and intriguing experience!

I decided to stay with my parents, who were now living in Glenageary, because they had a telephone, and we settled down to wait, playing cards to pass the time. The next day, I visited Georgina – and the day after that. There was still no sign of the baby.

'I could have jumped out the window with the pain,' she told me.

I felt completely helpless – and impatient! Finally, on the third evening, the call came. It was just before midnight on 3 December 1966. I had a son! My father opened a bottle of whiskey, to celebrate. For all of us, Derek's arrival was the climax of an extraordinary, wonderful year.

But I was uneasy. I was back in the 'real world' – I had found work with a new engineering company near Dun Laoghaire, fitting and repairing air-conditioning systems in schools and hotels. It was a big comedown from filming – and I was bored. The pay, too, was paltry in comparison to film work. Then, without warning, the factory workers went on strike, and for the first time in my life I was in the dole queue! The dole money wasn't enough to cover the mortgage. Georgina went back to work in her mother's shop, and I took care of Derek.

When *The Blue Max* was released, we went to see it in Dun Laoghaire. I had spent most of the previous year behind the cameras, helping to create the scenes that were unfolding on the screen. While my body sat in the cinema, my heart and mind were up there amidst the gunfire and explosions, the planes and the flying aces. I wanted to be making films as part of a platoon of respected technicians, where my worries vanished and the riddle about what my future held, which had haunted me in childhood, was solved. I was beginning to regret having declined my supervisors' invitations to work abroad. But I had bought a house, I had a wife, my parents lived less than ten minutes' drive away – and now, Derek was unwell.

The doctor examined him, but didn't seem to know why exactly the baby was lethargic and not feeding. Nevertheless, he prescribed medication. Two days later, the baby was still in distress and, not knowing what to do to comfort him, I took him to Georgina at the shop. I was just about to leave when Georgina came running after me, screaming: 'The baby's dead!' In the kitchen, behind the shop, I found her mother amidst a group of women, tapping the baby on the back, passing him from one to the other, and holding him under the cold-water tap.

'Oh, God!' one of them was saying.

'Oh, Holy Mother of God and Saint Joseph, come back, son, please come back!' another pleaded.

He had stopped breathing and was absolutely still. I realised that nothing was working. I grabbed him and laid him on the floor and instinctively began to try to resuscitate him. As I blew into his mouth for about the fourth time, I felt his tongue move! Then his head moved slightly, and his little body shuddered back to life. The women rushed forward.

'Oh, thanks be to God and His Blessed Mother!'

'Oh, Holy Saint Joseph!'

'We'll say the Rosary,' Mrs Ladley said.

The Rosary was in full swing when Georgina arrived back, still weeping, with Mr Taggart, a neighbour, in tow. He had phoned for an ambulance. A ramshackle red vehicle from the local fire station arrived. I held Derek tightly in my arms, trying to stop myself from bouncing off the roof, as the 'ambulance' rattled through the streets on the five-minute journey to St Michael's Hospital. Derek was kept in for a couple of days for observation and then we took him home, apparently none the worse for his ordeal.

He must have been about six months old when it happened again. One afternoon, we were driving home along Rochestown Avenue when his body went rigid and his breathing stopped. I pulled over and Georgina jumped out of the car and ran about, screaming. I tried to revive him.

A passer-by managed to calm Georgina down and escort her back to the car. As luck would have it, he was an ambulance man! Straight away, he sat into the front seat and took the child.

'Go on, drive!' he ordered.

With Derek lying across his lap, he began resuscitation. The child's head was partially obstructing the gear lever but I managed to shift into second gear and put the boot to the floor! At St Michael's, Derek was admitted, and detained for twenty-four hours, after which we took him home.

At night, we were afraid to sleep in case Derek would stop breathing again. I was back at my air-conditioning job, and *The Blue Max* and film work was becoming a distant memory. Sean Corcoran and his uncle Vincent were filming on a few commercials, and I was now keen to hear Sean's news from the film world, hoping for another break. Months went by. My father bought a motor boat; I helped him build a wheelhouse on board, and we took her for short trips around the harbour. We took Derek along on some of them. He was at the crawling stage, making brave attempt to stand. Still wary, in case he would suffer another breathing crisis, we never ventured too far from the shore.

I was restless, and money was tight. Georgina and I talked about emigration again. England was still gladly accepting the Irish and, provided that we met the criteria, the Canadian and Australian governments would also pay our way, find us jobs and subsidise our first month's rent. Some of Georgina's family were thinking along the same lines, and we were contemplating going to Australia as a group. But Georgina's mother complained about being left alone, and Georgina's sister-in-law worried about leaving her cats in quarantine. The cats won the debate: we decided to stay.

Then an unexpected break: I received a phone call from Colonel O'Kelly, an Irish army colonel with whom I had got along very well while working on *The Blue Max*. 'Young Johnston, I want to see you!' he said. 'Some big Hollywood actors are coming in. It's going to be along the lines of *The Blue Max*, so you'll know the ropes. You did a good job, so get yourself together and get some gear.'

The film was called *Darling Lili*, and was the story of an English/German music-hall entertainer living in London who is also a Mata Hari-like German spy. She is on a mission to extract military secrets from an American, Major William Larabee, with whom she falls in love. Lili, the showgirl, is played by Julie Andrews, who, in real life, had just married the director, Blake Edwards. Major Larabee was played by Rock Hudson and Jeremy Kemp was back – this time in the role of Lili's 'assistant spy'. The film called for authentic World War I aircraft and air sequences, similar to what we had created in *The Blue Max*, and O'Kelly said that we would be using the same planes and pilots as before. But I wasn't sure if I had learned enough about effects, or if I'd know what to do. O'Kelly seemed to think that I had it all under control. 'First thing you need to do is go out to Ardmore and give them your details,' he said. In fact, the first thing I needed to do was quit my job!

At Ardmore, I presented myself at the office, where I gave my name and address. I was told that I would be on the studio payroll. I was given an office and a phone, pens and notepads, and left to ponder my next move. I hadn't a clue where to begin! Fortunately, I had taken reams of notes while working on *The Blue Max* – a year's worth of information. I rushed back home and retrieved my diaries, then went to Baldonnel, where the World War I planes were in storage. O'Kelly met me and took me on a tour of the hangars. I met Johnny Marr again, and we took up where we'd left off two years earlier.

The planes were stored among modern Spitfires and helicopters in two hangars. In a third hangar, I found a small office and a team of air-force engineers. These were the guys who had assisted the effects crew during the filming of *The Blue Max*. I was introduced: I remembered some of the people; others were new to me. For this film, they were checking over the planes and making up fittings for the guns that would be mounted on board. I was already intoxicated – on the smell of aviation fuel and the sweet splutter of World War I aircraft engines!

It would be another four or five months before the rest of the department showed up. 'They're doing tests in Burbank Studios, in

California,' O'Kelly said. 'I've told them I'll have my man getting stuff ready back here at Ardmore!'

For the next couple of months, 'O'Kelly's man' busied himself ordering and buying, travelling between Baldonnel, Weston and Ardmore. Weston had taken in the surplus planes and turned a hangar into a workshop – complete with 'Radio Luxembourg' and all the sixties hits blaring all day!

My notes included a list of suppliers. I phoned one of these to place an order, but they were shutting down. I was given the name and number of a 'contact'. 'I'll meet you at the supply depot,' he said.

It was 1968, and there were no motorways in Ireland. Having driven for hours, around by-roads and country lanes, I found it: a hut in a field in the middle of nowhere! It was open. Cautiously, I stepped inside, to find shelves packed with reels of detonator cord and all manner of high-explosive materials! My contact was nowhere to be seen! After about ten minutes, he arrived. 'I was just across the way there making a phone call,' he said. 'Mr Johnston, I presume?'

We shook hands and, together, went through my list, selecting each item from among the shelves and boxes. However, the hut didn't have certain items that I needed, so it was back to the Colonel.

'They'll have some of that in the Curragh,' he said. 'I'll just clear that with the lads down there. The paperwork won't be a problem.'

We were up and running, and the Curragh Military Camp was added to my list of suppliers.

Finally, the Americans arrived, with all the usual state-of-the-art equipment: trunks on wheels with sliding drawers, each one stamped with the owner's initials. The veteran effects crew, led by Danny Lee, took over command of the film, and I became the trainee again. Lee's second-in-command was a gregarious, six-foot Texan called Bob Peterson, to whom I took an immediate liking. The pace revved up, and I was soon absorbed into the fold. I was in my element once more! In no time, the preparation for the filming began in earnest.

At Ardmore, long trestle tables were set up outside the studio workshops. We weighed, measured and packed our explosive cocktails into paper bags. Papier mâché was made up and moulded around the packed bags, and these were spread out on the tables to harden.

'Now we're going to erect a line,' Bob said.

At Weston, he took me to a pile of stakes, which we hammered, in a row, about five feet apart, into the ground; we then strung a length of washing line between them, about five feet off the ground. As we worked, I was reminded of my fishing days on the beach! Nearby, several large barrels held a strange red liquid, into which we dipped the hardened 'footballs'.

'That's called dope,' he said. I recognised the liquid as the hardening agent used on *The Blue Max* to stretch and harden the aircraft wings. After the papier-mâché 'footballs' had become solid, they were dipped into the 'dope', left to drain over the barrels on a wire tray and then pegged to the washing line to dry. Finally, they were sorted into batches and labelled 'No. 1's, 'No. 2's, 'No. 3's, and so on. I was now learning about the manufacture of the bombs that would be attached to planes or be fired at planes, from mortar pots or guns, on the ground. For now, only the trained effects crew knew what was inside them. I was still a trainee and it would be another couple of years before I would know enough to put the likes of these bombs together. Indoors, others among Danny's team were busy engineering: constructing aircraft simulators for the interior shots against blue screen, welding, cutting, hammering and grinding.

The studio was buzzing, and at the end of the day the crew headed to the 'boardroom' for a well-earned beer. Out at Weston, marquees became our workshops and trucks were used to store equipment. The fields around Weston also provided a delicacy – fresh mushrooms – which we fried up and had for 'elevenses'! On the first day of principal photography, the caterers wheeled in, and we were treated to four-course lunches and everything in between. I settled in, soaked up information like a sponge, and made enough money to cover my mortgage for the rest of the year. I learned more about pyrotechnics composition and felt that this would be my speciality. I also learned about the hazards of using pyrotechnics – first hand.

I was part of a second unit, shooting on location at the back of the Sugarloaf Mountain, overlooking Bray and Dun Laoghaire to the north and Greystones and Wicklow to the south. It was a calm day with intermittent cloud:typical of an Irish summer. We had the body of an aircraft, loaded with explosives, on a pulley suspended from a mobile crane. Bob was directing camera positions: three or four in all. I held the firing box – a radio-controlled, battery-powered firing device – with the mechanism primed and ready. The shot would be an aircraft exploding in mid-air and crashing in a ball of fire.

'Don't do anything after I tell you to "go hot", Gerry,' Bob ordered. ('Going hot' meant that the wiring was connected to the battery, and a green light on the firing box indicated that we had power.)

Darling Lili: I worked from the skid of this chopper at a few thousand feet!

Suddenly, there was an unmerciful bang and the plane left its mooring and started to 'fly' downhill, with the charges on board exploding along the way!

'Run!' Bob roared.

Crew scattered as the plane trundled to a stop in a pile of rocks and burst into flames. Immediately, Bob came running up to me.

'What did you do?' he demanded.

'Nothing,' I said.

We were bewildered — until someone told us that a group of model-aircraft enthusiasts, using radio-controlled units, had been flying models about half a mile away on the other side of the Sugarloaf. From that day to this, I have an aversion to radio-controlled or computerised devices when using pyrotechnics. Call me old-fashioned, but I like to be in control. The director will have only one chance to capture an explosion, and usually, like a surgeon's first incision, the pyrotechnics crew will have to get it right first time. For an explosion such as this, 'Take One' is the only take! As far as I know, some of the cameras had picked up segments of the unscheduled explosions, as the plane careened towards the rocks, and these were later edited into a sequence in the film.

This film also gave me my first chopper ride — a hair-raising jaunt above the city and out over the green fields around west Dublin. I had volunteered to operate the on-board firing mechanisms. Half of the chopper's glass dome had been removed and the front portion of a mock-up plane had been fitted on board. A propeller spun on the nose

Darling Lili: At the controls of a World War I plane at Weston, near Dublin

— just like the real thing — and two big guns protruded from the front. A camera had been mounted in the rear of the chopper cabin, along with a couple of gas tanks, positioned just within my reach. There was barely enough room in the cabin for the pilot! He was French, a brilliant test pilot, and I was thrilled to be flying (or rather 'hovering') with him. I was given a headset, through which I would take his instructions: when to turn on the gases for the guns, about manoeuvres, and so on. I was fitted with a belt that was attached to a fixture on the chopper floor. Thus anchored, I sat on one of the skids, with my legs stretched out in front of me, until the chopper lifted off the ground. Then, with legs dangling, I looked down at the crew, all waving and smiling.

The pilot's voice, like a distant tinny radio, came through my headphones. 'We just stop for ze wezzer forecast.'

When we were alongside the control tower — to get the weather forecast — he slid back his window and spoke across to the traffic controller, his voice intermittent and barely audible above the deafening noise of the propeller echoing off the tower! Then, we swooped away, rising into the clouds. I had thought that we would be hovering at about a hundred feet, but we were now chasing a real World War I plane at a thousand feet, maybe more! I clung on, whipped by the wind, as the pilot's voice leaked into my ears from time to time. I couldn't understand a word of his French accent, and I don't know if I ever answered him. Wearing only a T-shirt and jeans, I was frozen!

Somehow, despite the chopper's acrobatics — banking left, then right, then diving, with the ground rushing up to meet us — I managed to fire the guns by remote control from my flying rag-doll position, and when, after what seemed like an eternity, we landed, I was fit only for hypothermia treatment! People were around me, unhitching my belt, lifting me to my feet, their mouths opening and closing, but no sound was reaching my ears. I was probably a candidate for an A&E department, but I was young, a rookie, and had to 'save face'. After a cup of hot tea, I got back to work.

Before filming ended, I managed a more sedate stint in one of the planes — over the River Liffey, flying towards the dropping evening sun, feeling at one with the sky. I sat in the compartment behind the cockpit, a tiny space where the navigator would have sat, and could only marvel at the crews who had flown these things, under fire, with only a few basic dials, pedals, a joystick and a couple of guns on board.

Darling Lili was a musical, and musicals were no longer popular among cinema audiences. Despite receiving several Oscar nominations and winning a Golden Globe award for Best Actress for Julie Andrews, the film was a flop at the box office. To me, it didn't matter. I had notched up another movie and another year's apprenticeship.

I was preparing myself for another lull when I got a call from Colonel O'Kelly. 'Get yourself down to Dingle!' he ordered. I didn't even know where Dingle was! It sounded a long way away, and I guessed I would be away from home again — although this would be my first time away from home since getting married. Georgina would not be too pleased being left alone with a toddler who had a history of passing out! We had spent nearly a year taking it in turns to watch him: endless nights of broken sleep. But he seemed fine now, and I felt it would be safe to launch myself into another long stint of film work.

'They're coming in for the storms!' O'Kelly said.

4

'LOCK UP YOUR DAUGHTERS!'

I hired a Mini and set out, at about 4 PM on a Sunday evening, to drive
to Dingle, County Kerry, in the farthest, most southerly tip of Ireland
– a journey of about seven hours, along pitiful roads. I made it, without incident, until I was west of Tralee. As darkness fell, I hit a dense
fog. Then, suddenly and without warning, the car shuddered to a halt
and died – engine, lights, everything. The dynamo, I guessed.
Wondering what to do, and not knowing where I was, nor how far I
had yet to travel, I sat in the car, enveloped in mist, in complete silence.
I decided to get out; something told me to be careful. I could feel,
rather than see, a tuft of grass under my foot. The mist clung to my
skin as I felt my way round the car, on to the middle of the road. I was
about to start walking when I heard a chugging sound, and then a faint
beam of light came through the fog! I shouted, to attract attention. A
tractor drew alongside and a man's deep, Kerry voice said, 'Are ye
losht?'

When he heard what had happened, my Good Samaritan jumped
down and rummaged about in the tractor-trailer and found some rope.
We hitched up the car and towed it into a nearby gateway. He then
took me to his house, which wasn't very far away. Over a cup of tea, I
learned that I was on the infamous 'Connor Pass'. An hour later, we
were in my saviour's car, on our way to Dingle.

In daylight, Dingle was the most beautiful place I had ever seen –
a sleepy village, at the mouth of a long, narrow harbour, where fishing trawlers came and went at a leisurely pace and nothing stirred
before ten in the morning. The main street climbed away in the distance, and out to sea the craggy Skelligs rose in splendid isolation from
the inky waters of the Atlantic. After that, the next stop was America!

I was staying in the lap of luxury on the mainland, in the new

Dingle Skellig Hotel, just outside the village. The builders of the hotel were frantically trying to get the place finished before the arrival of the visitors from America, but despite its unfinished state, the hotel offered delicious food. Lobster, cod and mackerel were the 'order of the day'. Being a fish-lover, I had landed in paradise!

The government had pulled out all the stops and had once more donated army personnel to handle the logistics, and had handed down orders that the film-makers were to have every facility placed at their disposal. During my four or five days at the Skellig Hotel, I had scoured the village, searching for a place to set up a workshop, getting to know who was who, and where to source materials. No one else from the effects department had arrived. In fact, I was the only crew member on location, dining alone every evening in the hotel restaurant.

Each evening, a group of four people sat at a table nearby. From their accents, I could tell they weren't Irish. One evening, during dinner, one of the men called over to me.

'Are you visiting?' he asked.

'No, I'm here working on a film,' I replied.

'Really?' he said, beaming. 'Come and join us!'

He pulled out a chair. 'My name's David Lean,' he said, putting out his hand. 'This is Robert Bolt and his wife, Sarah, and this is Anthony Havelock-Allan.'

They could have been four of the twelve Apostles for all I knew; the names meant nothing to me. Nevertheless, I sat down and, as the chat and the wine flowed, I discovered that I was in the most esteemed company – with the 'luminaries' at the helm of the picture: Anthony Havelock-Allan, the producer, no less; David Lean, the director; Robert Bolt, the writer; and Sarah Miles, the leading actress. David Lean had directed *Lawrence of Arabia*, *Dr Zhivago* and *The Bridge on the River Kwai*. He was one of the most famous directors in the business. I don't remember what I blabbed about but it must have gone down well because I was invited to join them every evening thereafter! All I can remember, from these evenings, is David Lean and Robert Bolt squabbling incessantly over the script. 'We've been writing this story for ten years,' Lean declared, 'and we're still arguing over it!'

Lean, a tall man, spoke with a soft English accent and used huge words! Much of what he and the others were talking about went over my head. I had never seen a film script, nor was I a writer, and 'theatrical drama' held little interest for me – at least in those days. I came into my own when we talked about *my* work, and as we talked, I began to understand what O'Kelly had meant when he told me they had come 'for the storms'. About the same time every year, the west Kerry coastline is subjected to high winds and pounding waves from the Atlantic. This time, pyrotechnics would take a 'back seat'; it would all be about 'atmosphere'. The film was *Ryan's Daughter*.

I had to vacate the opulence of the Skellig Hotel to facilitate the 'higher-ups' who had travelled in from the United States and other foreign parts. Thereafter, I would only see the 'luminaries' at a distance, until filming started. In the course of my walks around the village, however, I had met a man called Tom Ashe, a publican, who seemed to be *the* man about the place. Tom found me a workshop behind a butcher's – next door to a slaughterhouse! Through the dividing wall, I was regularly treated to the spine-chilling roars of dying cattle and sheep. This took a bit of getting used to, but the building was conveniently located: right in the middle of the village, and close to my accommodation – a room in a house nearby. I was back to 'self-catering' instead of breakfast, dinner and the director's fine wine at the Skellig! The room was a bedsit with a two-ring cooker. It may have been a shop at one stage: my bed was underneath a large, plate-glass, shop-type window, and the place was freezing! A gas 'super-ser' heater created more condensation than heat. This could prove a problem for Derek when Georgina and he came to visit.

But something else was bothering me in the meantime. One evening as I was frying up my evening meal, the door opened and the woman of the house walked in. She looked at the pan and then at me.

'You've got too much food there!' she said.

'No, I don't think so. I like my food,' I replied.

'Well, here, let me do it for you. You go and have a bath,' she ordered, trying to grab the pan. I held on to it, for dear life!

'No, that's OK,' I protested. 'I can do it myself, thanks.'

'Right, well I'll put the kettle on,' she said, and proceeded to take out cups and the teapot, making herself at home. For the next few hours, she quizzed me about my work, my family and the film. I was relieved when her husband appeared, to ask her something about the children, and she left.

I had mentioned that the cold was getting to me, and the following evening she came back with a couple of blankets that looked like they could have done with a good wash! I accepted them as graciously as I could, while deciding that I would fetch some blankets from home the first chance I had.

'I'll put these on the bed for you,' she offered. 'You put the kettle on!'

'No, that's all right,' I replied. 'I'll fix up the bed.'

'OK, so, I'll put the kettle on!'

And there she was, ensconced at the table, nattering away while she waited for the kettle to boil. Hours dragged by, and when she eventually took herself off, I lay on the bed, wondering what to do. The next evening she was back, offering to cook, telling me to 'rest', 'take a bath' and 'put the kettle on'. She sat for hours, talking.

Finally, I had to let her know how I felt. 'I'd rather be on my own in the evenings,' I told her.

She looked a little put out, but nonetheless she called again. It was time to see Tom Ashe. Tom listened patiently to my 'landlady dilemma'. Straight away, he hit upon the solution. 'Come with me,' he said. 'A couple of aunts of mine have a place down the road.'

The 'Miss Ashes', as they were known, were two sisters, neither of whom had the gift of hearing – or speech! What they did have was a fairly substantial house overlooking the bay. Downstairs, a large room housed a bakery along one side and a bar along the opposite wall. Upstairs, I was shown into my bedroom. The two sisters stood, one holding the door open, and I found myself gazing into a shrine to none other than Gregory Peck! Pictures of the handsome actor adorned every wall. From the sisters' gestures, I gathered that Gregory Peck had stayed here, in this very room. I later discovered that his paternal grandmother was Catherine Ashe, a relative of Thomas Ashe, who had fought in the Easter Rising. My new friend, Tom Ashe and his aunts, were all members of Peck's extended family!

The Miss Ashes' reputation for hospitality includes a report that Nora, one of the sisters, was the first person in Ireland to serve 'pub grub'. It happened by accident, when a few of the film's construction crew were in the bar and they got the smell of Irish stew wafting out from the kitchen. They asked Miss Ashe if they could have some, and she served them. Meanwhile, I was still catering for myself. I came and went as I pleased without fear of disturbing the landladies and was mercifully left in peace. At night, I drifted into sleep in a voluptuous, well-sprung double bed, part of a suite of polished-mahogany furniture. The only slight drawback was that the 'Gregory Peck Suite' didn't have a telephone. There were no mobile phones in 1969, and my contact with home was limited. As usual, Georgina wrote letters. The local post office was soon well up on who was connected with the 'fillum', and, eager to provide a good postal service, delivered the letters to me wherever I happened to be on a particular day!

I had been five weeks in Dingle when Georgina and Derek came to visit. I met them at the train station in Tralee, an hour's drive away. I'll never forget the feeling of absolute delight when I saw this little tot jumping down from the carriage and running across the platform! He had grown, and looked extremely healthy, and Georgina looked gorgeous as usual. Their presence was a breath of fresh air for me. I was keen to show them around and make sure they had a good time. By now I had made friends, among them Des Lavelle, a limber, craggy-faced man with salt water in his blood – and a great storyteller. Des was in charge of the Valentia lighthouse. He also had a couple of boats on Valentia Island and took visitors from Dingle to the Skelligs in summer. I had heard so much about the islands that I was itching to take a trip out there. But on this occasion, a trip to the islands was out of the question. The Skelligs is no place for a toddler! Instead, Des took us out into Dingle Bay for a cruise – in calm waters, the sun beaming down on us – and afterwards we dined at the Skellig Hotel. Georgina and Derek stayed for a glorious two weeks and then, after a tearful goodbye at Tralee, headed back to Dublin.

With the Skelligs still calling to me from across the bay, I watched, from my workshop, as the fishing trawlers came and went. By now I also knew the trawler men very well. I had asked them if they could get me some crab.

'What in the name of God de ye want with that vermin?' they laughed.

Each time I saw them, I'd ask. By now, it had become a joke. 'Ah, here he is again, lookin' for crab!'

Weeks passed, and then one day they said: 'Come down tomorrow and we'll have yer crab for ye!' I had brought a bucket, but when the Skipper handed me a large, heavy sack, it was obvious that the bucket was sadly inadequate for the task. I thanked him and left, struggling to carry the sack, and wondering if contained lumps of lead! Suddenly, I felt a movement, and something inside the sack started wriggling about. A claw ripped through it, and then a leg emerged! In a flash, the biggest crab I had ever seen tumbled out on to the road! When it stood up, it was almost knee high! Its companions followed suit and I was left with the ripped remains of a sack in my hand, while four giant crab made a break for it! They scampered across the road as if they were on stilts – like giant spiders – zig-zagging this way and that. A car was approaching, and I had to stand in the middle of the road and put my hand up, my crab scurrying about behind me! I will never forget the look on the driver's face!

I eventually rounded them up and herded them, still zig-zagging about the street, back to the Miss Ashes', where I corralled them in the back yard. I then had to 'execute' them – somehow! But first, Georgina and Derek were coming to visit again, and I had to drive to Tralee to pick them up. When Georgina saw the crabs, she jumped up on the table, screaming! For the next hour, the Miss Ashes' kitchen resembled the slaughterhouse next door to my workshop! I think a hammer was my weapon of choice as I wrestled with the crab one by one. Despite the inelegant preparation, I dined on crab meat for weeks. I'm not sure if it was due to my enthusiasm, but crab became popular, and the fishermen laughed for a different reason: their 'vermin' were now in demand.

Then I was introduced to another delicacy. Tom Ashe called on me one evening to see how I was getting on. He slapped a white paper parcel on the table.

'Here,' he said, with a smile. 'Put that on the pan.'

I unwrapped the parcel and found an odd-looking lump of . . . something.'

'What is it?' I asked.

"Tis cod's roe, lad. You'll love it!'

'How do I cook it?' I asked.

'Just throw a bit of butter in the pan and away ye go!' Tom said.

When it was cooked, it was indeed delicious.

'You can put the rest in the fridge now and have a couple of slices whenever ye want,' Tom said.

When cold, cod roe slices like pâté, and it's just as tasty as when it's freshly cooked. I loved this little place!

As the weeks passed, the buzz around the village mounted, and bit by bit the 'circus' began rolling in to town: carpenters, set-builders and painters. Not far away, another 'village' was springing up in Dunquin, a small fertile valley facing out to sea, overlooking the Blaskets – another cluster of small islands to the west. That summer, the valley echoed with the sound of hammering, sawing and drilling as the film village took shape, on land belonging to the Long family. Many years later, I would meet Joe Long, who must have been a child then, when he came to Dun Laoghaire as my bank manager! (It was Joe's colleague Joe Whelan who told me that *The Dawn*, the first Irish film with sound, was made in Kerry by an enterprising garage owner by the name of Tom Cooper, back in 1936!) Meanwhile, for our film, a steady stream of traffic flowed into Dingle, laden down with supplies, and every available room in the town was occupied by crew.

However, weekend traffic headed *out* of Dingle and across the country – to Tralee and Killarney, and further afield, up the coast to Clare and Galway – in search of entertainment. I sometimes went home to Dublin for the weekend, driving for seven hours on a Saturday and seven hours back to Dingle on a Sunday. When I was not travelling home, I drove around getting to know the area, the people and the customs – the most memorable being the Puck Fair in Killorglin. Although the fair is now famous, in 1969 I hadn't a clue what it was about, and I wondered why a massive male goat was prancing about on a platform about fifty feet in the air, in the middle of the town square.

Back in Dingle, the local hostelries soon realised that other towns were benefiting from the 'new money', and threw open their doors, arranging for big entertainers like The Dubliners to perform for the masses. Parties were the order of the day – or rather, the night – all over town! But not everyone welcomed the new arrivals. One Sunday, at Mass, I sat through a homily by the local priest in which he warned his parishioners about the 'evil' that had descended on his parish! 'Lock up your daughters!' he roared.

The priest's warning would, for the most part, fall on deaf ears. Hollywood was coming, and Dingle held its breath. Eyes popped when a plane-load of glamorous-looking American girls arrived from Shannon Airport. We heard that they were 'escorts' who had been flown in to entertain some of the big nobs. If the daughters of the parish had been locked up, they soon escaped. Romances blossomed, and many of the local girls ended up marrying men who worked on the film! The property master married a local girl, and after the picture was finished they bought a hotel in Spain.

As the town partied, David Lean waited for his storms – and waited. As fate would have it, for the first time in fifty years, there were no storms in Kerry. Instead, the effects department had to create much of the wind, rain and crashing waves. I was back to engineering and hard graft. The effects shop also became the 'machine shop', where we manufactured, modified and fixed everything, including camera gear and props! My effects supervisor was Robert McDonald, a small, balding man with glasses, from the US, whose objection to strong language I discovered when I hit my thumb with a hammer.

'Shit!' I yelled, nursing my thumb.

'Get out – now!' McDonald roared.

I stood for a moment, confused and in pain, and wondered if I had heard right.

'Get out!' he shouted again. 'I will not tolerate language like that in my workshop!'

I refused to leave, sure that he would fire me, but he calmed down and I got on with my work, my thumb – and my pride – still smarting. At some point, weeks later, we were on a tea break, and I offered him a sandwich.

'What's in it?' he asked.

'Pork,' I said.

'I don't eat pork,' he snapped.

It was the first time since starting in the industry that I'd heard a 'cross word' from someone in my own department. Otherwise, the crew bonded and the money was good; the craic in the pubs, and the constant parties, were a bonus.

Our workshop was in overdrive, making up 'Carley rafts' – rectangular boats, about eighteen inches deep, much like today's inflatables – that would carry crates of ammunition ashore. These rafts were made from fibreglass painted to look like timber. We built wind machines, and at one point the camera department requested a special rotating cover with a tiny motor to protect the camera lenses from the water.

When we were measured for wetsuits, I thought we were going diving. Instead, we were working in the water, shooting the night scenes, in which guns are being smuggled in on the rafts. We had to make up massive mechanical winches, run by Volkswagen engines, to which we attached long cables; we then connected the cables to the rafts and pulled them ashore – in a rough sea. Without the wetsuits, which were supplied from the States, we would have been soaked – and frozen. During filming of a scene involving the actor John Mills, his small currach overturned and, as it did so, hit him on the head. For a few moments, we thought he would swim to safety, but we soon realised that he was in trouble. I was among the crew who plunged in and helped the rescue team pull him out.

The work went on and on for almost a year, in what I would learn was typical David Lean fashion. We often waited for hours for an exact shadow or cloud effect! When the skies were overcast, shooting was suspended. While we created storms for some shots, Lean waited for his real storm: the 'big one'. He found one – more than fifty miles away, in Kilkee in County Clare! Lean's fastidiousness – choosing a number of beaches, miles apart, for some of the shots – necessitated the constant movement of machinery and equipment – as well as of actors and extras. But despite the combined efforts of nature and the special-effects department, Lean's big storm eluded him. It is said that he eventually shot his 'perfect storm' on the South African coast!

Robert Mitchum, the leading actor, said, in an interview: 'The trouble with David is that he shoots four versions of a film and then chooses the best!' During long periods of inactivity, Mitchum would fly back to the States for the weekend! He would sometimes be halfway across the Atlantic before he was missed! On a few occasions, he would be met on his arrival in America and put on the same plane back to Shannon, because the weather would suddenly have taken a turn for the better! Some said that Lean would simply use the weather as an excuse to get him back: Mitchum is said to have been reluctant to play the part of a quiet country schoolmaster to begin with – a completely different role from his usual tough, gun-slinging parts in Westerns and war movies. He was also given to throwing lavish parties at Milltown House, where he was staying, and playing practical jokes – including answering the phone and taking guest bookings! Everyone forgave him, of course!

It was a weekend towards the end of the shoot before I managed to visit the Skelligs, the spartan retreat where a group of hardy monks lived in the stone beehive-shaped cells at the summit of Skellig Michael. My guide was Des Lavelle, who would later write the book *The Skellig Story*. Since then, his vast knowledge of the islands, his passion for photography, and his visual presentations about the Skelligs have taken him on lecture tours all over the world.

Des and I stopped at various points along the climb up the 544 steps on Skellig Michael to rest, take in the views and marvel at the engineering skills of the monks who built the stone stairways and the monastery. We eventually reached the monastic site: I couldn't imagine how anyone could have constructed these buildings with such precision, with their bare hands, on these razor-sharp rocks jutting up out of the sea – like sandstone icebergs – in the Middle Ages! As I gazed out to sea, I realised that the west coast felt different to the east coast: it was more raw and more dramatic. Looking across towards Dingle, I felt reluctant to leave this sanctuary. I tried to ignore a gnawing fear inside: as my idyllic year on the edge of the Atlantic was coming to a close, the old worries about my future surfaced again.

Back on the mainland, *Ryan's Daughter* was winding down. The film had changed the face of Dingle forever. Every hotel, guesthouse and farmhouse in the area had been booked out for the year and every aspect of local trade had benefited from the arrival of the big spenders from Hollywood. People from the village had been employed as extras, and local tradesmen – even the fishermen – had earned 'a fortune' working part-time on the film.

Ryan's Daughter was released in 1970 – to a bashing from the critics. Nevertheless, it picked up four Academy Award nominations and won two Oscars, one for photography and one for the actor John Mills, who played the village fool. Sarah Miles won a Golden Globe for Best Actress and David Lean received an award from the Director's Guild. The film became a 'classic', and in America Dingle became known as 'Ryan's Country'.

Almost thirty years later, while filming in Tralee in 1996, I made a detour to Dingle and caught a glimpse of 'Fungi', the lone dolphin who, for twenty years or so, added a new dimension to Dingle's tourist attractions. I hardly recognised the place, with its new guesthouses, restaurants and service stations – not to mention its new, improved road surfaces! I didn't have time to explore, and maybe it's just as well: I could preserve my fond memories of Tom Ashe, the 'Miss Ashes', the trawler men, Des Lavelle and 'Ryan's Country' just as they were.

5

CHANGING TIMES

Derek celebrated his second birthday in December. By Christmas, there was much speculation among the film fraternity about what the New Year would hold. A slew of films scheduled for 1969 indicated that work would be coming my way. Sure enough, in early January I got a call – again from Colonel O'Kelly. The film was called *Underground* and featured the singer Robert Goulet as an American spy who is disgraced during World War II for 'squealing' on his fellow agents while being tortured. To redeem himself, he joins a French resistance group and parachutes behind enemy lines. His mission is to kidnap a Nazi general and smuggle him back to France. With guns, explosions, smoke, rain sequences and 'executions', the picture kept me on my toes. *Underground* was closely followed by another film in the same vein, called *The McKenzie Break*. It is essentially a battle of wits between a hard-drinking Irish ex-crime reporter and captain in the British army – played by the American actor Brian Keith – and a witty, fanatical Nazi U-boat captain, now a prisoner of war, played by the German actor Helmut Griem. The action centres on the escape of the POW from a military detention camp. I met many new crew on this film; my list of contacts in the business was growing.

By this time, I had become known among the effects people in the UK and I had got a call from Nobby Clark, who would be my supervisor on *The McKenzie Break*. Nobby was a joy to work with: easy-going and amiable, and always encouraging and helpful. John Howard, also from the UK, was his 'second in command'. I was once again on location, away from home, this time in Wexford. One evening, Nobby and John got a notion to get in some target practice, and invited me along. On a wall at the back of an old farmhouse Nobby lined up a row of tin cans, and the shooting started. Bets were laid: £1 for every three-out-of-four hits.

'I've never fired a gun in my life!' I said.

'Aw, come on, it's just a bit of fun,' John laughed.

As I watched, Nobby and John were not having much luck. Then it was my turn. I took aim, and grazed the first can. The next – and the next – were bull's eyes!

"Ere, mate,' Nobby said, 'I though you told me you couldn't shoot!'

'I swear, I never have!' I protested.

I didn't tell them that I'd been a dab hand at archery back in the park at Blackrock!

Most evenings, I joined some of the other crew for a game of cards. Anna Dolan and Toni Delaney were the film's make-up artists. A native of Wicklow, Anna was a striking-looking woman in her thirties and a keen card player. Some said she was psychic and that, if persuaded, she would 'read' the cards for people! I settled for a game of 'Forty-five'! Anna later married Michael Dryhurst, a production manager who would then co-produce the early John Boorman films. I would work with both Boorman and Dryhurst in years to come.

Toni Delaney has for many years been involved with the Dun Laoghaire College of Art and Design, now Dun Laoghaire Institute of Art, Design & Technology. The three of us teamed up with some of the crew from Wardrobe and Props, and played cards late into the night. It was a good way of getting to know the people who made up the film world and learning about the work of the other departments. I also came to know many of the stunt crew, among them Michael McNieve, who would later retire from stunts and take up a position as head of security at Ardmore Studios. Michael and I are probably the two people with the greatest number of years' experience at Ardmore. Today, his diligent handling of security, his knowledge and his discretion are legendary. It may have been Michael who bestowed on me Karl Baumgartner's dubious 'handle': 'Boom- boom!', which was later picked up by a couple of ADs. On many a set, I would hear, 'Hey, Boom-boom, can we have some smoke over here?'

The year was rounded off by a few days' work on a film with the lengthy title of *Quackser Fortune Has a Cousin in the Bronx*. This film was memorable for me on account of the main character's enterprising choice of business: collecting and selling horse manure to women for their gardens. Quackser's family tries to convince him to get a real job, but he is quite happy scooping up horse dung and selling it for flower gardens. He meets an American exchange student and falls in love with her. Then, horses are banned from Dublin, sending his business to the wall. His American lover is also leaving for America, facing him with a dilemma. The film was fun to work on – there were echoes of my childhood in Williamstown, when local women collected the cattle manure from the Rock Road – and introduced me to yet more new faces among the cast and crew.

From 1969 to 1970, I supervised a couple of small productions around Dublin, including *Black Beauty, Mother Mafia's Living Field, A Quiet Day in Belfast* and *War of Children*. In my mind, one production melts into the other, but I recall one from the early 1970s being dubbed 'the mafia picture'. I got a call, at 8 AM one morning, from the Irish production manager, telling me that the producers were pulling out – and I hadn't been paid. I was just about to tumble into bed after a night shoot, but I rushed down to the Burlington Hotel and approached some of the production team. A twenty-foot container stood in the car park, loaded and ready to leave – with some of my equipment on board!

'We don't have the money,' they said, when I asked for my wages.

'What about my equipment?' I asked.

'We don't know anything . . . .'

'Who has the keys to the container?'

'We don't know.'

I said I would call the police. They looked nervous, but still there was no co-operation. I walked outside and took a sledgehammer from the boot of my car.

'OK,' I said, 'if this container isn't open in five minutes, I'm breaking the lock!'

At that moment, a rotund, stern-faced man, dressed in a suit, arrived. 'What's the problem?' he enquired.

'Who are you?' I asked.

'I'm a producer,' he growled.

'I'm not leaving here until I have my equipment back – and my wages,' I said.

But he still wasn't budging.

'OK,' I said. 'I'm breaking the lock.'

And then, just for good measure, added, 'And I'm blowing this thing up!'

He immediately ordered one of his lackeys to open the container, dug a hand into a back pocket, and took out a wad of notes. I then had to battle through the contents of the trailer to get to my equipment, which was buried right at the back. I was getting a taste of another side of the business: I had moved from big-budget films where everything was laid on to working out of the boot of my car.

Within weeks, I was asked to work on another World War I movie. Peter Dawson, my colleague from *The Blue Max*, had called and asked me to come to Weston. Army sergeant Noel Gallagher was arranging the movement of explosives and handling all the paperwork on behalf of the effects department. The film was called *The Red Baron*. The director was Roger Corman, who had a string of horror movies to his credit. In later years, he would set up a facility in Connemara in the wilds of County Galway, churning out a string of B-movies, on shoe-string budgets, back to back.

I was delighted that Peter Dawson, one of the most respected and experienced technicians in the UK, was again on board. Peter's quick wit was a tonic, and his beaming smile would light up even the dullest day. Over the years, we have become close friends.

'It's a mini-Blue Max,' he told me. 'Nothing new. Same shit, mate!'

Indeed, the picture called for all the 'same shit' – dogfights, bullet hits, explosions and some daring stunts. I was raring to go!

The Red Baron was Corman's most ambitious project, with John Philip Law playing the lead role as the famous German flying ace Baron Von Richthofen, dubbed 'The Red Baron'. The second-unit aerial director was Jimmy Murakami. 'When you direct with Roger, you do everything!' Jimmy told me. Jimmy would later set up Murakami Wolf Films in the United States and return to Ireland to set up an animation studio in Dublin.

At Baldonnel and Weston airfields, we swung into action. Once again, the effects department was augmented by army engineers and mechanics, among them Jim Brady and Tommy Berry, who would later join me as part-time technicians. I also met Roger Corman's brother Gene, with whom I would work again in Israel. For me, it was a third stint at Weston and Baldonnel, and a third film about World War I. I was beginning to believe I was *in* the war! At night, my dreams were filled with the dogfights over Weston – overlaid with the radio voice from *The Adventures of Dan Dare, Pilot of the Future*, amidst strange scenarios, in which I found myself living back at my old home in

Williamstown! I realised that my daytime conversations and activities were leaking into my few hours of sleep; my home 'relocation' dream was probably triggered by the fact that, a couple of weeks into filming, Georgina had started talking about moving house.

Apparently, long discussions with her mother had been afoot for months, and it seemed that the pressure was on Georgina to move closer to Dun Laoghaire, as her mother tottered into old age. She was no longer able for the shop, and was talking about selling. Derek had started at Harold Primary School in Glasthule, so Dun Laoghaire was presented as the most convenient place to be – for everyone. Georgina and her mother had spotted a 'For Auction' sign outside a house on the seafront. I was invited to the viewing.

'Do you like it?' Georgina asked me.

'Let's go in and have a look first – before we're too late!' her mother said.

The house was massive; old – built in 1824 – in a terrace of imposing seafront properties stretching from Dun Laoghaire to Glasthule. It had been owned by an old lady, recently widowed, and before that had been one half of a hotel called 'Realt na Mara'. From the outside, Number 9, Windsor Terrace looked impressive. Inside, it was dark, with high ceilings, heavy mahogany furniture, black cast-iron fireplaces in every bedroom, a large marble fireplace in the 'drawing room', sombre embossed wallpaper everywhere – and no central heating. What it did have was potential, and Georgina and her mother seemed to like it – a lot. We decided to buy it. Sean and Catherine Corcoran offered to buy our house at Beechwood, sparing us the task of putting it on the market. With deposits paid and papers signed, we were excited about our new venture, but, taking another look at the property, I suddenly realised that the place needed a lot of work. I gritted my teeth and prepared to face the task ahead. Then the banks went on strike – and closed their doors for nine months. Nevertheless, we managed to secure the property. As filming of *The Red Baron* drew to an end, I was looking forward to getting my teeth into work on our new abode.

A few days before the film wrapped, I was having a cup of coffee and chatting to some of the drivers. We could hear the now-familiar sound of an aircraft overhead, the droning coming and going on the breeze. Then someone shouted 'Jesus!' We ran towards the airstrip, just in time to see one of our World War I planes in a nosedive, the pilot clearly struggling. He succeeded in taking the plane out of the dive and lurched in to land, skimming the ground. He almost made it,

My parents with Derek, on his First Communion Day
at No. 9 Windsor Terrace, Dun Laoghaire

but then the plane veered off to the right and the wing caught the side of a prop truck parked on the grass. The pilot lost control, the plane plunged forward into a thicket – and exploded in flames. Intense heat from the burning aviation fuel prevented any attempt at rescue. Christopher Boddington, the young British stunt pilot, had only been in the country for two days. Corman called a 'wrap' and cancelled the remainder of the aerial scenes.

Almost immediately, still shaken from this experience, I began work on *Zeppelin*, a World War I spy film starring Michael York and Elke Sommer. *Zeppelin* was shot mostly in England; then the producers came to Ireland to avail of the aircraft and the army and air-corps facilities and personnel – who were by now World War I 'veterans'. The dogfights were being filmed from a chopper off Brittas Bay. On the day of the shoot, I briefed Colonel Liddy, one of the air-corps pilots, on the pyrotechnics controls we had fitted in the cockpit, and then watched the five planes and the chopper take off and disappear eastwards. Hours passed, and there was no sign of their return. Then we heard the news that, as the chase was in progress, out to sea, off the Wicklow coast, Liddy, in one of the planes, had dived underneath the helicopter; when he rose out of the dive, his plane collided with the chopper and fell into the water. All four people aboard the helicopter – Skeets Kelly, the DOP; Burch Williams, the film's producer; the French chopper pilot and Colonel Liddy – died in the crash. It was a sombre conclusion to filming – and to my World War I career.

Needing a break, I took Georgina and Derek on holiday to Majorca. Back then, the Balearic Islands was an 'exotic' holiday destination which was just beginning to cash in on the tourist trade. We both loved the sun and it was our first trip to this part of the world. The two weeks away, among palm trees and sandy beaches, started a lifelong love affair with foreign holidays and travel for both of us. Europe was beginning to open up. Dana, an eighteen-year-old girl from Derry, had just won the Eurovision Song Contest for Ireland, with the song 'All Kinds of Everything'; Irish citizens were getting their heads around counting their money in 'decimals'; and trade agreements were being signed between the Irish and other European governments. Up the road, in Northern Ireland, the Troubles featured at the top of every news bulletin, and in February, a British soldier was shot, the first British casualty since the Forces of the Crown arrived in the province in 1969. In the south, unemployment figures were rising, and the country would stagger into a recession. My world was different: an idyllic place of drama and make-believe; of enjoyable work and a nice new home. Derek was the apple of my father's eye, and 'Grandad Johnston' was Derek's hero. They spent a lot of time in each other's company and my parents loved to come over and babysit of an evening, or take Derek to their house and spoil him rotten.

In 1971, the American director Robert Altman came to Ireland to make *Images*, a psychological thriller about one woman's schizophrenia. Susannah York played the very impressive lead. During the film, someone discovered that Susannah liked table tennis, and so after work some of the cast and crew would team up to play doubles. Susannah asked me to be her partner, and for a couple of hours we would leave the work behind, amid the whoops and hollers of the players and the reveille of bats on table-tennis balls. The effects on this film were pretty basic: bullet hits, stabbings and a bit of atmospherics – until the director called me with a 'special' request. It was 4.30 PM on a Friday and I was looking forward to a game of table tennis after work. Standing outside the door of the sound-stage with a few of the crew, I was feeling relaxed, and happy with the way the picture was going.

The First AD appeared. 'The director would like a word, Gerry,' he said. 'He's on the set.'

Altman wanted an actor's stomach 'blown out', the work of a double-barrelled shotgun.

'OK,' I told him. 'When do you want it for?'

'Tuesday,' he said.

'That's grand,' I replied.

'Thanks a lot, Gerry,' Altman said. 'Have a good weekend.'

In fact, it was not 'grand'. I didn't have enough latex in stock to make up the 'stomach' and wondered where I would find some – between now and Tuesday morning! I tore over to the production office.

'I need about fifty packets of condoms – urgently!' I blurted out. 'What's the quickest way I can get them?'

The production secretary, a woman in her late forties, stared at me in silence. A smile gathered about her lips and then she started laughing. 'Gosh, you must be planning a good weekend!' she joked.

'Not exactly,' I said, and briefly explained why I needed an ass-load of condoms – yesterday! I had a lot of work to do – light-years from the purpose for which condoms were invented!

Condoms are ideal for making blood bags for bullet hits, but they were illegal in Ireland in the 1970s, and up to then our only means of supply was through the UK effects crew, who shipped them over, stashed in among the rest of their equipment. I had some in stock, but not nearly enough to create the effect Altman wanted. Special-effects 'wizardry' was a bit like the magicians' magic circle: tricks were closely guarded secrets. Nowadays, our secrets are out there – thanks to books and TV programmes that go behind the scenes and reveal the techniques.

'OK,' the production secretary said, 'I'll see what I can do.'

She was still smiling as I left the office. I phoned the UK and asked a colleague to courier over some latex – ASAP.

'Not sure if I can get it to you in time, Gerry,' he said. 'I'll do my best.'

About midday on Monday, I was trying to piece together the makings of a blown-out 'stomach' – with what materials I had – when I got a call from the production office. The production secretary was waiting, drumming her fingers on the desk.

'Gerry,' she began. 'You and your bloody condoms!'

'What's up?' I asked.

'There's murder!' she declared. 'You're to go and see John Collingwood!'

Collingwood, the production accountant, was a quiet, fastidious Englishman who always dressed in a smart suit and carried a briefcase

Images: With my table-tennis partner, Susannah York

everywhere. His office was just down the hall. I knocked on the open door.

'You wanted to see me, John,' I said.

He was standing behind his desk, a cup of coffee halfway to his lips. He took a sip, left the cup on the desk and flopped into the chair.

'My young man,' he said.

I sat down and waited.

'I got a call in London at 4.50 PM on Friday, asking me to buy a selection of ladies' underwear – and a *gross* of bloody condoms!'

I was curious to know why he was buying ladies' underwear, but said nothing. Collingwood put his elbows on the desk and propped his weary face in his hands.

'I break my neck to go out on Saturday morning and buy these things,' he continued. 'I have to buy an overnight case to put them into. I get to Dublin Airport this morning – and I'm bloody well *arrested!*'

I had a vision of my condoms sitting in some back room in Customs. I would have to get on the blower to my effects guy in the UK and find out if he'd shipped the latex! I had less than twenty-four hours to produce Altman's stomach: hours of tedious work lay ahead!

'I was stopped and asked to open my luggage,' Collingwood was saying. 'I was so embarrassed! All this ladies' underwear, and then underneath – a stash of *condoms!* "Come this way, sir", they were saying. Then the police arrived. I was there for an hour, trying to explain – about special effects! I was late for work!'

I wasn't listening. 'Where are my condoms?' I blurted out.

Collingwood leaned back in his chair and rubbed his eyes.

'Oh, they're in *Production*,' he said, exasperated.

I was at the door.

'Oh, and tell Production to get Miss York's underwear down to Wardrobe *immediately*!'

The scene was shot on Tuesday, as scheduled. Altman was delighted with the stomach. The film was released in 1972 and entered in the Cannes Film Festival, where it won Susannah York an award for Best Actress. A short time later, a group of Irish women travelled by train from Northern Ireland, carrying cases full of condoms, and changed Irish legislation – and Irish society – forever!

When *Images* wrapped, Altman presented every member of the crew with a painted egg bearing the title of the film. Mine sits on my desk to this day, reminding me of changing times.

6

DRINKS WITH JOHN HUSTON –
AND I CAUSE A BOMB SCARE!

After *Images*, I did a short stint on *A Fistful of Dynamite*, directed by the Italian director Sergio Leone and starring James Coburn – who plays an exiled IRA man with a knack for explosives – and Rod Steiger as a Mexican bandit. Rehearsing for a scene in which James Coburn is shot, I listened to about five minutes of animated conversation, in Italian, with much arm-waving and bits of strange-sounding English words, until it dawned on me that the actor was scared! Leone wanted me to 'take the hit'. I stripped to the waist and shot myself, to demonstrate for the director – and the actor – that the bullet hit on bare skin could be done safely. 'Mmm, that-a will-a be good,' was all Leone said.

Sergio Leone was born into the cinema. His mother was an Italian actress and his father was one of Italy's cinema pioneers. In his teens, he began working as an assistant director. Towards the end of the 1950s, he began to write screenplays and eventually began directing. His second film, *A Fistful of Dollars*, launched the former TV cowboy, Clint Eastwood, to cinema fame in 1964. Leone later declined offers to direct *The Godfather* (1972) so that he could pursue his own dream project, which became *Once Upon a Time in America* (1984). To me, his biggest film was *Ben Hur*, which I had loved way back in the days before I had any interest in how movies were made – and even less interest in who made them! Now, working in the film business, I had to get to know these people – and what they wanted from me. Again, I found myself working with a man who had made famous films, and all I was worried about was trying to understand his accent!

A short time after finishing *A Fistful of Dynamite*, my first supervisor, 'Ronnie' – Ron Ballanger – showed up for *The MacKintosh Man*, starring Paul Newman and James Mason. His co-supervisor was Cliff Richardson, with whom I had also worked on *Zeppelin*. The English technicians Joe Fitt, Bob Nugent and Alan Bernard made up the rest of the effects crew. This time, we were in the cold war, on a story about a spy (Newman) who is taken prisoner, escapes and ends up in Ireland. I found it boring. But then I'm not paid to like the script, I just provide the 'action'! The legendary John Huston was directing this one, parts of which were shot in Galway, where we had to 'burn' a huge mansion: an old derelict house, as big as a castle, dressed to make it look habitable.

Given the times that were in it, many considered Ireland unsafe. Huston was regarded as being particularly brave to come here. But then, he was interested in Ireland for reasons other than as a cheap filming location. I had bumped into him in the canteen at Ardmore Studios, and we got talking. 'I love Ireland,' he told me, 'and I want to see the industry flourish here.'

Huston had already made *Sinful Davey* at Ardmore in 1968, starring a very young John Hurt and a host of popular Irish actors. In 1972, he sat on the board of a company that had bought Ardmore Studios, and I believe he submitted a report on the industry to the then Minister for Industry and Commerce, George Colley. Colley introduced a Film Industry Bill in parliament, but the recommendations of Huston's report never saw the light of day. Following a general election, Colley was replaced as Minister by Justin Keating.

Huston was sympathetic towards film workers, whose skills and patience, along with their good humour, he admired. He wasn't giving up. 'As a technician, you can keep your ear to the ground,' he told me. 'Ask the production to give you my office number in America and let me know what's happening.'

I didn't see him again until we started shooting *The MacKintosh Man*. It was winter, and the light faded at four in the afternoon. The shooting crew wrapped early – they were the shortest working days we had ever done. Some weeks into the shoot, I was privileged to be among a select few who were invited for drinks at Huston's house, the eighteenth-century St Cleran's Manor, now a luxury hotel.

On account of the Northern troubles, extra security was required, during both preparation and shooting. Being the 'local', I got the job of arranging for the movement and storage of explosives. I found out the name of the sergeant at the army base, and storage was sorted. We were now obliged to have Garda escorts when transporting materials from storage to location. I had to liaise with the local Gardaí to arrange for escort duty and security on location. I was also on the trail of something else. The hills of Connemara are famous – in story and in song – for their poitín stills: clandestine 'manufacturing and retail outlets' for the local brew, which is purported to cure all ills! I didn't need poitín for medicinal purposes; I just wanted to try it. Since it was believed that nothing moved in the Irish countryside without the local 'constabulary' knowing about it, I thought the Garda station would be a good place to ask – but not yet; I had more serious business to attend to first.

At the Garda station, I was told that I would be assigned an escort and asked to wait. After about fifteen minutes, a lanky individual, standing at about six foot four, appeared. He was dressed in civvies. 'I'll be thravelling with you,' he growled.

I looked up at him: the thought of travelling for the next week with this character filled me with dread. He seemed to have been born with a scowl. Sure enough, the journey was painful; trying to make conversation was like trying to get blood out of a turnip! His height forced him to sit in the car with his head bent over to one side: it was comical.

On the third day, as I was leaving him back to the station, I struck up conversation with him.

'I hear the poitín's great around here. I wonder if I could get some?' No answer. By now, I was accustomed to his silence.

'That's *illegal*!' he growled.

I nearly jumped out of the seat with the shock!

'I used to go out to the islands. I'd shniff these lads out. The shtills were in caves, in farmyards, and I confishcated the lot! There's none of it to be had. I made shure there was nothin' left!'

'Oh, I see,' I said.

He was now in full flight. 'I'd go out in a shmall boat, with me oil-shkins and wellingtons – sometimes in the dead o' night, with the wind howlin' and the waves throwin' me about. I nearly losht me life on the rocks around some of them islands… I'd get the coils, maybe, but the resht of the shtills would be hidden all over the place. Them black-guards would know when I was comin'. But I got them all in the end!'

In no time, we were at the station, and I dropped him off. Next morning, dense fog had descended. Driving back to the station that evening, I could hardly see where I was going. With no road markings,

I was relying on the dry-stone wall to my right to guide me and was doing about ten miles an hour, dreading the time it would take to get to the station and be rid of the cop, who might as well have been a tailor's dummy in the passenger seat!

'Terrible fog,' I said.

No answer.

'I hope the weather will be better tomorrow,' I said.

No answer.

'Shlow down!'

My heart nearly stopped. I shifted the car into second gear and slowed to a crawl.

'Now, when I tell you to shtop, you shtop!' he said.

Chills ran up my spine. We were in the middle of nowhere, enveloped in thick, swirling mist.

'Shtop!'

I stuck the car to the road. My passenger opened the door, unfolding his lanky frame, and got out. Then his face suddenly reappeared inches from mine. 'You wait here!' he ordered, pulled up the collar of his big overcoat and disappeared.

I hit the hazard lights and waited. Then, through my wing mirror, I saw two shadowy figures by the dry-stone wall, about fifteen feet behind the car. One was the plain-clothes Garda, the other was a smaller man, dressed in a dark overcoat, the collar up around his ears, and wearing a flat cap. I waited nervously, the engine ticking over. The figures parted. The small man disappeared, like a ghost, into the fog. My travelling companion approached the car, opened the boot and dropped something in. He then came up alongside the car, opened the passenger door and folded himself into the seat.

'Prosheed!' he said.

When we reached the station, he uncoiled himself again.

'I'll shee ye tomorra.'

'OK,' I said. 'Don't forget your stuff in the back.'

'What shtuff?' he said. 'Go on, now, and I'll see ye in the mornin'.'

Afraid to argue, I put the boot down — fog or no fog — and headed for the Corrib Hotel. This guy gave me the creeps!

Back at the hotel, I opened the boot. Inside, I found a heavy plastic bag containing six bottles of what looked like crystal-clear water. For a second, I thought he'd given me holy water. Maybe he thought I needed it! I unscrewed the cap on one of the bottles and sniffed. It didn't smell like water. Then, I realised I had a boot-load of 'illegal' poitín! Over dinner, I told the story to my colleagues. They were gagging with laughter!

'What's poitín like?' Cliff asked, recovering himself

'I believe it's like firewater!' I told him. 'Great for rheumatism – and great for your sex life!'

'Cor, I could do with some of that, mate!' Cliff laughed.

The following day, as I drove to the Garda station, the sun was beaming down over a sleepy Galway city, but an icy wind blew down from the north. 'Longshanks' folded himself into the passenger seat.

'Lovely day,' I said.

No answer.

'By the way, thanks very much for the poitín.'

He never took his eyes off the road.

'What poitín?' he growled.

'The poitín you left in the boot last night,' I reminded him.

'I left no poitín in the boot!' he said. 'I don't know what ye're talkin' about!'

On location, the boys were in fits! Cliff joined us as we huddled around a Burko, trying to warm ourselves on hot coffee. He was probably in his early seventies, frail and plagued with aches and pains, and feeling the cold. I fetched a bottle of poitín from the car, opened it and poured some into a mug.

'Here, try that,' I said, handing it to Cliff.

He took a sip and almost choked!

'Jeez, mate! That's de-de-deadly!'

'Would you like to try some?' I asked Alan.

'OK, mate – can't be that bad!'

But he too nearly asphyxiated himself, knocking it back, like a tough cowboy in the spaghetti Westerns. Bob decided to try some, sipping it carefully as if it was boiling tea. Within minutes, their faces were glowing – and the weather didn't seem so cold, after all! The word was out: 'moonshine' could be had!

Paul Newman was staying, with his wife and children – and the children's nanny – at our hotel. My sister Barbara had been badgering me to get him to sign a picture of him which was one of her treasured possessions. One evening, I approached him in the hotel lobby and asked him to autograph the photo.

'I'm afraid I don't sign autographs,' he said.

'It's for my sister,' I said, lamely.

Newman paused, his vivid blue piercing.

'Well,' he said at last, 'I will make an exception, this time.'

Later that evening, I offered him a bottle of poitín, as a 'thank you' gift. He smiled and accepted it graciously. As far as I know, Huston was already a connoisseur, with his own supply — an appropriate accompaniment, I would imagine, to a fine cigar of an evening.

One evening, halfway through the shoot, I was back at the hotel when I discovered I had forgotten to leave my firing equipment — batteries, pyro-testers and rolls of tubing — at the army storage unit, along with the pyros. Thinking it would be too risky to leave the box in the car overnight, I took it in to the hotel and asked the hall porter if he would keep it somewhere safe until the morning.

'Certainly,' he said. I'll put it away before I go off duty.'

I left it with him and showered, changed and went down to dinner. In the middle of the main course, a uniformed Garda appeared in the dining room and shouted: 'Everyone out! Bomb scare!' The whole hotel was evacuated. Various people, including Paul Newman and his family, were gathered in the car park — some wrapped in blankets over their night attire — in the bitterly cold night air. The Gardaí herded the crowd to a safe distance, traffic was stopped, and the area was cordoned off. I noticed a member of an army bomb disposal unit, padded like Billy Bunter in layers of protective clothing, carrying a black box out the front door of the hotel.

'That's my box!' I said to Cliff.

'What? Jeez, mate! You'd better tell them!'

I approached one of the Gardaí, who took me up to a Garda sergeant, who in turn took me to the army sergeant.

'This man says that's his box,' he said.

'What's in it?' the army sergeant demanded.

I described the equipment inside. He ordered me to open it. I flipped the catches and opened the lid, to reveal the contents. We learned subsequently that the hall porter had gone home, forgetting to put my box away. When the night porter came on duty, he spotted it behind reception — and immediately called the Gardaí. With the danger over, the shivering staff and guests began to troop back inside. In the foyer, Cliff nudged me in the ribs.

'Could do with some of that moonshine right now, mate!'

7

ZARDOZ

In 1972, I found myself on a very unusual film called *Zardoz*, directed by the English director John Boorman. John had come to Ireland in 1969 for post-production on his film *Leo the Last*. He and his German wife Christel bought a house, on impulse, at an auction, and following the success of his film *Deliverance* they set up home in Annamoe, a tiny village in the Wicklow Mountains. I had been called in by producer Charles Orme and asked to 'run' *Zardoz*. I hired a team of technicians – colleagues from the UK – and we set up shop at Ardmore. *Zardoz* is a futuristic fantasy, set in the year 2293, when the world as we know it has disappeared. There is a genteel world of elite intellectuals, and a world of abject poverty and mayhem – the world of the 'Brutals', ruled by 'Zardoz', a terrifying stone head that flies across the land. But a 'new and perfect breed' of man emerges from among the Brutals, in the form of 'Zed', played by Sean Connery. Zed succeeds in penetrating the idyllic and unnatural world, where the elite have closeted themselves – safe from the war-torn, polluted world outside – and destroys it.

The costumes, designed by John's wife Christel, were sparse; Connery is dressed only in a loin cloth and fishermen's wader-type leather boots, his torso draped in bullets, and a revolver always at the ready. This rough, macho character was a strange departure from the suave James Bond we had been used to, and there was a lot of speculation among the 'experts' on the crew as to how Boorman had managed to entice Connery to work on the film. But I had other things on my mind. I had my first credit as a supervisor on *Images* and I needed a few more credits to qualify for my supervisor's ticket. *Zardoz* would be my second such credit, and I was keen to make it work well.

Some reviews have considered the on-screen effects on *Zardoz* to be minimal. Behind the scenes, it was another story – everything from a giant flying head (where the 'Vortex society' are residing) to tons of 'mud' in which two actresses wrestle – stark naked! In between these two scenarios, the film called for skeletons, dust, cobwebs, bullet hits, fires, atmospherics and weather – both interior and exterior. Every page in the script threw up something out of the ordinary.

Recently, I was browsing through a glossary of film terminology at the back of a publication about film-making. Beside 'Special Effects', I found: 'Trick photography and miniatures, to give a realistic effect'. I was rather disappointed, particularly as there are more comprehensive and more up-to-date descriptions on the Internet these days. Ten or fifteen years ago, I could have papered the walls of my workshop with applications from young students wanting to get into special effects who had absolutely no idea what the production of effects involved. For a number of years, I often toyed with the idea of setting up an effects training facility, and during the late 1990s, I was asked by two separate institutions to submit proposals and course outlines. This I did, but heard nothing in response. Back in the 1970s, when John Boorman became chairman of the new National Film Studios of Ireland, he wanted to set up a film school. Before him, Huston had harboured the same idea, and before Huston, other individuals wanted to establish a facility with proper technical training. It never happened. Ardmore Studios had been through several hands and was plagued by financial problems. In 1969, John Boorman took his newly made *Leo the Last* into a rundown facility that no longer employed a full-time workforce, with clapped-out equipment that couldn't be used. Three years later, as he went into production with *Zardoz*, little had changed, and training facilities remained a pipe dream. Film schools later offered three-year training courses in every aspect of film-making, and although I believe that their 'effects' modules have been expanded, they still offer only a smattering of physical and pyrotechnic effects.

As far as the Irish trade union SIPTU was concerned, Effects was lumped in with the 'Art Department', SIPTU having ignored submissions setting out the criteria for effects as established by BECTU (the Broadcasting Entertainment Cinematograph and Theatre Union) in the UK. Consequently, without adequate training and grading in place, Irish insurance companies wouldn't touch special-effects technicians, beyond a blanket policy covering the whole production. Many years ago, one Lloyd's underwriter offered me public liability for a premium of £9,000 a year – sterling! In truth, because I lived and worked in Ireland, he didn't want to know. For more than twenty of my forty years in Ireland's film industry, it was a haphazard business – awash with bureaucracy and ignorance – with special effects as the 'poor relation' to all the other departments. It was through my membership of BECTU that I finally qualified for public-liability insurance.

My first production meeting as a head of department (HOD) on *Zardoz* was held in a green hut on the lawn at Ardmore. In a large timber-panelled room, the meeting was about to start. Geoff Unsworth was the DOP, Tony Pratt was the production designer and Simon Relph was the first assistant director. These were the key people – my direct links to the information regarding production requirements. I needed to work closely with them, under the director's instructions – particularly with Tony Pratt – in order to work out what I would have to make up. We all sat around the long trestle table. Boorman, with his hair pulled back in a ponytail, walked in.

'Good morning, everyone,' he said.

After we had introduced ourselves, Boorman flicked through a sheaf of paperwork and then addressed himself to Geoff.

'So, let's talk about how we'll light it,' he began, then stood up and walked out of the room! Geoff followed him out to the corridor. We waited. From the corridor, we could hear a muffled discussion. After about ten minutes, they reappeared. Boorman paced the room, explaining shots – what the lighting entailed, and so on – then said, 'I want to talk about some of the sets, Tony' and walked out again! Tony Pratt duly rose and followed him outside. This scenario was repeated with another HOD. I hadn't been privy to any of the discussion – all of which was relevant to my work. I hadn't seen the drawings of the sets and hadn't a notion about costumes, or what effects would pertain to actors. Having read the script, I had a million questions. Boorman reappeared. He paced up and down for a few minutes.

'We'll talk about the special effects,' he said – and again walked out. I remained at the table. Seconds later, he was back at the door.

'I'm talking to *you*,' he said, glaring at me.

'Mr Boorman, with all due respects, this is a strange way to have a meeting. I need to discuss the script with the other HODs as well as yourself,' I began.

'Who employed you on this picture?' he shouted.

'Your associate producer, Charles Orme,' I replied.

After a long pause, he sat down – and the meeting continued.

Zardoz: With Sean Connery on the set;
stills photographer Johnny Morris is in the background

Around midday, we were distracted by a commotion outside on the lawn. There was a knock on the door and one of the assistants came in.

'We have some people for you and the director to see, Simon,' he said.

'Oh, yes, thank you. John,' Simon Ralph said, turning to John, 'shall we have a look?'

'Yes, sure,' the director said.

Simon nodded to the assistant, who disappeared outside. The director and his first assistant went over to the window and stood looking out. On the lawn, a crowd of young men and women, most of them wrapped in rugs or blankets, hopped around in bare feet, trying to keep warm! The director opened the window and called out: 'Have them move around a bit.' The assistant issued instructions and the crowd of about forty immediately began prancing around, arms waving, bending forward, affecting dance movements. Blankets were slipping, revealing the odd flash of a bare bosom, or a bare bottom! Boorman stood and observed, pointing to various people in the crowd.

'We'll go with her . . . and her . . . and him . . . and that blonde over there . . . ' he was saying.

Simon was nodding. 'OK, I'll tell the AD to hold on to those and let the rest go,' he said, and hurried off.

I still wondered about sets and costumes – and why the 'nudist' auditions on the lawn? It transpired that my most challenging effects on this picture would involve naked bodies floating in midair. I had to make steel uprights: each one a single rod with two footrests. The naked actors stood on these, the rod hidden behind them, suspended from a hook just behind their heads. In a shot of naked bodies on a glass roof, the camera, looking from below, sees the naked bodies lying against the glass. On top of that, the director wanted water running down the glass. Cold water was out of the question, and so the water had to be heated to body temperature.

Well into filming, we were shooting a scene at Hollybrook House, less than a mile from the studios. Effects had built a machine that spewed out bread rolls – much like a tennis-ball machine – through circles of steel tubes, to create the effect of bread falling from the sky: 'manna from Heaven'! From behind this giant machine, my crew were operating steam and smoke machines, while I supervised from my position 'on the floor', beside the camera. We had done several rehearsals and then we 'went for the take'. Simon, the first AD, called 'Action!' However, our machines, which had been running smoothly right up to that second, were now producing neither smoke nor steam.

'What's happening back there?' the director called.

'I'm not sure,' I replied. 'Give me a minute.'

Behind the set, one of the electricians was checking the generator.

'The genny spiked,' he told me. 'I think the power surge has blown the fuses.'

Zardoz: With one of the flying heads

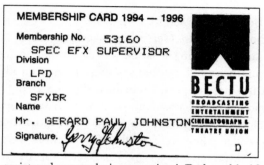

A registered pyrotechnic supervisor! (Red-card holder)

As I was heading towards my crew, I heard 'Special Effects . . . bloody idiot!' echo loudly around the set. The whole crew fell silent.

Gathering my wits, I informed my staff of the genny problem and they set about replacing fuses and doing repairs. It would take several minutes. I needed a cup of tea or coffee to settle my nerves. Near the catering wagon, I met one of the ADs.

'Did the director just say something derogatory about me?' I asked.

'Gosh, Gerry, I don't know,' he answered, looking at the ground.

I nursed my hurt – and my pride – until after we got the shot. As the cameras were setting up for the next shot, I approached Boorman.

'John, you made a remark about me earlier in front of the whole crew. Right?'

He looked away, with a wry grin, and said nothing.

'We had a problem back there, but it wasn't our fault.'

He still said nothing, just looked at me in stony silence. I pulled the burnt-out fuses from my pocket and showed them to him. He remained silent.

'Well, John, if I don't get an apology, I'm taking my crew and my equipment off this picture at four o'clock this afternoon.'

Just then, another AD appeared. I turned and walked back to my crew. One of the cameramen caught up with me and told me that the cameras had gone down at the same time.

'But we couldn't say a word!' he said. 'Freaky, or what?'

Just after lunch, Boorman sought me out. He threw his arms around me and made some joke about 'mishaps' and being 'under pressure'. We shook hands.

In the weeks following the incident, I was working late into the night, back at the studios. It must have been after 2 AM when the door opened and Boorman walked in.

'How's the work going, Gerry?' he asked, casually.

'Fine,' I said, wondering what he was doing here in the middle of the night. From then on, he would show up unannounced at all hours, to talk about the effects shots. I remained on my guard.

But the picture had its moments of fun. A scene, once again in the grounds of Hollybrook House, involved a male and a female baboon – and a chap called Mick, in a gorilla suit. All three were ensconced behind bars in three separate cages. I had made up the front bars of these big animal cages, using light tubular steel. Inside, only light wire mesh separated the three compartments, with the 'gorilla' in the middle. A few minutes into rehearsal, the male baboon began to act up, trying to reach the female! With bared teeth, he began chopping at the wire mesh! The keeper was off the set, having a coffee. Before he could be called back, the male baboon got an arm through the mesh. Mick grabbed the bars, pulled them apart, King Kong-style, and tumbled out onto the ground! The crew scattered in all directions and Mick made a run for it, the gorilla suit coming undone at the back as he ran. With the baboon still in hot pursuit, Mick's bare bottom disappeared among the crowd. The love-struck baboon shinned up a tree. Time dragged on, as the keeper tried to coax him down. Eventually, he was sedated with a tranquiliser gun and recaptured.

Some weeks later, it was the director who found himself at the centre of another drama – at the wrong end of a gun barrel! We were filming in the mountains. In the scene, Zed shoots a row of the 'wild' people in a trench. Boorman decided that he would stand in as one of them!

'Keep your head down, John,' Connery laughed, as he took aim.

Boorman's head popped out of the trench – just as Connery fired! The director was peppered with powder from the blank and had to receive medical assistance! I could imagine the newspaper headline: 'BOND SHOOTS MOVIE DIRECTOR'.

Engineering, prosthetics, plumbing water and water heaters, making up two heads – one measuring three feet by six feet, the other a giant flying head, suspended from a crane above the cliffs at Luggala – all necessitated long hours in my workshop, working closely with Construction, and long days and nights on the set. At Luggala, the wind, humming along the wires, elicited a remark from one of the drivers: 'Now, you're a musician as well, Gerry!' I needed a holiday. But three or four weeks before the end of the picture, I got a call from

Zardoz: On the mirror maze set, photographing a bullet hit on the glass

Bernie Williams, a line producer. Bernie had a film running in Waterford. 'When can you start?' he asked.

'Well, it'll be about another three weeks before I finish this picture,' I told him.

'Great,' he said. 'Look forward to seeing you then.'

Later that day, I was on a sound-stage at the studios when a call came through. I was standing next to the phone and picked it up. A man's voice asked if he could speak with John Boorman.

'Can I ask who's calling?'

'My name's Kubrick,' the voice said.

'Hold on a minute.'

John was standing, talking with the cameraman.

'Telephone call for you, John,' I said.

'Who is it?' he asked.

'A Mr Kubrick,' I replied.

'Tell him I'll call him back in ten minutes.'

'He'll call you back in ten minutes,' I told the caller.

'Much appreciated. Thank you.'

A few hours later, as fate would have it, I was again standing by the phone when it rang: 'Mr Kubrick' was calling for Boorman.

'I can't talk to him just now!' John snapped.

'Ahm, Mr Boorman is busy right now,' I told Kubrick.

Wrapping for the day, one of the 'sparks' joked about my 'hobnobbing with famous directors' – and I discovered who Kubrick was! 'He's about to shoot a picture in Waterford,' I was told.

Three weeks later, just days before my contract finished, I went to say goodbye to John.

'Where are you going?' he asked.

'I'm starting work on another picture in Waterford,' I told him.

His face took on an odd look.

'I have more effects scenes for you,' he said.

The next day, I arrived at the studios to find that an extra week of effects work had been added to the schedule. I phoned Waterford to explain, hoping that I wouldn't lose the picture. Bernie understood; I had another week's grace.

Now a freelance technician and having worked on several projects, I had amassed quite an amount of equipment: firing boxes, smoke machines, wind machines, and a good supply of tools. Storage and working space was becoming a problem. But *Barry Lyndon* was well under way, and I packed my bags once more and headed south-east to Waterford.

8

BARRY LYNDON – AND A ROYAL HANDSHAKE

Starring Ryan O'Neill, the film – about an Irish eighteenth-century rogue called Redmond Barry who changes his name to 'Barry Lyndon' and joins (and deserts) two warring armies – almost didn't make it to the screen. The production had encountered problems from the start. I heard that the director had been at loggerheads with the British union over pay – 'country allowances' – and had moved the film unit to shoot on his own land. When that didn't solve the problem, he finally shipped it to Ireland.

In Waterford, an air of uncertainty still hung about, as I began to get acquainted with the crew, find out what was needed, and take stock. I was told that Stanley Kubrick was a stickler for detail and would walk off the set on the slightest whim. His unrelenting demands of commitment and perfection from cast and crew had by now become legendary. Actors would be required to perform dozens of takes with no breaks. Almost every week, someone from among the cast or crew was fired: Kubrick was God. I was still finding my feet in the business, and although I wasn't the effects supervisor on this one, I was keen to do my job well. I learned that the work of the effects department would involve weaponry and battle materials such as muskets and gunpowder charges – on top of explosions and fires, and 'blood and gore'. I now had to take my mind out of the twenty-third century and into the eighteenth – and this time, the English were fighting the French, instead of the Germans!

Kubrick seemed to have graduated from the 'David Lean Academy of Directing', taking all day to shoot a scene, turning up at a location, where everything was set up and ready to roll, then deciding that he didn't like the location. We'd all have to dismantle our gear and spend the next couple of hours moving the wagons half a mile away, to another spot. On a particularly trying day, a duelling scene wasn't happening; the muskets wouldn't fire, and the director wasn't happy with the distance between the actors.

'We'll try and get this tomorrow,' he said.

They didn't work the next day either. I was asked to take a look at the muskets and see if I could do something. I worked late, modifying the chambers and the firing mechanisms, and the following day I presented a new theory about the shot to the director.

'The actors can stand within six feet of each other,' I said.

'Really? Are you sure?' Kubrick asked.

'Trust me,' I told him.

'OK, let's see what you've got,' he said.

I went to fetch the muskets, and as I walked back to the set I came upon someone from another department – banging his head against a car! Other crew members rushed to him, holding him, trying to calm him down.

'He's had it,' someone said. 'This picture is getting to some people!'

The man was exhausted. I continued back to the set; 'God' was waiting. We did a rehearsal. I was one of the duelling pair. The muskets worked a treat, with a very impressive flame, and Kubrick was happy. From then on, he seemed to take a keen interest in the effects department.

At one of our early meetings, Kubrick, standing on the set, asked me for a full inventory of the pyrotechnic materials and equipment being used by the effects department on the film. I listed off the dozens of smoke bombs, mortars, squibs and so forth that I had in stock. Kubrick looked as if he was in a trance, the soup he was swigging from a mug dribbling down his beard!

'OK, double that,' he said, and wandered off, leaving me to recover from near-nausea. But despite his culinary imperfections, his eccentricities and temperamental ways, and the exhaustive working days he demanded of people (with production meetings called at 5 AM, and long hours on set), I got along very well with him. His curiosity and attention to detail was a little unnerving at first, but I soon understood his ways and what he wanted.

A scene filmed against a tree and lit only by a candle was shot using a 50mm lens which was built by the Carl Zeiss Company for

NASA and is used in still cameras. This lens, modified with a Kollmorgen adaptor, resulted in stunning shots. Rumour had it that Kubrick had bought the lens from NASA. Whether he had or not, he knew how to use it; he was a true craftsman.

But another scene, involving the Irish actor Godfrey Quigley, didn't go as well. We had a new, sophisticated sonic firing mechanism. Godfrey was wired up with a bullet hit, and we went into rehearsal. Just as the charge was set and the power switched on, Godfrey got a fit of coughing. The charge went off, and 'blood' spewed out of his shirt! It was a replay of the incident on *Darling Lili*, the plane exploding prematurely due to interference from model-aircraft controls half a mile away. Wardrobe replaced Godfrey's shirt, and we went again, but for me, it was another reminder to avoid the newfangled firing equipment.

Meanwhile, a new twist to the Troubles in the North, this time a spate of bank robberies, bomb hoaxes and kidnappings, brought an abrupt end to filming. We were back in Dublin, and as the unit set up for a night shoot at a location near the airport, news reached us that there had been number of bomb hoaxes around the city. Some time in the late evening, the production manager asked me if I'd seen the director. I hadn't. He then asked someone else, and then someone else. Three hours passed as we hung about with nothing to do. Eventually, we were told to 'wrap'. Speculation about the director's disappearance was rife. It was not until the following day that I learned that he had left on the ferry for England. According to rumours, he'd received a 'suspicious' phone call and had vanished without warning. Apparently, Kubrick and his family were no strangers to threats, and took them seriously. They had received death threats following the controversy surrounding his film *A Clockwork Orange*, and when they travelled, they travelled separately.

Following Kubrick's unscheduled departure from Dublin, the production's publicity department issued a press release saying that the shooting schedule in Ireland had been completed and that the final scenes would be shot in England. The film *was* completed in England, and was released in 1974. It picked up three Academy awards — for Art Direction, Costume Design and Music. For me, it was simply another job done; time to move on to the next one. I was thirty-one years old and was on my way to becoming a graded supervisor within BECTU.

My BECTU membership card

At home, Georgina had been feeling a bit down and had been having some irregular bleeding. The doctor told her she'd had a miscarriage. For weeks, she was depressed. I thought a holiday might help, and we booked a short break in Cyprus. The alluring beaches and vineyards, olive trees and ancient ruins offered the right mix of otherworldliness, and we explored old stone villages and lay in the sun, savouring every minute. Georgina loved the place and vowed to return. But in July 1974, Turkey launched an air and sea-based invasion of Cyprus, and the resulting instability in the country put us off going there again.

I counted myself lucky to be able to take my family on holidays such as this. If only a few more productions like *Barry Lyndon* would roll in. But we returned to a lull in film work. Ardmore Studios was still in limbo. A group called the Irish Film Workers' Association was formed to try to save the studios from land developers. Ardmore was a prime piece of real estate which had caught the attention of speculators. We feared that it would be turned into a shopping centre. Film unions as such did not exist in Ireland; the only general union was the Irish Transport & General Workers' Union, and carpenters, plasterers and electricians belonged to separate unions. I had joined the Film Workers' Association, feeling – like everyone else – that we needed strong representation, not just to save Ardmore but to promote the growth of the industry in Ireland.

A delegation from the association met with SIPTU representative Mick McEvoy at Liberty Hall. 'You're all potential employers!' he argued, then suggested that we apply to the Union of Journalists. This cemented my conviction that we were in the backwoods as far as union support went: England, mainland Europe and America were light-years ahead of us.

In the outside world, two years of bomb hoaxes had desensitised the population and left the citizens of Dublin unprepared when the real bombs went off in the heart of the city, in May 1974, causing deaths, injuries and thousands of pounds' worth of damage to city-centre business premises. And as the Troubles raged on all over the North, foreign film-makers were put off coming to Ireland. I was lucky to find work on a couple of smaller productions, including a small-budget production called *Give Me Your Poor*. Otherwise, I occupied myself with doing DIY around the house and keeping in contact with colleagues in the UK.

My closest associations were with England, as I had trained — hands-on, mostly with English supervisors — on enough feature films to earn membership of the British union the ACTT (the Association of Cinematograph Television and Allied Technicians, later BECTU) as a technician. The ACTT had a grading system, which also carried affordable public-liability insurance, and the slew of high-profile productions and well-known directors I had worked with — most of them award-winners at Cannes, the BAFTAs and the Oscars — stood me in good stead. Kubrick and *Barry Lyndon* were the icing on the cake. The ACTT was a professionally run outfit with hundreds of members throughout the UK. Thanks to my Grandfather Johnston, who was born on the Scottish–English border, I held a British as well as an Irish passport and was eligible for ACTT membership — in the London region! As a registered technician, I was also eligible to work anywhere in the world. I travelled to London to find out more about the union and its working relationship with producers. I was also applying to be graded as a supervisor. At ACTT headquarters, a committee of supervisors and ACTT officials viewed my credentials. But some weeks later, I heard through the grapevine that my application for a supervisor's ticket was being blocked.

'Why?' I asked my 'source'.

'Because you'll be taking work away from the guys over here!' he said.

'Who's blocking me?'

'Can't tell you that,' he said.

I decided to pay the UK another visit.

Pinewood Studios was the HQ of film-making in Britain, a beautiful building with ornate carved ceilings and a restaurant with white linen and real silverware. Producers, directors and their advisors often held meetings in a bar just off the restaurant, while in another building, a canteen with Formica tables and tubular steel chairs was for the 'rank and file'. When I arrived at Pinewood, a film was in progress, and I knew that most of the special-effects fraternity would be working on it. It was just coming up to lunchtime, and I reckoned I would find them in the restaurant. I spotted one of the supervisors and approached him.

'Oi, what are you doing 'ere, mate?' he said.

'I hear someone from among the UK supervisors is blocking my supervisor's ticket!' I said, cutting to the chase.

'I don't know what you're talking about, mate,' he said.

'Well, I just want to make it known to whoever's blocking me that I'll take my case to a higher authority and . . . '

At that precise moment, a member of the studio security staff walked in. For a moment, I thought he was coming to remove me from the premises.

'Everyone!' he called. 'We have a very important visitor, so I'd like you all to move into the bar for a few minutes. This won't take long, and could you be very quiet for a little while. Thank you.'

We were duly assembled in the bar, and then a couple of uniformed policemen strode in, closely followed by several burly bodyguards and, in their midst, Queen Elizabeth! Her Majesty approached the line of people along the bar and began shaking hands, getting closer and closer to where I was standing. And then she was there, with a limp, gloved hand holding mine! I vaguely remember mumbling something about being Irish. A flicker of an eyelash, and the Queen moved on. Minutes later, the royal tour was over, the entourage swept out of the room, and everyone headed back to work. Two weeks later, my supervisor's ticket arrived in the post. I smiled. Maybe Her Majesty had put in a good word for me!

In July 1975, Ardmore Studios was bought on behalf of the Irish government by Radio Telefís Éireann (RTÉ), the National Radio and Televison Broadcasting Service. RTÉ would manage the studios in a caretaker capacity, pending the establishment of a body by the then Minister for Industry and Commerce. This was reportedly intended to safeguard the employment of skilled Irish film workers, thus ensuring their continued service to the industry, with a promise, yet again, to set up a film school to train Irish technicians. For the first time in years, the studio had begun to make a profit, largely due to commercials made by RTÉ, and some work on *Barry Lyndon*. Finally, a new board of directors was formed, and Ardmore's name was changed to the National Film Studios of Ireland – with the director John Boorman as chairman. Sheamus Smith, who had been a cameraman and later a producer with RTÉ, was appointed managing director. Other members of the board included the cameraman Vincent Corcoran, who in recent years had turned to directing films. Dermot O'Sullivan was caretaker manager; his first task was to sort and overhaul any salvageable equipment and get rid of the rest.

During *Barry Lyndon*, I had been renting a section of the construction shop to store my growing collection of effects equipment. Ever the optimist, I anticipated more work coming in, and I felt that I needed a workshop. Before it fell into the hands of the film moguls, Ardmore was part of the Meath Estate, owned by Lord Meath's family, with a working farm and an orchard. The orchard and walled garden were a bit like the *Secret Garden* – untended, yet still producing fruit: beautiful apples, pears and plums, and red and black currants. Next to the orchard, the cowshed, hayshed and dairy languished behind shoulder-high weeds. The farm had supported a herd of the finest Jersey cattle, one of a small number of Jersey herds in Ireland. Gilbert (Gillie) White kept a pig farm nearby, and he was a frequent visitor to the estate, collecting the slops from the kitchen at the big house, and then later from the caterers who serviced the film industry. Gillie and I got acquainted, and he loved to reminisce about the 'old days', when Ardmore was in its heyday.

'By the way,' I asked him one day, 'is it haunted?'

'Why do you ask?' he said.

I told him about a recent strange experience I had had while alone one evening in the toilets – which were located, along with the bar and kitchen, in the basement of the house. I was washing my hands at a basin when the door behind me started opening and closing and the temperature plummeted. I ran! Minutes later, as I drove out through the main gate, I stopped at Security and, still shaken, blurted out my story. The guard just smiled. 'Ah, yeah, sure the place is haunted. Even the guard dogs won't go into the basement!' he said.

'So they say,' Gillie said, with a laugh, when he heard my story.

One legend had it that one of the owners, a sea captain or a military dignitary, then in his old age, married a young maidservant. Before he died, he requested that his ashes be sprinkled on the estate. But lo and behold, the flighty young widow ran off with the gardener and, in a fit of bravado, sprinkled the ashes up the mountains at the source of the Dargle river! The dead husband came back to haunt his house.

But in 1975, it wasn't the house that interested me. On a warm afternoon in the autumn, I pushed open the creaking door and stepped into the farmyard; time stood still. A rat scurried across the yard, a flock of swallows burst out from underneath the corrugated roof of the cowshed, and then there was silence. I peered through the cobweb-covered glass in the dairy and saw a couple of old buckets and some farm implements. The tin roof had caved in, and in the centre of the yard sat old, rusted machinery, half-hidden in the weeds. The last of the winter's hay occupied the hay shed, to the rear, and the back gate led out into deserted, open pasture. The old farmyard, bad and all as it was, had plenty of space. There and then, on that autumn afternoon, I decided that I would rent the farmyard and the semi-derelict buildings, which would be my workshop. Gillie took the hay away. Now at least I had space for working and storage.

Between films, I now had two projects running in tandem: my house at Windsor Terrace and my workshop at Ardmore – both of which were in dire need of repair! I had bought a VW dome-topped van and used it as a mobile workshop on location. Between the cowshed and the van, I was well organised. In the cowshed, I cut away the iron bars from the stalls and feeding troughs. In the dairy, cooling pipes had to be removed, and a fifteen-foot-high tree had grown

The Cowshed:
We cleared the forest of
weeds and fitted a new door!

through the roof and needed to be cut down. I hired skips to remove the rusted ironmongery from the yard and flung a few sheets of felt over the gaps in the roof. The cowshed boasted one electric light bulb, and I found a water tap on a wall in the yard. When it rained, the yard flooded, but that problem, along with other building and repair work, would have to wait, because *The Purple Taxi* rolled in.

The film is the story of an ageing doctor, played by Fred Astaire, who travels around in a London taxi – painted bright purple! The cast also included Charlotte Rampling and Peter Ustinov. The twelve-week shoot took me to seven counties, including Galway, where the French production company put us up in Renvyle House. When I arrived at the hotel, I was told to go and pick a room, and so I took myself on a tour and came upon a door which I found was locked. At Reception, I asked why this was, and was told that this particular room was never used, as it was haunted. Barry Blackmore was the First AD. Barry and I had been to school together, and we were now working together, living it up on lobster and the best Chablis! A couple of nights into the shoot, I swaggered into the plush lounge, which had a log fire roaring in the grate. Two wing-backed armchairs faced the fire, and as I approached, a hand came out and rested on the arm of one of them – frightening the daylights out of me! It was not the hand of the resident ghost, however; it belonged to Fred Astaire.

'Ah, Fred. Nice fire,' I said.

'Yes, it is,' he replied.

'How are you settling in Ireland?' I asked.

'Oh, fine. My daughter lives here – in Cork – and I come over to visit,' he replied.

We chatted for a minute or two, about this and that.

'Gosh, it must have been great making all those films with Ginger Rogers. Those great dance steps . . . so fit and so graceful . . . .'

He sat up. 'I don't want to talk about any of that,' he said emphatically.

Feeling a bit stung, I turned and left.

Filming was on schedule, and all was going well until one afternoon, while working on the set on a location in the wilds of Connemara, an assistant came running up to me.

'Gerry, there's an urgent call for you. Can you come to the production office?'

The production secretary looked grave. 'Gerry, your father phoned. Your son is very sick.'

Several hours later, back in Dun Laoghaire, I called my parents and learned that Derek had been taken, that morning, by ambulance to the National Children's Hospital in Crumlin. Georgina was with him. When I arrived at the hospital, I found a skeletal little figure, hooked up to an array of tubes and machinery, receiving blood transfusions. Over the next few days, his condition improved, but the diagnosis flattened us: Derek had diabetes.

I limped back to work in the West, and after another week on location in Galway, returned to Dublin and then to Bray – back to Hollybrook House, the large period residence where we'd had the debacle with the bread machine on *Zardoz*. Part of the house was intact; the rest had fallen into disrepair. The French director, Yves Boisset, wanted it all to go on fire; it would be a night shoot. The construction department got to work making a false roof, and the art department dressed the derelict section to make it look as though it was being lived in. A return building housed stables, into which the fire would spread, and from which horses – some of them on fire – would be rescued. The shoot involved days of intense preparation and a large effects crew, a stunt crew and specially trained stunt horses.

In the previous weeks, Georgina had fallen into an exhaustive routine, learning to administer insulin to Derek and introducing a new dietary regime to manage his illness. Anticipating some excitement and needing a bit of a break, she asked if she could join me on set. My parents were only too happy to take care of Derek and drive her out to Hollybrook House, where, in the frenzy of preparations for the fire scene, I had caught only a glimpse of her, chatting with one of the make-up crew.

About thirty fire crew and Civil Defence members were on standby. Everyone had been cleared from the set, with the exception of the fire crew, the effects crew, the director, the director of photography, the sound technician and the stills photographer. The fire crew and I rushed around doing final checks. Then there was a delay of about half an hour while the director and camera crew had further discussions. We waited.

'Are we readee to start ze fire, Gerree?' the director called, at last.

'All clear?' I asked the fire officer in charge.

'All clear, Gerry,' he replied.

I gave my crew the order to start pumping smoke into the building. The cameras were rolling. I was just about to give the order to start the fire when we heard a shout – from inside the building!

'Cut the smoke!' I roared.

The set fell silent. The front door opened and out staggered Peter Ustinov, Charlotte Rampling – and my wife! Ustinov launched into some hilarious banter. I rushed forward and learned that the three of them had moved quietly inside during the delay in filming and had been sitting inside in the drawing room, drinking champagne, lost in conversation. Despite the presence of two famous partners-in-crime, Georgina was embarrassed, but everyone assured her that it had been a humorous interlude, and 'sure wasn't it great that she was the centre of attention for a change'!

When filming finished, the purple London taxicab became a familiar feature around the roads of Wicklow – driven by John Boorman's wife, Christel! It was ideal transport for their four children and all their school friends. When Christel purchased a new VW Variant in the late seventies, the purple taxi found a new owner, who drove around with an Irish wolfhound parked in the back seat. Locals were now well-used to the odd-looking vehicle, which could be seen winding its way around the mountain roads well into the eighties. The movie itself, filmed in English and French, quickly faded from public view, although the French version, *Un Taxi Mauve*, sparked a substantial interest in Ireland among French tourists, boosting the Irish tourist industry, at least.

The Purple Taxi was quickly followed by *The Last Remake of Beau Geste*, a period comedy directed by – and starring – Marty Feldman, and also starring Ann Margaret. I was hired by Johnny Stears, another of the UK supervisors. Again, I would source local trades and services, and buy the materials and equipment. One of our requirements was a harness, to suspend Marty Feldman from a roof at Kilmainham Jail in Dublin. I engaged the services of a Dublin saddle-maker to make up a body harness. I was so impressed with the finished product, complete with sheepskin padding, that I ordered a second one! While helping Marty into his harness, or talking with him, I could never be sure if he was looking at me. At meetings, no one knew who he was addressing. His eyes moved away from each other, in two different directions!

An interior shot involved Marty being hoisted up to about the fourth floor, where the hand of a prisoner protrudes from a cell. In one last take, Marty swung up, the hand shot out, and all was well – until he descended and watched the replay on the monitor. The sleeve of the actor's costume had slipped up his arm, to reveal a modern Rolex watch!

'You're fired!' Marty shouted.

9

A MIDNIGHT RAID

Despite his illness, Derek was a bright, lively ten-year-old, who delighted in taking his friends out to Ardmore at weekends and during school holidays, to help me with the clean-up operation. At home, they scampered about scaffolding and shinned up and down ladders as I battled with ancient, flaking plasterwork, rotting floorboards and layers of heavy, peeling wallpaper. Derek and the boys had hours of fun steaming off the paper. I was sure they would tire of it in no time, but they surprised me by working hard – motivated, no doubt, by the thought of how they would spend their pocket money!

In the yard at the cowshed: Derek and his pals loved to come out and help.

Georgina was four months pregnant, and excited about the arrival of our second child. We had talked about a contingency plan – in case the bottom fell out of the precarious Irish movie-making industry. As

a former hotel, our house would be ideal as a bed-and-breakfast business, but it would need upgrading. I enlisted the help of Tommy Berry,
an army sergeant and engineer whom I'd met on *Darling Lili*. He was
strong and fit, and willing to drive all the way to Dun Laoghaire, from
the west of the city, after work, and thought nothing of starting with
me at 9 or 10 PM and working until 1 or 2 in the morning. Tommy
would help me to install central heating, Paschal Jones and his team of
riggers from the studios had erected a maze of scaffolding in readiness
for my next task: an assault on the exterior paintwork. Indoors, every
room had been gutted; walls were stripped, and old curtains and fur-
nishings had been disposed of. We slept downstairs, in the drawing
room, and lived in the kitchen, where Tommy Berry and I had also just
installed new units.

In the midst of this domestic upheaval, I attended regular meetings of the Film Workers' Association. The association had learnt that
Ardmore was again up for sale and that moves were afoot to petition
the government to save the studios from developers. I wanted to keep
abreast of the news and make some contribution towards the goals of
the organisation. Fortunately, meetings were held in the Royal Marine
Hotel, just a stone's throw from our house. One evening, leaving
Derek finishing his homework and Georgina clearing away the dinner
dishes, I had to make a dash for the car, in torrential rain, to attend an
eight o'clock meeting. When I returned home after the meeting,
Georgina was sitting up in bed, flicking through a magazine.

'Tommy Berry phoned,' she said. 'You're to ring him back, immediately.'

'What did he want?' I asked.

'I don't know, he just said it was very urgent.'

Tommy's wife answered the phone. 'I'll get him,' she said, coolly.

'Tommy, what's up?' I asked.

'Gerry, I've just spent hours in the Garda station. Your van's been
used in some sort of a robbery! What's going on?'

I just laughed.

'C'mon, Gerry, what's the story?'

'That's impossible,' I told him. 'The van's parked outside!'

Tommy didn't sound convinced. I assured him that my van had
been parked in the back laneway since the previous day and hadn't
been moved. 'If the Guards get back to you, tell them to ring me,' I
said.

Georgina and I mulled over the bizarre phone conversation but soon concluded that if there were any further developments, I would be contacted. Right now, we were both exhausted and in need of a good night's sleep.

Just as we were about to doze off, the room was lit up. Through the curtain-less bay window, a flashing blue light shot about the ceiling. I jumped out of bed. A Garda squad car was pulled up at the front gate. In pyjamas and bare feet, I went to answer a loud hammering on the front door. Through the glass panels, I could see a number of dark figures hovering on the steps. I had just undone the lock when the heavy oak door was pushed in against me and a bunch of uniformed figures stormed past, like ants – up the stairs and into every room. 'Get out of that bed!' one of them roared at Georgina.

At Ardmore with my VW van – my first mobile workshop –
which got me arrested!

A tall, heavy-set Garda – who seemed to be in charge – strode into the hallway. 'Is this about my van?' I asked him. 'I got a call about my van being in a robbery, but my van's out the back.' He grabbed me by the collar and jammed me against the wall, pushing me and thumping me in the ribs. I was then hauled through the house and out into the back yard. The rain had stopped and a full moon silhouetted a row of dark figures, armed with what looked like rifles, along the top of the wall! Out in the back laneway, more figures – armed to the teeth – were lined up against the walls of the neighbouring houses. The stones underfoot dug into the soles of my feet.

'There's some mistake . . . ' I began. 'My van's been here . . . '

The response from the 'boss' was another box in the face!

'I'm reporting you, you bastard!' I said, nursing my jaw.

'You won't find any numbers on me,' he sneered.

Sure enough, his epaulettes bore no identifying numbers. I was pushed back through the house and straight out the front door, pleading, in vain, to see Georgina. Still in pyjamas, feet wet and bruised, and with Georgina's screams ringing in my ears, I was bundled into the back of the squad car. Two hefty members of the force wedged me between them, and the car sped away. Minutes later, we were at Dun Laoghaire Garda Station.

A surprised-looking local sergeant in the front office recognised me. 'How'ya Gerry. What are you doing here?'

I was pushed past him and thrown into a cold, drab room. Before the team left, I asked for a cup of tea. I got no answer. I asked to phone Georgina and was told 'No'. I asked to call my father and was again refused. For the next three hours, I sat alone, huddled and shivering, wondering what had happened to my family.

It was sometime around 6 AM when the door opened and three men, in civvies, walked in.

'Gerry,' the first one said, all business. 'I'm so sorry. There's been a bit of a mix-up!'

I didn't recognise him. Disoriented and freezing, I went for him! The torrent that came out of my mouth has faded into history.

'Come on and we'll take you into Jury's Hotel for breakfast,' the strange man was saying.

I wanted to get home – yesterday! I also wanted answers. I was led to a waiting car and, accompanied by the three detectives, taken home. On the way, I heard the story. An attempted abduction had taken place at the home of a bank manager somewhere in west Dublin. The bank manager hit an alarm, which was connected to his local Garda station. Within minutes, a SWAT team arrived, and the criminals jumped into a blue VW van with a dome roof, identical to mine, and sped off. A chase ensued, during which the van broke a red light and collided with another car, coming out of a side road. Someone in the van smashed the rear window and fired shots, causing the car to crash into a lamp-post. The van, with its occupants, got away.

Back outside my house, the driver turned around to me. His voice dropped. 'D'ye remember, there was an armed bank raid in Dun Laoghaire a while back? The guy's name was Johnson!'

Georgina came running from the house, in floods of tears, closely followed by my father. I almost collapsed onto a chair in the kitchen, where my mother made tea. My 'rescuers' were getting an earful from my father in the hallway: 'You had no search warrant. You beat him up. You harassed his wife.'

It didn't make sense. The geniuses who had abducted me could see that the windows in my van were undamaged, and that the ground underneath was dry, despite an evening of heavy rain. I simply couldn't take the story at face value. I don't know what I must have looked like, but I felt done in. Two days later, urged on by my father, I went to the garda station to lodge a complaint. Behind a desk, in a back office, a lanky superintendent leaned back in his chair, looking me up and down. 'They weren't from here, so they didn't know you. And after all, sure they were only doin' their job!' he drawled.

I called Tommy and told him what had happened. 'Listen, I'm sorry,' he said. 'I think I signed for the new tax disc last week and that's how they got my name. I had to tell them it wasn't my van.'

So many unhappy coincidences.

Early the following week, Georgina complained of searing cramps. By evening, she was bleeding. I took her to Holles Street, the nearest maternity hospital. In another shiny green-walled hospital lobby, I was told to wait, and she was wheeled away. Hours dragged by. Every hour or so, a heavily pregnant woman, moaning and crying, her face creased up in pain, came in and hobbled away, on the arm of a nurse, the husband told to go home. Hospital rules hadn't changed since 1966. As nightfall came, a doctor came striding in to the lobby and over to where I was standing. His face told me he had bad news.

'Mr Johnston,' he said. 'I'm afraid your wife has lost the baby.'

My throat went dry. The doctor turned and strode back the way he had come.

'Excuse me,' I called.

He stopped and turned to face me. 'Yes?'

'What was it?' I asked.

'A baby boy,' he replied, and continued on his way.

Our world had been turned upside down. Desperate to get back to normality, we pressed ahead with plans for the B&B. With the house finally ready, we registered with Bórd Fáilte. I became the cook and Georgina the waitress, and we shared the 'housemaid' chores. We had accommodation for ten to twelve guests at a time – and they arrived, in their droves! A couple of days a week, I took myself out to Ardmore to continue repairs on the workshop. Derek had learned to inject himself with insulin, which seemed to hurt him at times. It was hard for me to watch. I needed another film, but Ardmore was like a ghost town. *The Purple Taxi* and *Beau Geste*, both consisting of more drama than action, had provided me with a few weeks of work here and there. At the time, given my other commitments, it was enough. I needed to get my teeth into something bigger, but there was nothing on the horizon.

To film workers in Ireland, it seemed that producers were more inclined to bring in foreign craftspeople, and as the eighties approached, the vast majority of TV commercials began to go abroad. The advertising agencies said that Ireland didn't have 'qualified' directors! The Film Workers' Association had to try and come up with something to stop the work going elsewhere. Meanwhile, I heard that a publishing company in Belfast planned to put together a directory, listing all sections of the industry: who was who in the business, north and south of the border. It sounded like a good way to generate publicity. A group of us travelled to Belfast and met Stan Mairs, who headed up Adleader Publications. Stan had been in the publishing business for years and had a clear vision of his market: film producers in mainland Europe, America and the UK. Our listings would carry pictures, banner headlines and movie credits. Over the next few years, Stan succeeded in getting a large proportion of Irish film services to advertise, and 'Filmscan' was launched. In late 2004, Stan phoned and asked me for an interview about special effects in Ireland, to mark the directory's twentieth anniversary. In the course of the interview, it dawned on me that 2005 would also bring me to forty years in the business!

10

AER ARANN TO THE RESCUE

In 1976, BBC's drama programming began to incorporate more comprehensive effects. Bigger effects would call for more extensive health-and-safety measures. The BBC approached ACTT, which had a long list of effects supervisors, who, between them had years of experience, but in order to comply with national health-and-safety regulations in the workplace, the supervisors would have to upgrade their knowledge in this area. I was selected by the union to take a course in health and safety, and for three days I waded through reams of work, in the company of about a hundred other course participants, at a TUC conference centre in London. Hands-on experience was a doddle; studying was something else! Fortunately, over the years, I had worked extremely hard to improve my reading and writing, studying on my own – everything from newspapers and magazines to holiday brochures – and as a supervisor, I had to learn to read a film script and find the effects scenes in order to produce an effects budget. Now, I was fortunate to be studying in the company of colleagues.

Reading through the material, we discovered that the health-and-safety 'Factory Acts' did not cover much of what we did and that new criteria would have to be written, passed and incorporated into existing legislation with regard to film work. On completion of the course, I was among a small group of freelance supervisors and technicians – the others were Ray Harryhausen (already a legend as a film-maker and a wizard in stop-motion animation and miniatures), John Markwell, Ian Scoones and Brian Shemmings – who were co-opted on to a health-and-safety committee that met with BBC effects designers, producers and directors from a number of television networks, on several occasions, at BBC headquarters in London. In the end, it was Brian

Shemmings who went on to specialise in this area and become a health-and-safety consultant in film and television.

At home, Georgina's mother had been pestering her to take the lease on the shop. I wanted nothing to do with it, but the B&B was hard work and business was slow in winter. Georgina was also afraid that if I went away, to work on a picture, she would be left to run it on her own. Looking back, I believe that she wanted me to quit the film business altogether. For the moment, she seemed to get her wish, because, although there was some sporadic activity, nothing was coming my way. I gave in, and the late spring of 1977 saw me, with the sterling help of Tommy Berry, ripping out the interior of the shop on Patrick Street. Within a month, we had a new shop-front and a new, Mock Tudor-style interior, sporting freezer cabinets, a sandwich bar and seating accommodation for up to eighteen people. The business took off, with customers from local banks, offices and schools queuing up outside. Derek had a new after-school venue and would come and help – and his pals were enthusiastic customers!

Then I got a call for 'a few days' work' at Ardmore. John Boorman was back, 'finishing off' a film he'd been making in LA and New York, called *Exorcist II: The Heretic*. At Ardmore, the crew walked around on eggshells. While shooting in the US, the film had been plagued by a succession of problems, both technical and personal: accidents and sudden illnesses, culminating in the director's illness. People were afraid that they'd catch the film's 'virus'! 'The bloody picture's jinxed!' they were saying. A couple of days into the shoot, I happened to be in Dun Laoghaire buying supplies for the film and called in to grab a sandwich from the shop. I looked out the window, just in time to see Derek run across the street – straight in front of a passing car. He flew up in the air, like a rag doll, landed on the ground in a crumpled heap and lay motionless. I ran out to him. He jumped up, looking dazed! The driver of the car took us to St Michael's. On the way, Derek collapsed in my arms. X-rays revealed no broken bones, but he was detained for observation and remained in hospital for two days. Thankfully, although shaken and badly bruised, he was not seriously injured. Maybe the timing, coinciding with the beginning of my work on *The Heretic*, was just a freak incident, but I was cautious nonetheless.

Sets for *The Heretic* were built on three sound-stages – enormous, fake, eerie landscapes, with tons of sand, a cityscape and a couple of other interiors. The effects requirements for the film were unusual, including a swarm of locusts, for which I had to build special cages with air-conditioning fans. Either the males or females (I can't remember which!) had been extracted beforehand, to avoid reproduction – and possible infestation – but once they were free, those that we used managed to infiltrate every nook and cranny in the studios. For months after the film was finished, the odd scream could be heard from people working on the sound-stages who had suddenly found a dead locust in the coleslaw! One of the scenes required a special lens to fake the windscreen in an aircraft, with locusts crashing into it, leaving blood and cracked glass. I never saw the film, but I understand that one reviewer described the locust scenes as 'a bunch of leaves, released by a prop man in front of a gardener's leaf-blower'. So much for special lenses!

Another scene involved a visible, beating heart! Down I went to the local abattoir, in Bray.

'When will you be killing the sheep?' I asked.

The butcher just stared. 'What d'you want to know that for?' he demanded.

'I want two hearts – still beating,' I told him.

'Two hearts,' he repeated, sardonically.

'Yes. I need one as a spare.'

I wasn't sure if he would laugh or go for my throat! After the words were out, it dawned on me that maybe he had visions of some sort of impending cult sacrifice; that I was some kind of weirdo. He continued to eye me suspiciously as I waited for the hearts. With the aid of tiny pumps, fake blood and yards of medical tubing, one of these hearts went on to live forever on the big screen. One of the girls from the accounts department was poured into a body stocking and sat behind a glass screen, massaging her chest. The beating heart was superimposed, through the screen. The scene took most of the day to shoot. *The Heretic* also called for earthquakes, collapsing columns and buildings, windstorms, heat haze, steam and a plethora of other effects. I needed extra manpower. I approached Boorman. The budget was minuscule. It took him all of two seconds to come up with the solution: fifteen minutes later, someone from production, wearing a smart suit, was up a ladder, with a smoke machine. The 'few days' work' had turned into weeks, with little sleep.

Given the difficulties he'd encountered in the US, including problems with the effects people there, I expected Boorman to be awkward. However, this time, he and I got along very well, and I actually enjoyed working with him. We shared a keen interest in the 'look' of a scene, and he would frequently ask 'What do you think, Gerry?' when designing a sequence. John knew the business from the ground up and he and I worked long hours on the complex shots. This 'reconciliation' seemed to give rise to remarks from the floor. Each time Boorman appeared on set, I heard 'Here's Gerry Johnston's mate!' from among the crew. I began not to care; I was developing a thick skin!

Starring Richard Burton as the tormented Father Lamont, the exorcist priest, *The Heretic* was said to have started out as a sequel to the blockbuster *The Exorcist*. However, film-goers, expecting more torture and gore, were let down by the movie, and at the box office, *The Heretic* was an all-time flop. But I was still on a high, when I got a call to work on another picture, called *The Flame Is Love*, directed by Michael O'Herlihy and starring Linda Purl and Timothy Dalton. My job? To make up a functioning, life-size golden eagle, for a cult scene in front of a flaming altar!

Meanwhile, Morgan O'Sullivan, who was now heading up his own company, Tara Productions, at Ardmore, had done a script deal with NBC Television in New York. The script was by the British writer Frederick Forsyth, who lived up the road in the picturesque village of Enniskerry, near the Powerscourt demesne. The protagonist is a former Green Beret, played by Rod Taylor. The much-loved Irish actor Cyril Cusack played the rumpled, Columbo-type Garda Inspector. *Cry of the Innocent* − a conspiracy story, involving a plane crash in the west of Ireland − would be my second film with Michael O'Herlihy.

I got a call to accompany the director on a recce to the west. We would travel with Aer Arann, a small airline which had been set up a few years previously to provide an island-hopping air service from Galway to each of the three islands of Aran, just off the coast.

'I need to blow up a plane, in mid-air,' Michael was saying. 'How do I do that, Gerry?'

I told him what we had done on *The Blue Max, Darling Lili* and *The Red Baron*, but the budgets for those films were way out of our league. This time, we'd have to compromise. So I explained the procedure, beginning with the acquisition of a plane. Below us, the scenery changed from mountain ranges to open country, with fluffy white clouds whipping past us. I had created similar scenes a dozen times.

'Where do we get the plane?' Michael asked. And then we both exchanged looks. We were sitting in it! Paddy Robinson was the pilot, and when he heard he was going to be swooping and diving for a couple of days, over Galway, in a plane rigged with black smoke, he broke into a big smile.

Instead of a mid-air explosion, the small, private plane, en route from Rome, would go into a nosedive and crash into a house. From the camera's point of view, the plane would dive, disappear behind a hill, and explode. From my point of view, I could feel the adrenalin rush as I watched Paddy in rehearsal. He could make that plane dance, and for a moment I wanted to be up there instead of building and tending a fuel dump (which would look like the exploding plane) on the ground. On the day of the shoot, I listened to the plane in the distance, waited for the approach, then the dive; the moment the plane began to climb behind a hill, I hit the button. The explosion rose over a hundred feet in the air as Paddy glided safely back towards Galway, out of sight of the camera. Surrounded in black smoke, my crew and

Cry of the Innocent: Paddy Robinson dives over Galway

I waited. Minutes passed as the camera rolled, and then my walkie-talkie came to life.

'Bloody hell!' O'Herlihy shouted. 'That was absolutely fantastic!'

One chance, one take: has to be right. These were my moments.

Cry of the Innocent: With director Michael O'Herlihy

The chauffeur, Eddie Dunne, who had taken me, in his black limo, to Ardmore on that memorable day in 1965, was retiring. His son Arthur was taking over and expanding the fleet. Arthur was transport captain on *Cry of the Innocent* – and he had a problem.

'The director wants a Ford Granada to go up in smoke, Gerry,' he said gravely. 'I can only get a loan of a feckin' brand-new Granada, straight out of the showroom, and I have to bring it back the way I got it!' I had my hands full, with the tail of a plane and a wrecked building to burn – the aftermath of the plane crash. I needed time, but time was not on my side. I consulted with the art director and came up with a plan. While my crew cursed me to hell and back, we took the car aside and began the transformation, beginning with the application of a light foil skin. The painters were busy on the 'plane' and the derelict house, so I had to do the 'artwork' on the car myself – working all hours to get it finished. Then we wheeled it out for Michael to have a look.

'That's very impressive,' he said.

We put our fire equipment in place, and the cameras were set up to film the fire.

'OK, stand by,' the First AD called. 'Ready, Gerry?'

'Ready.'

'Cameras rolling!' the First AD shouted.

'Start the fire, guys!' I said.

Flames gutted the tail of the plane, which was protruding from the burning house. In front of the house, smoke poured from underneath the Granada, which was parked between the camera and the house; then flames leaped up from behind it. From the camera's point of view, the car looked like it was burning.

'Keep the cameras rolling,' the director ordered.

We all stood in silence and watched. I prayed. Arthur Dunne was white as a sheet.

'OK, cut!' the director finally called.

The car looked a mess. Arthur appeared at my side.

'Bloody hell! The feckin' car!' was all he could say.

Camera checks – and then the First AD said, 'OK, we got that. Thanks, guys', and rambled off.

'Right, lads, let's get this car off the set!' I said.

Ahead lay a good two hours' car 'valeting'! That evening, one of Arthur's drivers sat into a sparkling Granada, in 'showroom condition', and drove away. My final act of destruction on the film took place back at Ardmore. The studios, doubling as a secret weapons compound, rocked to the sound of explosions! Fortunately, at that time, it was isolated, set on acres of open ground.

During *Cry of the Innocent*, Michael O'Herlihy entertained us with stories about *Hawaii Five-O*, the series he had directed for television – a fast-paced action series that I loved at the time. He told me about his first trip to America, with a couple of friends – aboard a yacht, from Dun Laoghaire! It was a daring adventure, without the accompaniment of any escort or support vessel, or satellite navigation.

'Anyone who knew what we were up to told us we were mad – and of course we were!' he said to me.

Michael had been a theatre designer with the Abbey Theatre, and he soon found work as a director in theatre on Broadway, before working his way to America's West Coast, and Hollywood. His later successful TV credits included *The A-Team* and *Miami Vice*. Working with him had been a pleasure.

Success was also on the cards for Aer Arann, which is now an international airline, servicing many UK and other European destinations from Galway and Dublin. One day soon, I hope to travel on one of their new fleet, for old times' sake!

I was back working with a foreign director for a film called *The Outsider*, about a disillusioned Vietnam veteran, of Irish descent, who comes to Belfast to join the Provisional IRA. In real-life Belfast, the Provisional IRA was engaged in a real conflict, and the film had to be shot in Dublin. An area of Ringsend was chosen. The other 'wizards': construction, plasterers, painters and set dressers, got to work and the Ringsend street was transformed into a working-class district of Belfast. The director, Tony Luraschi, wanted a riot; it was my job to create it – complete with Molotov cocktails, rigged guns for firing CS gas, bullets (rubber bullets this time), bullet hits, armoured cars on fire, smoke, and gallons of blood. One evening, an elderly couple – residents of the street – took themselves to the pub. The street was 'dressed' – strewn with litter – my smoke machines were cranked up, and we were ready to roll. Suddenly, the director announced that he could see a couple of normal (instead of 'dressed') houses in the shot. Panic! Set dressers scattered, and within minutes sheets of corrugated iron, lengths of timber and cans of paint materialised from nowhere. Availing of the break, we dived on the coffee, while a frenzy of hammering and banging went on down the street. Finally, we heard: 'First positions, everyone! We're ready to start shooting!' The crew, actors and extras took up positions, and the 'riot' began.

All went well until closing time in the pubs, when the elderly couple – who had vacated their house, at teatime – arrived back. The set was eerily silent as a dialogue shot was filmed.

'Jaysus, Mary and Joseph – where's me house?' the husband shouted.

Heads turned. The couple stood, dazed, in the middle of the street. 'What's happened to me house?' the husband wailed.

'We can't find our house!' the wife whimpered.

Luraschi hurried over. 'Can I help you?' he asked.

'We can't find our house,' the husband said again.

The wife looked as if she would faint. The unit nurse was summoned. A sheepish-looking set dresser sidled up.

'What number is it?' he asked.

The first AD took charge, and gently ushered the couple towards their 'derelict' home. Construction crew hurried ahead to dismantle the corrugated sheets and timber and allow them to re-enter the house. I'm not sure if they ever put their noses outside the door for the remainder of the week! In any case, I never saw them again. When the shoot ended, I was headed for England.

11

CONNERY DICES WITH DEATH,

BUT HE'S NOT THE CASUALTY!

The call had come from Eric Rattray, the associate producer on something called *The Greek Tycoon*. He said that Peter Dawson had given him my home number.

'What can I do for you?' I asked.

'Would it be possible to get hold of a couple of minesweepers?'

'Excuse me?'

'A couple of minesweepers. The British navy has been of no help, I'm afraid.'

I racked my brains for a moment. 'My uncle was in the British navy,' I said. 'I'll ask him.'

Uncle Frank gave me the name of someone in the Irish navy. But all Irish vessels were on active duty. I called Eric.

'Well, we'll find some somewhere. Are you available for work?' he asked.

'Sure,' I told him. 'When do I start?'

Before travelling to Portsmouth, off the south coast of England, I had to report to the production office at Pinewood – and meet Eric Rattray. He was in his forties, wore glasses and was dressed in a suit. He appeared very much at ease, and I was pleased to hear I would be working with Ron Ballanger again, who had been my supervisor on *The Blue Max*. Next day, in my hotel room in Portsmouth, I got another call.

'Do me a favour, Gerry. I've set up a meeting at a facility near you,' Eric said.

At the facility's security hut, I was directed to an office, where a tall, flamboyant man, dressed in overalls, shook my hand warmly.

'I'm Jim,' he said. 'I believe you're looking for a couple of minesweepers?'

'That's right,' I replied.

'Come with me,' Jim said. 'I'll show you around.'

We emerged into a maze of corrugated buildings and, beyond them, a massive dry dock. I was looking at a whole fleet of ships: minesweepers, destroyers and cargo vessels! I was in a sort of used-ship lot: there were more ships here than in Cork harbour!

Jim was talking at a mile a minute.

'Do you want an aircraft carrier? Do you want a captain? A crew?' he was asking. 'You want tanks? Aircraft? Cannon?'

He took me into a hangar. Tanks were lined up in a row, and beside them was a row of turboprop aeroplanes. Back at the hotel, I phoned Eric.

'I think I've found what you're looking for,' I told him.

A week later, painters were working on the minesweepers, and I resumed sourcing other items on my effects list.

The Greek Tycoon: Standing on the iced-up deck of a tanker
on loan from the Onassis fleet

The Greek Tycoon is the tale of a wealthy Greek businessman called Theo Tomasis, who courts and marries the lovely young Liz Cassidy, widow of a slain American president. It is based on the story of Aristotle Onassis and Jackie Kennedy. Anthony Quinn plays 'Tomasis' and Jacqueline Bisset plays 'Liz Cassidy'. Years later, I read somewhere that Aristotle Onassis expected that a film would be made about his life and requested that Anthony Quinn play the part. The two met, some time before Onassis' death, and Quinn agreed to take the role. My 'role' involved icing up a massive oil tanker, which had appeared out in the harbour (it was on loan from the Onassis fleet) for a scene in which the tanker, on its way from the frozen Arctic, comes under fire – from a flotilla of minesweepers.

On the first day of preparation, we were taken out by one of a fleet of tugs, of the kind that service ocean liners. Rising out of the water, the hull of the tanker looked like the Berlin Wall, with four massive rusted funnels rising from her deck and, hanging over the rails, rows and rows of dark-skinned sailors in overalls. The huge vessel was said to take four miles to turn around and about a mile to come to a stop! On board, we were introduced to the Pakistani captain and the ship's engineer. The engineer, a man in his fifties, was the only European on board, and didn't have much to say. None of the crew had been ashore for months! Adjustments to the rough-and-ready regime included new orders from the captain, including one that women among the crew would be accompanied to the bathroom – for their protection – and that men would go in pairs! It was said that the food on board was 'not the best', and so a catering company was employed. Back on board our tug, we had our meals flown out by helicopter; our sandwiches came towards us swinging through the air in five lunchboxes, suspended from the chopper's winch.

Supervisor Ron Ballanger and technician Ron Cartwright joined us on day two of preparations and I had my mate Tommy Berry flown out a few days later. When filming started, it was 'all hands on deck' for the scenes in which the tanker is attacked by shells and gunfire. I found myself laying charges in the water, traversing the channel in a tug, which was skippered by a man wearing a naval cap, with an insignia. He was a former German U-boat captain, with very little English, who operated out of Jim's dry dock.

Finally, on day three, the barrage began. The first charge sent up a twenty-foot plume of spray.

'We can't see it from the boat, Gerry,' the First AD informed me. 'Can you move closer?'

We set up again, and my tug shot forwards to within about eighty feet of the tanker. I was nervous. This time, the plume of spray rose to about forty feet. We rolled about for a few minutes and waited.

'Can you move a bit closer?' the AD called.

'I'm not sure. I'm worried about safety,' I replied.

'Try it!'

The third charge sent a sixty-foot wave into the air. The tug rolled and heaved in its wake and, through the spray, I could see the shock waves 'rippling' along the tanker's massive hull! I held my breath. My walkie-talkie crackled into life.

'OK, Gerry, we got it!'

The director and DOP were happy, but many of the ship's crew, off duty and below deck, did not take too kindly to the thundering explosions that woke them from their sleep! The next two days pushed others to the limits of endurance, as our tug scurried about in the Bay of Biscay, chasing the tanker. Aboard the tug, the crew, including my U-boat captain, were throwing up. One other crew member and I were the only people whose stomachs seemed to stay where they were, as we filled the air with gunfire.

The Greek Tycoon: With my U-boat captain, aboard our work-boat

Back on dry land, we had just tucked into dinner one evening at a local restaurant when, suddenly, Tommy Berry started coughing. His face reddened and he began choking. One of the crew jumped up, grabbed him from behind and yanked. Tommy slumped forward and spat out a fish bone. I had just witnessed my first 'Heimlich Manoeuvre'!

In Dun Laoghaire, Georgina was running the shop almost single-handedly. It was a lucrative business, but the hours were long, and Georgina told me that she was feeling sick. I put it down to exhaustion and we talked about giving up the business. A visit to the doctor confirmed that she was pregnant – as good a reason as any to quit the shop. I suggested that she take a break, and a week later the production arranged for Georgina and Derek to fly out from Dublin to join me. They spent a week visiting the sights, including the Isle of Wight. Rested after the break, and no longer feeling sick, Georgina seemed a lot more relaxed and happy to become a stay-at-home mother, closely monitored by her medical team. When filming on *The Greek Tycoon* moved indoors, I returned home. Within days, I got a call about a big picture. Sean Connery was back in town.

The First Great Train Robbery, based on the novel by Michael Crichton and set in Victorian England, is about a sophisticated criminal who is planning to steal a shipment of gold being transported to the Crimea. He plans to execute this robbery on board a moving train. Connery plays the upper-crust gent who is the brains behind this daring project, and Donald Sutherland plays the working-class comic relief. Dublin was picked as the location because the city has some of the world's best-preserved Georgian buildings; ideal to double as nineteenth-century London. At Ardmore, coaches were built for the Victorian train and were transported from the studios down to the local railway station in Bray, loaded onto sets of wheels supplied by the national railroad transport system (CIE), and pulled by a vintage steam engine from Dublin's Transport Museum. Bray was used for testing. Heuston Station in Dublin was one of the actual locations, where the effects department fitted pipes along the bottom of the carriages – to carry the steam back from one of our steam machines, which were mounted in the engine compartment – and created smoke to block out any modern backgrounds. We made rain for street scenes, pumped smoke from chimneys and created the 'pea soup' fogs for which London was famous. I would also be providing wire rigs and harnesses for the later scenes, on top of the moving train.

The unit then moved down to Mullingar in the midlands – doubling as the English countryside – where most of the exteriors, apart from station and street shots, would be filmed from a helicopter. We also had cameras on board the train for interior shots. Most of the time, I was on the roof of the train, calling out 'Bridge coming up!'; at the last minute, Sean Connery and I would fall on our backs and hang on to the air-vents protruding up through the roof as the train passed beneath a bridge or a tunnel. For hours each day, we were deafened by the engine noise echoing from inside the tunnels, the stone roofs just inches away from our noses. We were smothered in black smoke, blowing back at us from the furnace, and by the end of each day we were as black as coal miners, our hair and eyebrows singed from sparks. Directing operations from the pile of coal at the front, Crichton was as black as the rest of us by the end of each journey! The designated speed was 35 mph, but the chopper pilot told us later that he was travelling overhead at 55 mph all the way along the line. Travelling downhill for much of the time, the engine driver had to try and gauge the speed as best he could by counting the seconds between telegraph poles, because the old relic from the museum did not include a speedometer!

Back on terra firma, the word had come down the ranks that there were problems in the production department. During a break, Connery strolled in to our temporary canteen and helped himself to a coffee. 'You mightn't shee me tomorrow, boys,' he announced with a grin.

Next day, sure enough, he was missing. We hung about, waiting for news. Someone said that there was a problem with his contract, but no one could be sure. Next morning found us in Wardrobe, dressing up as extras. We boarded the train and trundled up and down the line while the chopper filmed overhead. On the second day, the 'strike' was still on! Paddy, the 'Standby Props', a dapper individual, always alert to the needs of the artists, and nicknamed the 'Road Runner', got wind that the soccer fraternity was gearing up for the World Cup in Argentina – and Scotland were among the hopefuls, hoping to progress to the second round, for the first time in their history. A 3–1 defeat to Peru and a 1–1 draw with Iran meant that they needed to beat the Netherlands, finalists in the previous tournament, by three goals. Our famous Scot, who, according to some sources, was an ardent soccer fan, couldn't be in Argentina, but he couldn't be left wanting, either! Paddy was on the job.

A television set materialised and was set up in a house which was used during filming as a production office, close to the railway station in the village of Moate. Connery was summoned, and he, along with those of us who had more than a passing interest in the game, settled in to watch the match. In Argentina, Glasgow-born Kenny Dalglish cancelled out a Rob Rensenbrink penalty. We held our breath. Connery's eyebrows formed a single black line. At half-time, the 'Road Runner' wheeled in the coffee. At the start of the second half, mid-fielder Archie Gemmill gave the Scots the lead with a penalty. The room erupted, every Irishman rooting for 'Connery's team'! With twenty minutes to go, Gemmill weaved his way up the field, leaving three Dutch players in his wake. The goalkeeper came out and Gemmill flicked the ball into the net, bringing the score to 3–1. One more goal would be enough . . .

'Are we making a movie, here?'

It was the voice of the producer, John Foreman. All eyes fell on Connery, who just raised an eyebrow. The producer left. When the next goal came, it was scored by Dutchman Johnny Rep. The Netherlands went on to finish the World Cup as runners-up, while Scotland went home – too soon. If they had won, we might have been going home too soon as well!

We then moved back to Dublin, and the sedate tranquillity of the Phoenix Park, where we took over an area close to Áras an Uachtaráin. In the grounds, the film provided a daily spectacle: actors strolling around in their Victorian finery, women with their parasols and men in top hats, evoking scenes from another time – a time when the 'refined' classes strolled in the grounds of the Vice-regal Lodge, in the company of the future king of England and other dignitaries, representing our government of the time. But beneath the glitz of state visits by British royalty, insurgents were busy, trying to oust the British presence, and in 1978 a new generation of 'insurgents' were still at it – in Northern Ireland.

This time, another state visit was in progress, amid a heavy security presence, but it was so low-key that I was unaware of anything out of the ordinary. Sitting on a bench, at a trestle table in the dining tent, I was about to tuck in to lunch when a soft male voice enquired: 'Do you mind if I join you?' I looked up into a face I recognised, but I couldn't put a name to it. The man, dignified, in dark suit, left a cup of coffee on the table, sat down, and shook my hand.

'My name's Paddy Hillery.'

'Pleased to meet you, Paddy,' I said.

'Great weather we're having,' he went on.

'Yeah, we're very lucky to have a bit of fine weather for the film.'

'Indeed,' he replied. 'And what is it you do, on the film?'

'Well, we're doing a bit of atmosphere, for a few of the shots.'

Then the penny dropped: I was chatting to the present incumbent of the Áras – none other than President Patrick Hillery! He talked away, completely at ease. I don't remember if I finished my lunch, but I recall leaving the tent with him, still chatting. As we emerged into the bright sunshine, a couple strolled towards us.

'Ah, Your Highness,' the President began. 'This is Gerry. He's working on the film.'

A delicate hand was extended and I looked into the smiling face of Her Serene Highness, Princess Grace of Monaco! Beside her, Prince Rainier put out his hand and said, 'Nice to meet you.' Her Highness said she hoped that the weather would 'keep up' for us and wished me well. Then the three dignitaries strolled off to have a look around the set and meet the actors. When I'd gathered myself, I found one of the crew who had a camera, and we managed to get a couple of photographs of the royals. Four years later, Grace Kelly would meet an untimely death. I'm not sure if 1978 was her last visit to Ireland

The First Great Train Robbery was coming to an end. My father, in retirement now, was experiencing the making of a film, this time as an extra. Ever the charming gent, he looked the part and had managed to secure himself a full two weeks' work, as a member of a jury in a court scene and as a passer-by in various street scenes! All that was left for me was a shoot at the level crossing, over the railway at Merrion Gates, ten minutes from home. The shot involved Sean, standing on a twelve-foot-high scaffolding platform with fireworks going off all around him – a lighting-effects shot – just before dusk. The rest of the unit

The First Great Train Robbery.
With Sean Connery, director Michael Crichton and his wife
on the roof of the train in Westmeath

was shooting elsewhere in the city and, at extremely short notice, I had to string about a hundred fireworks around the scaffolding tubes on my own. Each mechanism involved two movements: two pins to be released, one at a time. But I knew this was impossible; I didn't have the manpower. I devised a set-up whereby all the pins were in the upright position, attached to a wire cable. The wire cable would then be pulled, releasing all of the pins together. In rehearsal, Sean was standing a bit too close to the fireworks. I handed the cable to an AD and went over to ask him to move. Just at that moment, the platform lit up; fireworks erupted! Instinctively, I slapped my hand over a sparking charge nearest to the actor. Pain tore through me. Then, someone ran to me with a tin of hand-cleaning gel and I plunged my hand into it.

'Get my car!' Connery ordered.

Minutes later, I was on my way to St Vincent's Hospital – accompanied by '007'! In Casualty, it took seconds for the word to spread: Sean Connery was in the building. Nurses appeared from everywhere. My hand was treated and bandaged in record time! Back in the lobby, Connery was nowhere to be seen. His driver had whisked him back to the set before his adoring fans in the Irish medical profession could find an excuse to detain him! But he had sent his driver back to pick me up. When I was discharged, the driver was waiting for me and took me back to Merrion – to strip down my handiwork and 'wrap'. The night car ferry from Holyhead was pulling into Dun Laoghaire harbour as I drove home – hand stinging, bleary-eyed – and fell into bed.

The First Great Train Robbery: With Sean Connery, in the days following my accident at Merrion Gates. (My hand is still bandaged.)

12

A New Baby – and U2 Is Not
a German Submarine!

Georgina's pregnancy lasted full term, and on 4 April 1979 the labour contractions started. I took her to St Michael's Nursing Home in Dun Laoghaire. This time, I was allowed to wait until she was settled. By that evening, nothing had happened. By the evening of the next day, I was hoping against hope that there were no complications. At about 6 PM, I called the nursing home and was put through to Georgina's room. A male voice answered.

'Who's that?' I asked.

'It's Jimmy here. Who's that?'

'It's Gerry. Can I speak to Georgina?'

'Ah, congratulations, Gerry, you have a baby girl!'

At the nursing home, I found Georgina in tears – upset that her brother hadn't waited for her to tell me the news! I was just happy that the baby was born and that all was well. She was wrapped in a blanket, in Georgina's arms. I sat down and took my daughter, and counted her little fingers and toes. She was beautiful – the image of her mother. Georgina was a big fan of the actress Audrey Hepburn, and Peter Dawson's wife's name was Audrey. She and Georgina had become close friends. Our daughter would be called Audrey.

We had a new daughter and I had a new film; *The Big Red One* was in town – another World War II film, covering the war from the perspective of the men on the ground: in this case, a group of raw recruits in the First Infantry Division, nicknamed 'The Big Red One'. The film was directed by Samuel Fuller, and the cast was headed by Lee Marvin, as the sergeant, and future *Star Wars* star Mark Hamill as 'Private Griff'. Roger Corman's brother Gene was the producer. The effects crew – Kit West, Peter Dawson and Jeff Clifford – had been working on the film in Israel, which had been the principal location. I was on board for a two-week stint in a few Irish castles and stately homes, including Trim Castle in County Meath and Carton House in County Kildare. We had just finished shooting at Trim, and six of us, including Lee Marvin, Sam Fuller and Mark Hamill, were holed up in a pub, having a quiet drink after work. Marvin, ever the raconteur, was in full flight. It promised to be a good session. It was interrupted, however, by an item on the evening-news headlines blaring from a television set sitting on a shelf in one corner:

'The actor Robert Shaw died today, at the age of fifty-one . . . '

Lee's glass stopped halfway to his mouth. A picture of Robert Shaw filled the screen. The newsreader continued:

'Robert Shaw was an accomplished writer and supporting actor. His literary contributions include *The Man in the Glass Booth*. His films include *From Russia with Love, A Man for All Seasons, The Sting* and *The Taking of Pelham One, Two, Three*. He is best remembered as the character Quint in *Jaws*.'

The next news item took over. I turned to pick up my glass and looked over at Lee. Tears were streaming down his face! He plonked his glass on the table.

'My old buddy,' he was saying. 'I gotta go.'

In the following days, the schedule had to be re-arranged to allow Lee to attend his fellow actor's funeral.

'A grown man, crying like a bloody baby!' someone said. 'Bloody evening ruined!'

It was then that I realised I had never before seen a grown man – never mind a famous actor, with a tough, violent screen persona – reduced to tears.

Hot on the heels of *The Big Red One* came *North Sea Hijack*, about a gang of criminals who hijack a Norwegian supply vessel, carrying supplies to two North Sea oil rigs. With limpet mines attached to both rigs, they then demand a ransom of £25 million sterling from the British government – headed by a woman prime minister. The oil company's insurers, Lloyds of London, call in Rufus Excalibur Ffolkes and his team to resolve the situation. Roger Moore played Ffolkes, Anthony Perkins played Lou Kramer, the lead hijacker – and James Mason showed up again, as Admiral Sir Francis Brindsden. Within a year, in real life, a British general election would put Margaret

Thatcher, the first female British prime minister, at the helm of Her Majesty's government!

The director, Andrew McLaglen, had previously worked in Ireland, as a second assistant director on John Ford's *The Quiet Man*, and although *North Sea Hijack* was set in England, much of the film was shot in Ireland. Needing to simulate a Norwegian port, McLaglen and his location manager found the ideal spot in Galway, which also doubled as Scotland. Other locations stretched as far as the Aran Islands and the Burren in County Clare. I teamed up with supervisor John Richardson and technician John Morris, and headed west. Martin Grace, a young Kilkenny man, was Roger Moore's stunt double. Martin, another close friend of mine to this day, has a string of impressive screen credits and is still working as a stunt co-ordinator and lecturer.

North Sea Hijack: With James Mason.
The director, Andrew McLaglen, is in the background.

The effects agenda included gunfire and explosions, and on board the supply vessel we made rain, fog and wind, as well as bullet hits for shoot-outs between the hijackers and the ship's crew. I also got the job of standing by, in a rescue boat, alongside the ship, to pick up another stuntman, doubling as a crew member who is shot and falls overboard. On the first day, filming had to be abandoned because of bad weather. I had chugged the four miles out to the vessel in a rusted tub, skippered by a trawlerman who insisted on cooking breakfast. I was treated to a plateful of sausages, rashers and black and white pudding, swimming in grease, while the supply vessel, with the rest of the crew on board, cruised back to Galway – to showers, a change of clothing and a slap-up lunch.

For three days, I was fed on greasy breakfasts in the tiny wheelhouse, and chugged around Galway bay, freezing, in the wake of a massive cargo ship. Eventually, the First AD's voice crackled over my walkie-talkie.

'Stand by, Gerry! He's coming over!'

'Standing by,' I answered.

'OK, Gerry, camera rolling . . . And Action!'

The tub chugged towards the big vessel. I scanned the black, rolling waves but could see nothing! I asked the trawler captain to move closer, and I made ready to jump. Then I spotted the stuntman, swimming for his life, towards us. We inched closer and he scrambled aboard, heaving and spluttering, teeth chattering.

'Jeez, m-mate, the w-w-water's facking f-freezing!'

'Got him, Gerry?' the First AD's voice asked.

'OK, got him.'

'Great,' he said. 'You can go now.'

The shoot lasted five weeks, during which we were again reminded that the Troubles were never far away. A Union Jack had been hoisted on top of the ruined Kinvara Castle, doubling as a castle in the Scottish Highlands. One morning, we arrived on set to find the flag riddled with bullet holes! Some sort of 'negotiations' took place between the production and the locals, and we were allowed to hoist the flag for a designated number of hours, in order to film, and then take it down!

Rough weather caused more delays: a lot of hours were spent 'on standby'. During one of these periods, I was sitting on a rock, overlooking an inlet, waiting to do some small explosions in the water, when Roger Moore joined me. He raved about the scenery and talked a little about growing up in London; how different it was from where we were sitting: a tranquil spot that was light years from the hustle and bustle.

'How did you get to be a famous actor?' I asked him.

He looked at me with a twinkle in his eyes, and said: 'There's nothing to acting, you know. I don't know why they pay me!' A quip I

North Sea Hijack: With Roger Moore, admiring a motorcycle
on location in Galway

believe he has since repeated in media interviews. His friendliness and
easy manner lifted the 'doldrums' of bad weather and hard graft – and
my growing resentment, for which there were two reasons. One concerned the fact that many films made in Ireland – even those with an
Irish storyline – were released as 'British' films; the other irritation,
closer to the bone, was that I was noticing that my name did not
appear among film credits on many of the films I had worked on! But
for the moment, it seemed that there was very little I could do about
either situation. Down the road, in County Clare, Richard Burton,
Cyril Cusack and Kate Mulgrew were in a love triangle in *Tristan and
Isolde*. I finished work on *Hijack* and immediately joined my school-
mate Barry Blackmore and one of my crew, who was already on location in Clare, making rain for a scene on *Tristan*.

In August, a last-minute invitation from a diving colleague took me to
Donegal, near the border with Northern Ireland. When I arrived, my
friend informed me that he'd lost the trailer, on a bend in the road! But
he managed to get the inflatable and the diving equipment to the
water, and we spent a couple of days exploring the depths of Donegal
Bay. As we prepared to leave – minus the diving club's wrecked trailer
– we loaded the inflatable and the diving bottles into the back of my
estate car. About ten miles south, I had to cross into Northern Ireland
– past a British army checkpoint. Just before the checkpoint, I was

hailed by two soldiers, who were armed to the teeth, and was escorted into the army compound. I was ordered to unload the inflatable, the bottles and my overnight bag. The car was turned inside out, and for the next hour I was questioned and re-questioned. 'Just my luck', I was thinking. I was completely unaware that, while holidaying as usual in his summer home in Mullaghmore, in County Sligo, the queen's cousin, Lord Louis Mountbatten, his daughter's mother-in–law, the Dowager Baroness Brabourne, his grandson Nicholas and a local lad of fifteen had been killed by a bomb planted in his boat in Donegal bay! The Provisional IRA admitted responsibility for the bomb. On that same day, eighteen British soldiers were killed in a bombing at Warrenpoint in County Down. The border counties were bristling with heavily armed British forces and police and, on the southern side, Gardaí and Special Branch. To the combined security forces, a Southern-registered car, laden with diving equipment, travelling south, probably looked highly suspicious.

Between 1979 and 1981, Ireland was teetering between tradition and progress. In Dublin, a heated debate about the building of a new office block on the site of a Viking settlement at Wood Quay was raging as Pope John Paul II arrived in the country, to a tumultuous welcome. Across Ireland, there was a resurgence of Catholic fervour, and a million people flocked to the Phoenix Park for his first Mass on Irish soil. They cheered and waved as a type of golf cart, dubbed 'the Popemobile', carried him on a tour of the park. A helicopter took him from Dublin to Knock Shrine in County Mayo, where the faithful rallied to his call and came out in droves. While the Gardaí were busy controlling the pope's fans, a little-known rock band released its first single: 'Out of Control'! The band had a strange name: when I first heard it, I thought people were talking about German World War II submarines. But the lads in 'U2' would soon be as well known as the pope, sweeping to dizzying heights on the world stage. Rock videos and rock concerts had become all the rage, and effects were now in demand in the music industry. Flames, fireballs and other pyrotechnics formed a dramatic background to the gyrations of the big bands. In 1979, however, U2 were just starting out, performing warm-ups for other bands, and a group called Thin Lizzy was hitting the big time.

My first rock concert would come in 1981. Thin Lizzy was the 'big band', and U2 would be warming up the crowd in the grounds of Slane Castle in County Meath. Paul McGuinness, U2's manager, whom I had first met when he was an AD on one of John Boorman's films, asked me if I would 'let off a few bangs' when the boys came on stage. The boys strutted out, Bono stared out across the thousands present, and silence descended. A rousing drum roll from Larry Mullen, to introduce the first chord on guitar by The Edge, the sound wave enveloped the crowd and my crew and I sent a line of 'flak' racing across the sky: sixty to seventy rockets exploded in rapid succession about a thousand feet in the air. The crowd, of about forty thousand people, went wild! When the boys came off the stage, the crowd was still shouting 'U2! U2!' My son Derek, who was with me at Slane, tells me the opening number was called 'With a Shout'. Backstage, we met the band, literally hopping with excitement, and Derek came away with a set of drumsticks — a gift from Barry Downey, Thin Lizzy's drummer. And this was one credit I would get. A few years ago, I was told that someone had mentioned my name on radio, recounting the 'bombardment' that launched U2, at Slane!

Fashion-show promoters were also jumping on the bandwagon, and atmosphere and pyrotechnics began to be photographed — lighting up the pages of fashion magazines. Backstage, in Dublin's Jury's Hotel, I had to jostle through hoards of semi-naked models, flapping hairdressers and make-up artists to lay cables and set up equipment, in preparation for a show with the theme 'Around the World in Eighty Days'. The idea was to show fashion for all seasons: rain lashed down, snow fell, leaves blew — and the show was a huge success.

My brother Terry, having worked in management for a number of years, had been suggesting that I set up an effects company. He talked about tax benefits, about claiming back expenses, about being in charge, about profits on equipment hire — all sorts of attractive reasons for going into business. Over the next few weeks, we came up with some figures and put a business plan together.

'And do you have anything else lined up, work-wise?' Terry asked.

As luck would have it, I had a call from a director at RTÉ. A lavish period drama production was in the works. I'd had a meeting with Niall McCarthy, head of drama, and John Baragwanath, head of sales, at Fitzpatrick's Castle Hotel in Killiney. The project would call for battles, injuries and armour. Terry and I put in a figure for the special-effects work and presented ourselves at my bank manager's office.

A small, sour-looking individual in his late fifties introduced himself. We shook hands.

'Have a seat,' he instructed. 'OK, now,' he said, pushing aside a folder. 'You want a business loan, I gather?'

'That's right,' I began.

'Have you a business plan?' he asked.

I handed over our carefully prepared portfolio. He studied the contents.

'Film business. Mmm,' he mumbled. 'I see you have a contract with RTÉ. Good.'

He then addressed himself to Terry. 'However, from what I can see, you don't know anything about this business!'

'Well, I can learn,' Terry said. 'I'm a fast learner.'

The manager didn't look impressed.

'Did you ever hear of a career change?' I interjected.

'Well, you know your business, but I'm afraid your partner might find it a bit of a challenge.'

Leaning across, I gathered up the portfolio, closed it and got up. 'Come on, Terry,' I said, 'we're leaving. There's another bank down the road.'

'No, no! Wait!' the manager said, rising from his chair. 'I'm sure we can work this out. Erm, would you like a cup of tea or coffee?'

A couple of weeks later, we had a loan of £21,000 to be invested in setting up a special effects company. In 1981, 'Special Effects Ireland Limited' was born and I would be a company director. Meanwhile, I had a new TV series waiting.

13

LEARNING IRISH HISTORY

The Year of the French was a six-part adaptation for television of Thomas Flanagan's novel of the same name. Set around the time of the 1798 Rebellion in Ireland, it was intended to portray the influences of the French Revolution in Ireland, chiefly among now-famous figures such as Theobald Wolfe Tone, the founder of the rebel United Irishmen, and Father Murphy, a rebel priest from Wexford. The oppressed peasantry had pinned their hopes for freedom from the British monarchy and its agents on the arrival of the forces of republican France. But only a small force of French soldiers sailed to Ireland to lend support to the Irish, now in open rebellion.

With a £2 million budget, *The Year of the French* was an RTÉ co-production with Britain's Channel 4 and FR3 in France. The series production had hired a British military advisor to oversee the cannon fire and choreograph the battle scenes. Sporting a 'handlebar' moustache, he looked every bit the 'Crimean-type' general.

'Are you familiar with filming?' I asked him.

'No, I arrange pageants,' he said gruffly. 'And cannon balls just plop on the ground when they're fired, by the way! We don't have bladdy big explosions.'

I turned to the director. 'The script seems to have cannon exploding. Do you want cannon to explode?'

'Yes,' he replied. 'And I want carriages blowing up . . . and gunfire!'

My team and I set out for the west of Ireland. Not two days into filming, the DOP wanted close-up action shots and, following discussions with the director, commissioned Effects as a second unit. The director suggested that I line up some 'filler' shots of cannons firing and the guns recoiling, some exploding, gunpowder barrels blowing up, and so on – while the first unit filmed armies marching.

As I was lining up the first shot, a camera operator appeared. 'What are you guys doing?' he asked. When he heard that we were a second unit, he trotted back to the director and complained. We had to suspend work and were recalled to the first unit. Two days later, we were given the go-ahead again. This time, one of the producers turned up – in a suit – and announced that *he* would be directing! As well as all the usual battle drama, effects included rain, wind and fires. Then, a last-minute request for a 'sinking' rowboat saw us hastily scrambling together wire cables to pull the boat down into the water. I was not happy with our frantic, ill-prepared effort.

The Year of the French:
Lining up a shot, as second-unit director. A dummy doubles as a rebel, hanging in the background.

There was a disturbingly casual feel to the whole thing, almost to the point of carelessness. One of the military advisor's men received minor burns when a keg of gunpowder, brought in by his team, exploded! Even as I observed the actors and extras – many of whom arrived on set in period costume and modern jewellery – I felt that this wasn't a serious production; it was more like a school play. However, Terry enjoyed himself, working with my team – and as an extra – and the locals plied me with wild salmon, which I cooked in milk and bay leaves and served to my crew on a table by the truck!

In the evenings, the only place to go was the local pub. One evening, I was introduced to Pat Kenny, a young man from Dublin. When he heard I was in special effects, he seemed very interested in what we were doing. He told me that he had trained as a chemical engineer and was now in broadcasting, working with RTÉ. We spent a pleasant hour or so talking about effects, before heading back to our respective lodgings. Pat's voice would become a regular feature on RTÉ radio. By the time I met him again, he had become as well known – and as successful – in TV.

The Year of the French was a flop, however. Although beautifully filmed in parts, and with the music of the Chieftains and Eugene McCabe's acting giving it quite a polished style, it was, by many accounts, a very flawed production. Bad and all as it was, it had provided me with a contract that secured my business loan!

Two years earlier, I had worked on a television series called *Strumpet City*, also an RTÉ production, and a really outstanding historical drama of the time. Indeed, it was declared the highlight of RTÉ's whole drama broadcasting history! A seven-part adaptation of James Plunkett's novel, it gave viewers a true taste of Dublin life during the years 1907 to 1914, a time of bitter confrontation between capitalism and labour, including the 'lock-out' of 1913. *Strumpet City* was RTÉ's biggest breakthrough on the international market, thanks to the casting of Peter Ustinov as King George V of England and Peter O'Toole as the labour-movement leader James Larkin. In his new 'acting career', cast as a smart Dublin Metropolitan policeman, my father excelled himself, while I supervised rain, a massive fire in a coal-yard, collapsing a tenement, and setting a pub on fire. It was hard, dirty work; I could empathise with the men who had worked in the coal-yards in 1913! Another scene involved lengthy preparation of a bloody, gory prosthetic limb – the aftermath of an accident. Donal McCann played the part of the unfortunate worker who has his leg severed. *The Year of the French* came nowhere near *Strumpet City* in terms of professionalism, but work was work, and I had learned to take the rough with the smooth.

Series such as *The Captains and the Kings*, *The Manions of America* and *Ellis Island* followed the fortunes of Irish emigrants making their way in America. Other series, such as *Against the Wind* and *Eureka Stockade*, concerned Irish rebels who were transported to Australia. The Australian production *Waterfront*, much like Strumpet City, portrayed Irish immigrants caught up in the class struggle on the industrial front, and *The Thorn Birds* centred on the more intimate aspects of the lives of the Cleary family, New Zealanders of Irish descent, now at the more affluent end of the Irish-Australian society. While I was at school, Irish history – or indeed the history of anywhere else – held little interest for me. But working on films, I had been exposed to two world wars and a variety of other historical material. Now, through my work on *Strumpet City* and *The Year of the French*, I was learning a smattering of history, which was being played out – albeit in a truncated form and out of sequence – before my eyes.

The Manions of America would introduce an important young Irish actor to American audiences: Pierce Brosnan played the lead role of Rory O'Manion, alongside *Starsky and Hutch* star David Soul as Caleb Staunton. Rory O'Manion emigrates from Ireland to escape the Irish potato famine. In America, he goes into business. Set in Ireland and Philadelphia in the late 1840s, the series also stars Kate Mulgrew as Rory's sweetheart, Rachel. For me, the assignment began with a call from Irish Production Manager Don Geraghty.

'There's a week's shoot coming up in the west of Ireland,' he said. 'How are you fixed?'

'I'm available,' I told him. 'What do they want?'

'It's about evictions. The British burning down cottages, setting fire to them. Battering rams, flaming torches – that sort of thing. American backers. They want to shoot a week in Ireland and the rest will be shot in Australia.'

Manions of America: With David Soul in Athy, County Kildare

Over the next week, I got a crew together and procured all the gas, fuel and other paraphernalia, and we took ourselves back to the west. Three days into the shoot, the word came back: 'We love what we're seeing on the dailies. Stay where you are!' The entire mini-series would now be shot in Ireland! The 'week's shoot' turned into the best part of

In the Border Country: Brendan Gleeson poses with 'gunshot wounds' at Dollymount Strand in Dublin, November 1990.

Richtofen & Brown (*The Red Baron*): World War I planes explode at Weston Airfield, Dublin.

Drinking Crude: The oil tanker goes up. (Later, it was towed back to Kerry, none the worse for wear.)

Christmas 1982:
Georgina with Derek and
Audrey, opening Christmas
presents at home

In the Name of the Father: Manning a smoke machine and wind fan in Dublin's inner city

Seawolves: (from left) David Niven, the author, Peter Dawson and Andrew McLaglen, in Goa, India

Manions of America: The 'gunpowder factory' blows up, but the old mill survives — a million bucks saved!

With Pierce Brosnan, who got his first big break on *Manions of America*

Derek, Chris (one of my technicians) and myself with our 'gravestone' and 'creature', from one of my own projects, *Key for an Epitaph*, abandoned due to lack of finance

Living Doll: Working on prosthetic models in a tiny workshop in London

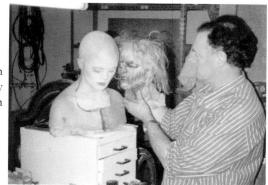

Interior D Stage at Ardmore Studios: A snow scene for a German biscuit commercial

Reign of Fire: The 'city of London' burns – at Ringsend in Dublin.

Covering a Dublin suburban house and garden in snow for an episode of *The Works* for RTÉ

Excalibur: director John Boorman strides among hanging 'knights', as we fill Childers' Woods with smoke

A Man Called Sarge: One of our explosions in the Valley of the Dead Sea

A Man Called Sarge: From half a mile away, oil barrels shoot into the air and the earth trembles from the exploding 'fuel dump'.

Angel (Danny Boy): A burst of flame from the door of the ballroom, shortly before the building exploded. The fake was mistaken for the real thing by the Special Branch.

Testing rain stands on a set in Monkstown, County Dublin

In my workshop, with posters of some of the films
I have worked on

Silver Lion Award: My childhod friend Sean Corcoran and I share the credits –
for a commercial on water conservation for Dublin Corporation (now Dublin
City Council).

The Last Days of Pompeii: The effects crew recreate the eruption of Mount Vesuvius. This is where I had a close call with a fireball machine.

Soweto: An armoured car runs the gauntlet of strategically placed burning debris, created by 'protesters', in a scene from the series, filmed at Jos in Nigeria.

Spacetruckers: With some of the crew and BMWs (Bio-Mechanical Warriors) on D Stage at Ardmore Studios

Like sentries: With Michael McNieve, head of security at Ardmore. He was responsible for giving me the name 'Boom-Boom'.

Allan Quatermain: The completed earthquake set near Victoria Falls, Zimbabwe.

Saving Private Ryan: Manning a 'bezzler', creating fog at Curracloe, County Wexford

Saving Private Ryan: With a technician, Andrew, and a couple of 'casualties' at Curracloe

Creating a hovercraft landing at Bray for a Guinness commercial

Soweto: Blowing up a truck beside the university in Jos, Nigeria

In the Name of the Father: Daniel Day-Lewis and fellow 'inmates' have a snowball fight in the exercise yard at Dublin's St Patrick's Institution.

A Man Called Sarge: With Peter Dawson (at right) in Israel

Zardoz: Rigging skeletons for the film at a workshop in Ardmore Studios

Roses in Dublin: Sending a flaming Morris Minor over the cliff at Howth, County Dublin. A short time later, I would be retrieving the car from the seabed!

two months. As far as I was concerned, this was as good as a feature film.

The evictions over, we headed back to Dublin. A week later, I got a call from one of the producers. 'We'd like you to come to Athy, in Kildare,' he said. 'We want to blow up a gunpowder factory.'

One of the most prominent landmarks in Athy is a towering mill on the banks of the Grand Canal, under the stewardship of the Office of Public Works. This was the gunpowder factory! I met American producer Stan Kaylis and his production manager Billy Ray Smith, a New Yorker, and went to survey the building.

'If we knock this building, it'll cost us a million bucks!' Stan said.

Several floors up, a crow flew from the parapet, dislodging a cloud of dust and debris.

'It looks a bit unstable,' I said. 'It may not be safe to be working around it.'

'Mmm . . .' was all Stan said. 'Come on, let's take a look around. We'll show you the part we want to blow up.'

And that's when I was met with the first challenge. The construction department had built a solid extension on to the front of the building, facing the canal. It was supposed to be a large warehouse and had a real slate roof, which was supported by heavy wooden beams and dozens of timber struts, criss-crossing in all directions. In fact, it looked more like a permanent fixture than a film set! A quick look around inside told me that a good deal of the construction department's handiwork would have to be undone. Stan and Billy looked worried.

'How much will it cost?' Billy asked.

'I don't know,' I replied.

I pointed to the crumbling stonework. 'We'll also need scaffolding erected on that corner of the building to prevent it collapsing!'

'Right,' Stan said. 'Let's go and find Construction.'

In the art department, designers Conor Devlin and Arden Gantly were putting the finishing touches to the drawings of the new construction's exterior.

'What? Dismantle it?' Conor asked.

'Well, a lot of those uprights will have to come out,' I told him. 'I have to get in steel tubes and tanks and gas piping. I really should have known about this earlier.'

'How long will it take?' Billy asked.

'About two weeks.'

Construction manager Joe Lee was called in, and I waited while they all conferred. I didn't envy Joe the task of having to break the news to his construction crew!

'OK, you got it, Gerry,' Stan said at last.

Just to make sure that there were no more surprises, I took myself on a tour of the vicinity. Less than fifty yards from this historic building, I found a private house. The owner, an elderly gentleman, greeted me at the door. Having explained who I was and what I was proposing to do, I was invited out the back. In the garden, he had a greenhouse – about half an acre of glass, a virtual 'Crystal Palace' – right in the line of fire! I high-tailed it back to Stan and the others.

'By the way,' I said. 'You'll need to add about half an acre of tarpaulin to the budget.'

Work began. Out came a portion of the timber uprights and roof beams; in went my steel tubes, tanks and steel plates. In each of the plates on the ground, we packed in our explosives: 'lifters', to launch the uprights, and lift the roof. Hundreds of gallons of fuel would go into the tanks, sending fireballs into the air. Piping was laid in to carry the gas that would create an inferno in the background. I would perch myself on a twenty-foot tower, with my firing mechanisms. Signs were erected proclaiming: 'Danger! Keep Out!' I asked Barry Blackmore, the First AD, to ensure that no one with walkie-talkies came within two hundred feet of the site in case their static ignited the powder charges, and that any filming in the building would be completed before I 'loaded'. By the day of the shoot, we had the pipe-fitting done and were making up our pyros. About a third of the warehouse was loaded by lunchtime. The town was buzzing, and locals were positioning themselves on various vantage points around the perimeter to get a good view of the activity. Extra cameras were hidden in barrels and perched on makeshift platforms – and one was on a barge on the canal. Coming back from lunch, I suddenly noticed a flicker through a window in the warehouse. A flame! Inside, one of the lights had caught fire – inches from one of my fuel tanks! I yanked the plug from the socket and carried the flaming light outside. A million bucks saved!

We packed and packed, progressing on schedule. Then Barry Blackmore appeared.

'Sorry about this, Gerry,' Barry said. 'We have to get in some interior shots while the place is still standing!'

Work came to a standstill. The hours rolled by. Finally, a close-up of Pierce Brosnan's steel-studded boot sparking against the concrete ramp was done in one take. The factory was supposed to go up at 8 PM. It was heading for 9.30 when I called for last checks and climbed on to my perch. One of my crew, along with Barry and a cameraman, joined me. We had a panoramic view of the set and the canal. Cameras rolled. Silence fell. Somewhere in the darkness beyond the town, crowds were gathered, their eyes trained on the glow from the film lighting. Otherwise, the town was in darkness. At 10 PM, I sent a fireball through the open doorway. A couple of stuntmen were 'blown out' by the blast. Two cameramen on board the barge ran for cover! I was engrossed in the ensuing barrage, firing, and watching; the adrenalin flowed, as fireballs leapt hundreds of feet into the night sky and explosions rocked the town.

When it was over, only the sound of crackling and the smell of burning fuel hung in the air.

'The sky's full of matchsticks!' Barry said.

I looked up. Millions of smouldering bits of timber and debris were falling in slow motion. I held my breath. Fire crews were standing by, primed and ready. We waited. I thought about 'Crystal Palace' next door. The cameras continued to roll. I felt sweat running down my body. The film unit broke into applause. The gentleman next door inspected his glasshouse. It was still intact. No injuries, no damage. Athy's flimsy old mill was still standing, and Stan's 'million bucks' was safe. Next day, I slept. That night, I was the 'VIP' at a champagne dinner in the hotel, hosted by the producers.

'That will be the biggest explosion ever seen on TV,' Stan said.

I was invited to work in Los Angeles. I had an open invitation to Stan's home in the Hollywood Hills. A few days later, I got a call from the Irish production manager: extra work. The Pine Forest near Rathfarnham was picked for the scene in which a team of horses is pulling a wagon loaded with barrels of gunpowder. The horses are spooked by a snake. They bolt, and the wagon comes adrift. As it tumbles down an embankment, the driver jumps and the barrels fall off and explode. 'A spectacular shot' was the verdict among the film's backers in LA.

A month later, as I was arriving home, with the family, from a visit to my parents, about to turn the key in the front door, I heard the telephone ringing. I grabbed the one nearest, on the wall in the kitchen.

'Hello, mate.' It was Peter Dawson.

'How are you, Peter?' I asked.

'Great. You sound puffed. You been out joggin', then?'

'No, just ran to the phone.'

'Listen, mate, get your shots done. You're going to India!'

It took a few seconds for this to sink in. 'When?' I asked.

'I'd say just after Christmas. You'll need time to let your shots take.'

The shots were inoculations against a whole range of strange-sounding diseases. I hated injections and wondered what these cocktails of drugs would do to me.

But I didn't have much time to dwell on it. Audrey was nine months old, and Derek was just about to start secondary school. With a baby crawling around everywhere, gates had to be fitted at the bottom and top of the stairs. With the winter setting in, the big, high-ceilinged rooms were eating up heat, so I installed several layers of roof insulation and new windows at the back. Georgina was now a full-time mother who also had a good business sense and good foresight. She always liked to have some other enterprise running, in case the entertainment industry went belly-up. Her latest idea was to turn the two floors at the back of the house into a separate apartment and let it out. More renovations!

At Ardmore, the former farmyard was constantly flooded. Water ran down the inside of the walls of the cowshed that I used as my workshop, and I was forever moving equipment and buying sheets of plastic and tarpaulin to keep it covered and protect it from water damage. Steel boxes kept electrical tools safe from the mice and rats that seemed to multiply, despite the presence of stray cats. I had an old radio, a present from my cousin Joe Byrne, just like our 'Dan Dare' radio in Williamstown. Having discovered the comfort of heated valves, the mice had set up home in the back.

Just before Christmas, my travel ticket arrived and my thoughts wandered to India. Despite the Christmas festivities, Derek was looking a bit downcast. I knew he would miss me.

'It's a bit far for your mum to come and visit, especially with Audrey,' I told him, 'but I'll ring as often as I can.'

Rumours of another film were flying around Ardmore. John Boorman phoned to say that he would be going into production with a film in January or February, wished me a merry Christmas, and said he'd be in touch in a couple of weeks. December came and went without another word from Boorman – or the studios – about the film. On the one hand, I was disappointed: I would have welcomed the opportunity to work with Boorman again. On the other hand, I had an assignment already 'in the bag'. I opted for India.

14

From Goa to *Excalibur*

I remember watching a jumbo jet landing at Dublin Airport for the first time and thinking that it was the biggest aircraft I had ever seen. Now, on board a huge British Airways jumbo, on my way to India from Heathrow, I walked around, stretching my legs, exploring. Hours passed, meals were served. Below, I caught glimpses of strange lands and blue seas. Overhead, sunshine. I dozed off. When I awoke, I felt warm. The cabin lights were off. It was night, and we were still travelling. I gazed out the window. I could see the curve of the earth, backlit by a halo of light, with 'flames' rising off its surface. I couldn't take my eyes off the shimmering earth, imagining that I was in outer space! Then, across the aisles and through a window on the far side, I could see the beginning of a few rays of light: dawn was breaking, and the cabin crew were serving breakfast.

On arrival at Bombay, my breath almost stopped when I stepped out into the Indian heat! In Arrivals, I spotted a European-looking man dressed in white, holding a placard with my name on it. Eagerly, I headed towards him.

'Mr Johnston, nice to meet you,' he said. 'Please, come this way.'

He seemed anxious to get away. Outside, crowds milled around the building, creating a deafening babble! For a moment, I felt like a celebrity! Then I noticed hoards of 'disabled' people – from children to young adults – on go-cart-type contraptions, pushing their way forward; some without arms, others without legs. Suddenly, out of the corner of my eye, I saw something: an object flying through the air – straight at my head! On impulse, I caught it. Through its filthy clothing, it felt odd, like a rubber doll, but I soon realised I was in fact holding a live baby! In an instant, my driver grabbed it and flung it back into the crowd! I couldn't speak. Carrying one of my bags in front of him, he pushed his way forward. I followed, struggling with the rest of my bags, feeling hands touching me, the noise doing my head in! Finally, we were in the car. I must have been as white as a sheet.

'They break the children's bones, or chop off their limbs, and thrust these maimed bodies under your nose to get money,' he said. 'They have maimed kids and kids with broken limbs going around the streets on those go-carts, begging.'

I felt my stomach heave. The driver looked at me sympathetically. 'Yes, I know . . . barbaric,' he said. 'You'll see some awful things here.'

We sped away from the airport and out of the city. It was not yet noon, but the temperature seemed to be already at boiling point! We were on our way to another airport, where I would catch my flight to Goa. On board the Air India 737, the first thing I needed was a strong coffee! As the plane touched down at Goa, I wondered whether more horrors awaited me. Feeling slightly uneasy, I made my way through Arrivals. A tall man was standing with a placard that read 'Gerry Johnson'. 'They can never get my name right!' I thought. I headed towards him.

'Hi, my name's Gerry Johnston,' I said.

'Ah, Gerry, good to meet you. My name's Euan Lloyd.'

I recognised the name from the unit list. Euan Lloyd was the producer. He asked if I'd had a pleasant flight. I told him about my experience at Bombay. He just shook his head, knowingly. We arrived in Panaji, the capital of Goa, and at the hotel I met the rest of the effects crew: Kit West, Rodney Fuller, Terry Glass, Kenny Gittens and Peter Dawson. Peter appointed himself guide and mentor, and over the next few days glued himself to my side. I welcomed his company. I soon got used to the temperature, which ranged from 25 to 33 degrees centigrade – in January!

Goa is divided into 'New' and 'Old' Goa. It is basically a triangular island with a coastline that is about sixty-five miles long – and, inland, mountains rising to thousands of feet. I learned that the region had been in the hands of various 'tribes' for hundreds of years before being taken over by the Portuguese in the sixteenth century. Then it was 'lost' to the British – who in turn lost it back to the Portuguese. A lot of people had Portuguese names and everyone spoke English, although some Hindus spoke another language, and some Muslims yet another. Beer was cheap, and of course there was a plentiful – and legal – supply of local 'hooch', as Peter called it. Tourism seemed to be the main money-spinner: the hotels were good, and restaurants and cafés catered for the needs of all segments of the tourist trade. Around the coastline, sandy beaches were crowded with foreign tourists – just like any Mediterranean resort. One of these was 'Baga Beach', where, according to Peter, the rich hippies hung out, and pot was readily available.

Sea Wolves: 'Cows are sacred,' Peter said.
Here, I wait while one has her lunch!

Our workshop was located on the ground floor of an old hotel, in the middle of a street market. Some of the actors were staying upstairs. On the narrow street, rickshaws jostled with oxen, and women peddled saris and exotic spices. Between the racket on the street and engineering downstairs, I don't know how the actors managed to live there at all! Our effects team was augmented by dozens of local men, who had a habit of disappearing every day at about noon! I asked one of the other locals where they went.

'They've gone for their "fix",' he told me.

I was puzzled.

'Come with me,' he said.

Outside, in a compound, he pointed underneath a line of trucks. I got down on all fours. There, curled up like snakes, were a couple of our workers – out cold! Every vehicle had a couple of comatose bodies suspended on the chassis! The 'fix' was a tobacco-type concoction which they wrapped in leaves and smoked. On another day, I lifted the lid off a laundry basket and discovered one of these guys asleep inside!

We came to expect anything and, indeed, were seldom disappoint-ed. The sight of cows meandering through the market was common-place.

'Cows are sacred here,' Peter said. 'You can't harm them.'

One day, as Peter and I strolled around the streets, exploring, three massive elephants rumbled towards us! I needn't have worried; these things were simply 'on their lunch' – like the cows – helping them-selves to a variety of fruit from the market stalls! Arriving back at our hotel that evening, we were met by the sight of an enormous brown bear! He was muzzled and was held on a flimsy chain by a little weasel of a young Indian man in a loincloth. People were throwing coins from a safe distance as they passed in and out of the hotel. The fol-lowing evening, I opened the door of my room to find clothes and shoes strewn everywhere. I thought I'd been burgled. Then I saw the culprit: a good-sized monkey, sitting on the floor of my bathroom, chewing my toothpaste! I picked up a shoe and threw it at him, where-upon he sprang out through the open window – still clutching the toothpaste! When I looked out, there he was, looking up at me, teeth bared as if grinning, as he sat on a branch of a palm tree, just below my third-floor window, chewing away on my tube of Colgate.

The film I had come to work on was a true World War II story, about a secret British military mission to destroy a Nazi radio ship. A group of retired soldiers, dubbed the 'Calcutta Light Horse', played by Gregory Peck, Roger Moore, Trevor Howard and David Niven, are hired to pose as civilians, on a fishing trip, but they are really trying to ascertain which ship carries the radio. The ships are in neutral waters, so the British government must deny any involvement, if the mission fails. The Calcutta Light Horse succeeds, however and blows up the ship. And so our department put together the usual 'arsenal'. Our tar-get, a retired cargo vessel, lay anchored out to sea, and we were ferried back and forth as we loaded her up with explosives. When we finally started shooting, a daily feast of the most sumptuous Indian cuisine was served on board.

By now, I had come to adore Indian food, still opting for fish as a first preference. I had caught thousands of fish in my youth and thought I knew all there was to know about fish – until one evening, as the sun was dropping over the horizon and we were cruising back to shore. We were nearing port when suddenly a flying object narrow-ly missed my head! My mind raced back to the stomach-churning incident at Bombay. I ducked – and then I saw them: flying fish, leaping out of the water, not unlike salmon, but much faster, remaining airborne for several seconds! Shoals of them swam quickly towards the surface and then jumped into the air. Once they were airborne, I could see wing-like fins and large forked tails, like outboard motors, as the fish gained height and glided along, sometimes for thirty feet, and as high as about three feet above the surface of the water.

Indeed, these waters harboured a huge variety of sea life. One of the film shots was a close-up of a limpet mine attached to the side of the ship. I got the job of fixing the flat disc – the 'mine lookalike' – in place. It was a night scene, and I would descend via a rope ladder and slap the thing on the bow, while a few smaller boats directed lights on to the ship. Clutching my 'mine', I was about to hoist myself over the side when I saw a seething mass of ominous-looking objects floating on the surface. It was a sea of crab – all with their claws in the air – probably drawn by the lights around the ship. I was scrambling down a rope ladder towards them, in T-shirt and shorts! I managed to remain down, inches from the water – inches from 'crab-land' – until the director, Andrew McLaglen, got his shot. After what seemed like about a year, the First AD shouted: 'Take it off, Gerry! You can come up now!'

Minutes later, a flotilla of hollowed-out tree trunks arrived alongside us, and a dozen or so young, half-naked men began diving from these boats, disappearing for minutes at a time, diving for barnacles. It looked dangerous but they seemed to be enjoying themselves – much like I had enjoyed my youthful fishing exploits back home. Finally, as dawn broke, the crew boarded the ferry back to shore. In the semi-darkness, I noticed that several of them had lit cigarettes, and I got a strange smell.

'What's that smell?' I asked Peter.

'Hashish,' he replied sleepily.

Two days later, Roger Moore, David Niven and I were sitting on deck, in the shade of the wheelhouse, during lunch break. David and Roger were sharing stories about London, their respective acting careers, and the directors they'd worked with. Then Gregory Peck joined the group. I'd been hoping for a chance to talk to Peck about Dingle. He sat down, stretching his long legs out in front of him, and I told him about having slept in 'his' room in the Miss Ashes' house in Dingle.

'No kidding!' he laughed, and for the next twenty minutes or so we reminisced about the Miss Ashes and Dingle. Later that day, he posed with me for a photograph – one of my treasured pictures, to this day.

Sea Wolves: Gregory Peck on the set in Goa

Goa was a long way from the windy beaches of Kerry, and danger seemed to lurk everywhere. I was out with UK effects technician Kenny Gittens, exploring life away from the towns. We came to a remote village some twenty miles from base. We had taken a walk, and as we strolled back along a narrow dirt road, we stopped to rest. I sat down on a grass verge in the shade of a dry stone wall. Suddenly, Kenny let out a roar.

'Gerry, get out of there, NOW!'

I turned around and came face to face with a massive cobra! I jumped to my feet. Kenny was pointing towards the wall.

'Look!' he said.

The entire wall was almost obliterated by snakes! We walked backwards until we were at a safe distance, and then broke into a run, until we were right in the village! Having gathered our wits about us again, we discovered that the place was full of market stalls. I spotted some silk shirts hanging inside a poky little tailor's shop. In a flash, Kenny and I were measured by the tailor, and after a few hours we'd collected some beautiful silk shirts and bought some spices and incense to take home. Most of these spices were still relatively rare in Ireland in

1980; nowadays, of course, they are available in every supermarket and health-food store.

When the picture wrapped, we had a two-day stopover in Bombay. The owner of our hotel took it upon himself to show us the sights, including what they called 'Cage City', an unbelievably sleazy area with makeshift cages, through which men handed money, before visiting unseen prostitutes inside. Cage City was perched at the top of a steep incline of busy streets, looking down on a communal laundry, where thousands of women were scrubbing and washing, non-stop. While we cruised, a sea of hands and faces were pressed against the windows. Fists banged on the roof. Our 'tour guide' firmly clasped a handgun!

'Don't open the windows!' he warned. 'And don't take pictures!'

When we returned to the hotel, he ordered his driver to swap cars. Within minutes, an open-top Cadillac nosed into view, and we were taken on a tour of the city's more refined areas. India was a land of extremes. I had a sense that there was much more to it: hidden mysteries that I might never explore. But it was time to leave. The picture had finished shooting, and a call had come through to the production office from Ireland. Mike Dryhurst, John Boorman's production manager, was on the line.

'Gerry, how soon can you get back to Ireland?' Mike asked.

John Boorman's picture was happening at last!

After months of Indian heat, I looked – and felt – like seasoned oak. At Heathrow, I skimmed my 'five o'clock shadow' and slapped my face with cold water. At Dublin Airport, one of Arthur Dunne's drivers was waiting, to take me straight to the studios. At Ardmore, laden with luggage, I reported to a new office block, nicknamed 'the synagogue', and was told to go straight into the production meeting. All heads turned. John Boorman rose from his chair.

'My, my, Gerry, you got a good tan!' he announced. 'Everyone, this is Gerry Johnston. Gerry, you're just in time for breakfast!'

Physically, I was shattered! Instead of food, I needed sleep. Mentally, I *was* asleep! But there was a definite buzz in the air, and after breakfast I got my 'second wind'; after all, an urgent summons from the director was a privilege! Then Boorman called for 'formal' introductions. I already knew most of the Irish HODs, but there were a couple of unfamiliar faces. One of them belonged to Peter Hutchinson, a stocky individual, wearing glasses.

'I'm the special-effects supervisor,' he said.

I was suddenly wide awake. For the next couple of hours, I tried to figure out why I'd been summoned back and whisked directly from the airport to a production meeting – presumably to supervise the effects. At lunchtime, I approached the director.

'John, I thought I was asked to supervise this picture!'

He just shrugged.

'Well, who asked Peter Hutchinson to work on the picture?'

'I'm not sure,' he said. 'I think maybe the art director.'

'Who's the art director?' I asked.

'Tim Hutchinson.'

Tim and Peter were brothers! Tired and downcast, I headed home. After a night's sleep, I felt better, glad to be working on home turf again. The budget for *Excalibur* was reported to be about $11 million – a major boost for Ardmore. The money came entirely from a Hollywood film company. Irish banks and Irish businesses were wary of investing in film – a situation which did not change until the late 1990s.

Based on Thomas Malory's classic *Le Morte d'Arthur*, *Excalibur* was a mixture of historical fact and romantic fiction. The cast – mostly theatrical actors from the London stage – was headed by Nigel Terry, as King Arthur, with Helen Mirren as Morgana, Nicol Williamson as Merlin, the American actor Patrick Stewart, of *Star Trek* fame, as Leondegrance, the Irish actor Liam Neeson as Gawain – and Gabriel Byrne, in his first feature film, as Uther Pendragon. The film begins with the stirring Siegfried's Funeral March and a visually stunning scene, showing horses breath in the night air, back-lit by fires, and their riders, Uther's men, doing battle with the Duke of Cornwall's army. The young, naive Arthur releases the enchanted sword Excalibur from a stone, goes on to become King Arthur, marries Guenevere played by Cheri Lunghi, and builds an empire with the court of Camelot as its epicentre. The film was a lavishly designed epic, against the picturesque landscape of the hills and forests around Wicklow.

When I finally read the script, I knew we were in for a lot of hard work.

'Can you pick up a couple of extra crew out here?' Peter Hutchinson asked. (I was always amused when the visitors referred to Ireland as 'out here'.)

'Sure,' I told him – and enlisted Mick Doyle and Gay O'Reilly, glad to have some 'home-grown' support, as well as some additional mechanical skills, on board. I wasn't running the effects department, but I was determined to do a good job. Fire-lit breath of the horses, acres of thick mist, the blood and gore of the battle scenes, sparks from Merlin's crosier, fires, flaming torches, and smoke, rain, wind and snow and effects weaponry were the order of the day – or in this case, the order of many a long, cold night. The weather in the Wicklow hills provided at least one real snow scene, with 'walls' of snow along the mountain roads. While scrambling about with a smoke machine, Alan Whibley, another UK effects technician, disappeared momentarily down a well-camouflaged bog-hole! Happily, he survived intact. The summer of 1980 brought some respite, but it was one of the worst on record, with rain almost every day, which caused shooting to run over schedule. At night, the heavy, dewy atmosphere brought out swarms of midges. The creatures seemed unaffected by the insect repellent doled out by the unit nurse. A more effective antidote was smoke – and as we had to pump in smoke constantly, to create the mist effects required for atmosphere and lighting, the midges were kept somewhat at bay.

The location was Childers' Wood, a deciduous forest on the Barton-Childers Estate, near Annamoe. For one sword fight – a night scene – as the rest of the effects crew worked four large smoke generators, fired by industrial gas burners, mounted on tractors, I was 'on the floor', running around with a twenty-five-pound smoke machine in one hand and a twenty-five-pound gas bottle in the other. The forest was enveloped in 'mist'. Boorman kept shouting: 'More smoke, Gerry! Run!' And so I ran – in and out, back and forth – covering about a quarter of an acre each time, stopping to duck in among the shadows to change over to a freshly filled machine and a bottle of gas.

'More smoke!' the director shouted.

This time, I didn't see the tree root. I was on the ground, writhing in agony. The nurse and the First AD ran over.

'My ankle' was all I could say.

I was helped up, but I couldn't stand on my right foot, which had swelled up like a balloon. Within minutes, I was being assisted to a waiting car, John Boorman's voice echoing in my ears.

'What's going on? I need more smoke on the set!'

'You need medical attention,' the nurse said.

The Casualty Department at St Michael's Hospital was quiet, and I was attended to immediately. I wanted something for the pain – fast!

'You've damaged your Achilles tendon,' the doctor began.

What was *that*?

'You have three options,' he said. 'I can put your foot in a cast – that's the first option.'

'Will I be able to work?' I asked.

'Not for about six weeks.'

Six weeks?

'Surgery is often an option of last resort,' he was saying. After that I heard only an odd phrase – 'Friction between the tendon', 'Recovery is slow', 'A temporary cast' and something about 'a rehabilitation program to avoid weakness.' I was already getting weak, and now my head was throbbing.

'What's the third option?' I asked. *Excalibur* and work were uppermost in my mind.

'A steroid injection,' he replied. 'But you'll have to stay off that foot for a few days.'

'I'll take the injection,' I said.

'Fine,' he said. 'When?'

'Now!' I said.

'Well, lie up there, face down,' he said, indicating the examination couch.

I clambered up and lay on my stomach. The doctor busied himself with instruments. He took hold of my throbbing foot.

'You'll probably feel this.'

I felt an unmerciful stab somewhere in the region of my afflicted ankle. I screamed.

After one restless day, in and out of bed, tanked up to the eyeballs on painkillers, I returned to work. Back on set, actors, extras, crew and caterers were milling about, chatting, rigging, rehearsing. The director gave me one of his 'surprised' looks, and smiled. I expected a bit of fuss; someone to ask how I was. No one did. It was business as usual.

As the weeks wore on, this picture seemed to throw up more than its fair share of hazards. A scene requiring the sword Excalibur to rise from the lake involved the lowering of a hydraulic rig, with the sword in place, into the black waters of Luggala Lake near the village of Roundwood. The rig was pulled out from the lakeshore with ropes, and dropped into the water. As it was lowered, it suddenly stopped about fifteen feet beneath the surface. Peter Hutchinson, Alan Whibley and I set out in a dinghy to secure it. Wearing a snorkel, I dropped into the water. Within seconds, I was in pitch blackness. My torch beam stopped only inches from my face! Momentarily disorientated, I was suddenly aware that the dinghy was circling overhead. I could hear the engine coming at me, but I didn't know from which direction; the vibration was all around me! Instinctively, I put my hands over my face. The propeller ploughed past, a hair's breath from my fingernails! I dived. Down at the rig, I could just about make out that it was perched at an angle on a ledge. I tried to gather the ropes to pull the rig upright, but it tilted and began free-floating down and down, entangling me in swirling ropes, one of them around my leg. I was sinking fast, deeper and deeper into the abyss! I fumbled about for my knife, which was strapped to my leg. I finally managed to pull it free and begin cutting through the rope. After what seemed like an eternity, I was free and floating to the surface, gasping for air!

The rig had disappeared. A second attempt, by a group of my colleagues from the diving club, failed to locate it, and a couple of days later, a team of professional deep-sea divers was called in. The divers did manage to locate it and, using inflatable air bags, brought it back to the surface. 'Gosh, that lake is some depth,' one of them said afterwards.

Luggala Lake, known as Lough Tay, in the shadow of Luggala Mountain, is part of the Guinness Estate and is visually stunning. The magical landscape provided a perfect location for the 'Lady of the Lake' shots in *Excalibur*. I have been back there, working on various productions since then but, despite the visible beauty, I am reminded each time of the 'shadow side' of Luggala: the frightening, never-ending depths beneath the surface.

Mishaps plagued the stunt department too. A team of young stuntmen – Dominick Hewitt, Alan Walsh, Paul Kelly, Eddie McShortal, Donal O'Farrell and Ken Murphy – provided the spectacular falls and the choreographed fighting, and we hoisted Mick (the 'gorilla' from *Zardoz*) up in a harness, to double as one of Arthur's knights, swinging perilously from the raised drawbridge of the massive silver Camelot Castle, built on the studio back lot. Eddie Kennedy, an accomplished polo player, Tony Doyle, Donal Fortune and Bronco McLoughlin were among the riders and stunt riders. Going for 'the take' in a jousting scene, Kennedy's lance pierced Bronco's visor and scratched the top of his head! But Bronco recovered, and a couple of weeks later he submitted himself to a further tortuous few hours, strapped, half-naked and upside down, to the back of a horse being walked by a knight through the forest!

By contrast, Boorman's son Charley, who was fourteen, seemed to be thoroughly enjoying himself playing the young Mordred, riding around in a golden mask. My son Derek, the same age as Charley, was behind a grotesque rubber mask as one of a community of 'little people': all children dressed as old people, who had to remain motionless for hours as I sprayed them with 'blood' and guts. I was worried, as Derek was a diabetic and I feared that he might hit a 'low'. But he was fine, and had a ball. For me, something had changed on *Excalibur*. For the first time since I had begun working in the film business, I felt dejected. On *Zardoz*, I had experienced rebuffs, dismissive comments and derogatory remarks, and on this film, my injury and my close call in the lake had left me with a feeling that I was just a cog in a machine. The promise of the role of supervisor on a big picture, the glittering vision that had sustained me on the long flight from India, was fading. But now, as I saw it, the most powerful man on the project – Boorman, my 'mate' – had, in fact, been powerless, outnumbered and over-ruled, ironically by his fellow Englishmen. I was angry – and I was not alone.

As shooting drew to a close, rumour had it that the Irish members of the crew were being let go. 'Typical,' people said. 'The Irish are always asked to do the donkey work, and then they're the first to be to let go!' Years later, another battle scene on the plains of the Curragh, and the words of an English monarch, echoed those feelings. Again, buried among a large English effects contingent on *Braveheart*, I heard Patrick McGoohan, as King Edward I, assessing his battle strategy and delivering the immortal line: 'Send in the Irish!' And in they went: brave, obedient – and dispensible.

From the point of view of the Irish crew on *Excalibur*, letting Irish go and retaining the foreigners made no sense: paying per diems, transport and higher wages must surely have pushed the budget to its limits. Collecting my second-last-week's wages in the production office, I met a few of the Irish crew. 'Ah, to hell with them,' they said. 'Just take the money and run!' I wondered if I would even get a credit for *Excalibur*. With a week to go, I eased off, no longer eager to make sacrifices for the picture.

15

FROM POLITICS AT ARDMORE
TO A CLOSE CALL AT POMPEII

A young Irishman was on his way up in the business. Neil Jordan had made a documentary on the making of *Excalibur* and was a fan of John Boorman. Boorman had teamed up with Sheamus Smith, the former managing director of Ardmore Studios, to establish the Motion Picture Company of Ireland, based at Ardmore Studios, to produce low-budget films. The company's first project was *Angel*, written and directed by Neil Jordan. Barry Blackmore was the producer. Set in Northern Ireland, *Angel* had an all-Irish cast, headed by Stephen Rea. In fact, only four of the film unit credited were not based in Ireland: a pleasant change! *Angel* is the story of a saxophonist called Danny, who sets out to avenge the murder of his band manager and a deaf-mute girl. As he searches for answers, he finds only more questions, illustrating the wider context of the Troubles, which was then still gripping Northern Ireland. It was the first film to receive funding from the Irish Film Board, of which John Boorman was a member.

Explosions, shootings and knee-cappings, rain and smoke were the effects required, depicting the horrors that were still raging less than a hundred miles up the road. In one scene, terrorists blow up a ballroom. We were using a semi-derelict building on waste ground, on the site of the present-day industrial estate at Sandyford outside Dublin. The British ambassador's residence stood in sylvan seclusion in nearby Leopardstown. In spite of brave attempts in the 1970s to bring hostilities in the North to an end – most notably the Sunningdale Agreement in 1973 – no real progress had been made, and the Troubles rumbled on, spilling over to the south, often resulting in death and destruction. The ambassador's residence was protected by a team of Special Branch security guards: 'watchdogs', with the memory of the assassination of the previous incumbent, Sir Christopher Ewart-Biggs, by the IRA in 1976 still fresh in their minds.

On the evening of the shoot, a couple of Gardaí were directing the mounting Friday-evening rush-hour traffic. I had done my duty: I had visited the local Garda station a couple of weeks beforehand and informed the sergeant of our impending explosion. I had then informed the film's locations department about our effects procedures and got on with the preparations. Blissfully unaware that I was about to blow up a building within yards of the spot where Sir Ewart-Biggs' car had been attacked, I was eagerly awaiting my fire cover – in the form of a 'green goddess' fire tender and crew. As we put the final touches to the building and the cameras were set up, there was no sign of the tender. At 6 PM, as darkness fell, I got a call on my walkie-talkie informing me that the 'green goddess' was stuck in traffic about a mile away! Barry Blackmore appeared at my side.

'Gerry, we gotta go,' he said urgently.

'I'm not going without fire cover, Barry,' I told him, my eyes glued on the road.

Just then, I spotted the fire tender, crawling along the narrow road, inching past the traffic, which was now halted and pulled over by a traffic cop.

'OK, Barry, stand by,' I said, and ran back to my firing equipment.

'OK, guys, going hot,' I called to my crew, indicating that the firing mechanism was powered.

'Camera rolling,' the First AD called.

Our 'IRA terrorists', in their costumes – balaclavas and black attire –exited our ballroom, fired off a few blanks, jumped into their getaway car and sped away, out of shot.

'Now, Gerry!' the first AD shouted.

I hit the button. Fireballs lit up the sky and the sound of the bangs filled the air. While the cameras filmed the aftermath of the explosion, the 'green goddess' pulled into the waste ground and the crew began pulling out hoses and connecting to the water supply.

Suddenly, unfamiliar black-clad figures appeared from everywhere. Some of them jumped over cars as they swarmed onto the set.

'Who's in charge here?' one of them roared, frothing at the mouth.

In seconds, the unit was surrounded by the real Special Branch, armed with machine-guns, their fingers on the triggers. There had been a glitch in communications between the Gardaí and the Special

Branch, and once again the fake had been mistaken for the real thing. But the drama didn't seem to bother Neil Jordan, who was as happy as a pig in the proverbial with the explosion, and *Angel* received critical acclaim at Cannes, with Chris Menges' photography and Honor Heffernan's acting as Deirdre, coming in for particular mention. The title of the film was changed to *Danny Boy* for release in America.

Another ballroom was at the centre of my next assignment. *Ballroom of Romance* is the story of a lonely farmer's daughter who hopes to find love at the local ballroom. Co-written and directed, on a shoestring budget, by Pat O'Connor, and set in the 1950s, it starred a young Brenda Fricker in the lead role.

Pat wanted rain. 'Come on and I'll show you the location,' he said.

Half an hour later, we were standing looking at a vast, desolate peat bog, stretching as far as the eye could see.

'This is where you want the rain?' I asked Pat.

'Yep,' he said.

'And where am I going to get water?' I asked.

He looked about and shrugged.

'I'll need a few thousand gallons of water, and that means a water tanker – and probably a fire tender,' I said.

'We don't have the money,' Pat replied. 'There has to be water around here somewhere!'

It probably took a day, clambering through miles of squelching peat and heather and prickly furze bushes, to find a decent stream. It took another half-day to dam it up, submerge the pumps in the dammed-up stream and run hoses across the bog, for the rain sequence.

Filming, even for TV, was slowing down again, and there was unease in the air. The government and the 'big names' associated with film-making were still wrangling about the future of Ardmore Studios. John Boorman came in for a bashing from some among the older film makers, who were aggrieved by the granting of Film Board funding to Neil Jordan's *Angel*. It was even claimed that Boorman 'took taxpayers' money to line his own pockets'. In April 1982 John Boorman resigned as chairman of the National Film Studio of Ireland – and as a board member of the Irish Film Board. The following day, the then Minister for Industry and Commerce, Albert Reynolds, announced that the studio would close and that a liquidator would be appointed. Ardmore would be auctioned off in two lots: the studio, on its five acres, as one lot, and the remaining twenty-five acres would be sold for development.

To our ears, it was the death knell for the film industry in Ireland. I talked with a number of colleagues, and we decided to try to purchase the studio. About eight people from the industry rallied to the call. Our optimism was boosted by the appearance of an investor, of considerable means, and a friend of my family, who would put up half of the £900,000, leaving the rest of us to come up with just £50,000 each. We decided to operate a 'four-wall' system, meaning that companies and individuals from within the industry, either in Ireland or from abroad, could hire the facilities. After our second meeting, however, the accountant called me. Some from among the group did not agree to our 'four-wall' system, complaining that these production companies would bring in their own catering services and technicians, depriving the Irish of work; they did not want competition.

'Let me think about this,' I told the accountant.

I didn't think for very long. Within twenty-four hours, I had stepped down from the consortium. I met with our chief investor and relayed the news of the breakdown of our group. 'Ah, I know,' she said. 'It's hard to get people to agree on anything.'

The studio workforce had organised an action group – whose spokesperson was property master Eamonn O'Higgins – and lobbied government and opposition parties to retract the decision to liquidate the studios. On the political front, the Film Bill, which had been debated at length since 1979, came into force. The Association of Independent Producers of Ireland opposed the bill, which echoed the aspirations of John Huston and John Boorman, among others, to set up a training facility at Ardmore. But Ardmore fell into the hands of the liquidator, and several big-budget films were lost to Ireland. Tiernan McBride, whom I knew from childhood, was appointed as a member of the Irish Film Board, and Michael Algar, another acquaintance, was appointed chief executive. Muiris MacConghail, head of television features at RTÉ, was the new chairman, and the board based itself in Dublin, rather than in Ardmore. Years later, a new board would relocate even further away – to Galway.

In front of my cowshed, a forest of weeds bloomed between the door and a sunken water-storage tank, which had been installed many years earlier as an emergency water supply. I was alone in the workshop when I heard voices outside. Beyond the 'weed jungle', I spotted several heads. One of them turned in my direction.

'Hi,' an American voice said.

A man came towards me, parting the long weeds.

'Golly, I never knew this place existed!' he said, holding out his hand. 'Hi, my name's Doug Trumbull.'

His companions gazed around in amazement at my rudimentary premises, fascinated by how much work I had generated in such a primitive facility. He bombarded me with questions about the history of the studio, and who was involved with it.

'OK, why don't you come to a meeting with us?' he asked.

Douglas (Dougy) Trumbull was a director who had also been responsible for the special effects on Stanley Kubrick's *2001: A Space Odyssey* and was now part of a company called Ardmore Completion Communications, which was considering the purchase of Ardmore with a view to using the studio as a multi-purpose facility: producing effects for films, processing film and manufacturing photographic equipment. I wasn't sure what exactly it entailed, only latching onto the word 'effects', but it sounded like just the sort of thing that would be a 'goer'. Doug took me around to one of the large units, which ran along between the sound-stages. This was a spacious unit, which had previously been used as a construction shop, and Dougy said that this would be my new workshop. Up in the big house, we stood at a bay window and surveyed the property: the Wicklow Mountains rising in the distance, and the studio buildings spread out, in what had once been the grounds of the large private estate – quiet now, devoid of any activity.

'This is your office,' Dougy announced.

It seemed too good to be true; as it turned out, it was. Soon afterwards, the Irish partner, Vincent O'Donoghue, unable to secure financial backing, withdrew from the deal. The other partners took themselves off to France to look at another facility. Before leaving, Dougy had said: 'You gotta come over. We got a fabulous place – everything you need. You'd love it!' Again, I toyed with the idea of going to America. Georgina and I talked it over and decided that, with family and all our friends here, and with Derek approaching his first state exam in secondary school and Audrey just three years old, we'd be better off staying put. Moreover, my father had not been well of late and my mother was not enamoured with our emigration idea. Once again, the 'American dream' faded, and I was distracted by a call asking me to work on a feature film. I welcomed it with open arms.

Educating Rita: We covered Trinity College Dublin in snow.

The film version of Willy Russell's play *Educating Rita* was to be made at Ardmore. However, the producers went to a studio in Paris and used Dublin for some outdoor location work in Dublin. It was a sunny August when I covered Trinity College – the building, grounds, trees and shrubbery – in snow! A national newspaper carried pictures, and an article headed something like: 'DUBLIN WAKES UP TO A SNOW-FALL IN AUGUST!' Within hours, we had wedding parties turning up at Trinity for photographs in the 'snow'; more arrived over the next few days, streaming on to the set to have their wedding pictures taken. Once the snow scenes were over, the script called for another seasonal change. This time it was rain! Our thirty-foot towers, where we had been perched with snow blowers creating the falling snow, now supported hoses and rain heads, dispersing rain. Still the wedding parties and visitors arrived, clamouring for 'the rain'! A combination of the novelty and lure of a film set – and probably because it was the hottest August in decades – had piqued public interest. Snow was also featured in another wedding scene at an old church in Dublin's city centre. In the early-morning shadows, cast by the huddle of tall buildings, it looked even more wintry. Arriving on set, the actress Julie Walters exclaimed: 'Ooh, it's cold. When did it snow?' '

The director, Lewis Gilbert, and the leading actor, Michael Caine, had worked together on *Alfie* in 1965 and had a great rapport, which rippled down to the floor crew. Throughout the picture, Michael was affable, courteous and always in good form – with the exception of one morning, when I happened to meet him on set, looking downcast. He told me that his wife was in hospital in the States: he was understandably upset that she had spent hours on a gurney in a hospital corridor! I was shocked when he told me that if patients there didn't have medical insurance, they could be left untreated and could die. I was grateful that hospitals in Ireland had a more humane attitude! Thankfully, Michael's wife recovered and all was well.

Julie Walters played Rita, a working-class hairdresser who starts adult-education classes and encounters Caine as the alcoholic Professor Bryant. The feel-good storyline added to the feel-good atmosphere on set; I felt proud to be working on a picture that everyone seemed to believe would be a winner. Indeed, Caine, Walters and Russell were all nominated for Academy Awards and the film was a major success.

Towards the end of *Rita*, I got a call to work abroad again – this time in Italy. It was a mini-series called *The Last Days of Pompeii*, starring Ned Beatty, Laurence Olivier and the British actor Nicholas Clay, who had featured in *Excalibur* two years earlier. *Pompeii* was a re-enactment of the eruption of Mount Vesuvius in 79 AD, in which the city of Pompeii and its unsuspecting citizens were buried by lava and ash. I would be involved in recreating the volcanic eruption, collapsing building, creating fires, and the general mayhem associated with one of the worst natural disasters in history. It began with a few weeks' preparatory work in Pinewood, with Peter Hutchinson. Peter then asked me to set up the on-location workshops and hire some local crew in Italy.

A driver took me from Rome to the studios at Cinecittà. Sitting on about eighty acres, the studio compound was strewn with the odd galleon and armoured tank left over from other films. I met with the director, the producer and the production manager and learned that there were two main locations, one near Rome and one in Pompeii. I would need to recruit an Italian crew and was taken to meet a special-effects supervisor who had a workshop in the studio compound. He was a man in his sixties, working in a tiny, dingy workshop that was infinitely worse than my cowshed, back in Ardmore. His place was cluttered with every conceivable variety of bric-a-brac, rusted equipment and antiquated machinery, all residing under a pitted-tile-and-timber roof, with a single fan suspended from a rafter. He said that he would bring in two or three of his crew to assist me. I wanted to know about rates.

'Ah, you do not-a worry,' he said.

I was thinking about Peter Hutchinson's effects budget: I wanted to try to keep within it.

'Well how much do I pay *you*?' I asked.

'Ah,' he said, with a shrug. 'You buy me a racehorse! Come, we go to lunch.'

Several hours later, we arrived back at the production office, where I took delivery of a minibus: my transport for the duration of the shoot.

In the ensuing weeks, the Italian entertained me to lunch every other day, every time in a different restaurant, each one more opulent than the last. He insisted on driving; we would pull up in his rust bucket of a car and be met by a uniformed attendant, who would park the sorry-looking vehicle amid the assembled gleaming Lamborghinis and Ferraris. I would die of embarrassment! In each restaurant, he was treated like royalty – just the same as people like the legendary Sophia Loren and a host of luminaries from the entertainment world, some of whom joined us. I was never allowed to pay. Much later, my host took me to his home, an estate with a stable yard – a state-of-the-art equine facility – and a string of thoroughbreds! He also had at least two other cars – one of them a Lamborghini – which were taken for the occasional spin. His son owned a large retail clothing chain; I wondered why on earth his father was fiddling about in a dingy shed at Cinecittà.

In Pinewood, Peter was preparing to ship the materials for the falling ash, the fake blood, the grain blowers and the hydraulic 'rocker' discs, which would be used to topple the giant pillars. I was becoming tired, dashing from place to place, covering hundreds of miles between locations, buying in materials and getting crews organised. Finally we were ready to do camera tests in Pompeii. My friend, the stunt co-ordinator Martin Grace, and the cameramen, Joe Martin and Shane O'Neill, made up the rest of the small Irish contingent. Five or six cameras would be shooting. The effects crew had set up three large tanks, with funnels rising twenty feet in the air. Barrels of paraffin placed alongside each tank contained wads of steel wool. These wads were then extracted with tongs and dropped into each tank, from where they would be blown up through a funnel and through a rotating, gas-fuelled ring of fire, emerging as flaming balls that would fall

The Last Days of Pompeii: Collapsing columns in Pompeii

from the erupting 'volcano'. In the background, several members of the effects crew were also busy, setting up wind machines and smoke generators to blot out the sunlight and recreate the black pall from Vesuvius that turned day into night.

At lunchtime, the director decided to retain two cameras and a handful of crew to get some extra footage. A couple of effects technicians remained on set and the rest of us went to lunch. On my return, I stepped in to man one of our fireball machines. Just as I was loading the wire wool, I got a waft of petrol fumes. Suddenly there was a bright flash, and I fell back, my clothing on fire! My next recollection is having my head and upper body under water! Some of the crew had dunked me, head first, into a barrel of iced water, which was used to keep the soft drinks cool. Then I was in an ambulance, on my way to hospital. I was treated for shock, and the pain from the extensive burns to my face, arms and hands kicked in. It turned out that someone had inadvertently put petrol into the tank instead of paraffin. The wire wool had ignited in the funnel, causing a blow-back – right in my face! Due to the quick action of the crew, I escaped with minimum damage, and three days later, still with arms and hands bandaged, I was back at work.

Georgina joined me for about two weeks. My parents took up residence at our house, to look after Derek, who was now seventeen, and Audrey, aged four. A friend took Audrey to and from school. On the first Sunday of Georgina's visit, we travelled to Rome and toured St Peter's and the city, mostly on foot; the following Sunday we visited

Capri, taking the hydrofoil across the bay of Naples. A cable car took us to the summit of the highest point, from where we could take in the views of the bay, with the yachts looking like tiny white toy boats below us. A few days after Georgina returned home, she called me with the news that my father had been admitted to hospital for 'routine tests'. He was discharged within a week but was not up to attending the wedding of his niece – my uncle Frank's youngest daughter – in Cork. Then I got another message from home, and the world stood still. Uncle Frank had delivered a speech at the wedding, sat down – and died! As far as I knew, Frank was a fit and healthy seventy-one-year-old, with years left in him. He and his wife Etta were very close to my parents and were regular visitors to my parents' house in Glenageary. My father was devastated. I had lost my hero: the man who had nourished my childhood dreams, helped me find work, taken me into his home and treated me like a son – and whose life at sea had sparked my own love of adventure. Coincidentally, my work would take me to many of the places where Frank had lived and worked during World War Two: Plymouth, the Middle East, Malta and other places along the Mediterranean. I would also holiday in places where he had been: Greece, Scandinavia and Hong Kong. Years later, I learned that Frank had written a memoir, packed with action and adventure, and I didn't know the half of what his career had entailed! He was in command of a destroyer called HMS Tartar, which was one of the ships among the British naval force sent to the North Atlantic to sink the great Bismarck. The film that recorded the event was taken from the bridge of HMS Tartar. Frank wrote that this image remained with him throughout his life and he prayed that day – every day since – for the men who had perished aboard the Bismarck. I remembered only snippets of the stories he had told me. Recently, his daughter Hilary told me that her parents would make the girls wait for the credits at the end of a film.

'There! That's your cousin, Gerry!' they'd tell them, when my name appeared.

'They were so proud of you,' she said.

I wish I'd managed to get to know Frank more, and that we'd had the chance to 'compare notes'. He and I had a lot more in common than I realised.

When Frank died, I had been working nights; Georgina's call had been recorded on a scribbled note in reception at my hotel, where it had escaped the notice of staff until the day of the funeral. While

Frank was being buried in Deansgrange Cemetery in Dublin, I was back on a day shoot, helping to stage a first-century gladiator contest, up to my shins in blood and gore! A row had broken out among the 'spectators': extras, some of whom were local, and others who had been hired and ferried in from Naples. The locals didn't take too kindly to the appearance of the Neapolitans. A few minutes into rehearsals, we heard gunfire, followed by someone on a loud hailer ordering everyone out of the arena! The police were called, and it was almost an hour before order was restored and filming could resume.

Although the destruction of Pompeii was committed to film at least eight times, this production, a three-part TV adaptation of Edgar Bulwer-Lytton's 1834 best-seller *The Last Days of Pompeii*, was said to be more faithful to its source than any of the earlier film versions. With a $19 million budget, it was certainly the most expensive. Mercilessly slated by the critics, it nonetheless received healthy ratings when it aired on ABC in the summer of 1984.

Back home, the first series of *The Irish RM* went into production. One of Channel 4's first commissioned dramas, the first of the six episodes was made by a consortium, including RTÉ. It starred the English actor, Peter Bowles as the 'Resident Magistrate', a classic embodiment of humourless, English sobriety, but with a strong sense of fair play and common sense. The production also featured a whole host of Irish actors, headed by Brian Murray, as Flurry Knox, who was typically stage-Irish, charming, devious; full of superstition and given to drunkenness. The series was a joy to work on in the laid-back atmosphere and peaceful surroundings of the locations – one of which was again, Luggala.

I then went to work on an Irish-French co-production, *Roses from Dublin*, a mini-series about a French photographer who comes to Ireland and falls in love with a comely Irish 'colleen'. It involved about a week's preparation before shooting, rigging a Morris Minor and laying a thirty-foot steel track down a perilous cliff, overhanging the sea, near the Howth Lighthouse, for a scene in which the Morris Minor falls over a cliff, exploding as it falls. The preparation and the shoot went well and then, while wrapping, I was approached by the production manager, who told me that a trawler had been commissioned to retrieve the car from the sea and asked me to help.

I drove to the harbour and met the trawler crew, who were

making ready to cast off – there and then. All I had with me was a wet suit and a snorkel. They said the car wasn't far down, but they needed someone to go down and pinpoint the location. When I dived on the spot, I found the wrecked Morris sitting on rocks and about to be swept away by the current. There wasn't time to call in help: I had to guide a heavy, inch-thick, steel cable down through the swaying current and attach it to the car, a procedure that was tiring, dangerous and awkward and would normally require two people to do it. However, I eventually managed to hook the cable on to the car and it was gradually hoisted aboard the trawler. The car was shipped away and I drove home, my energy spent.

Two feature films, *James Joyce's Women* and *The Country Girls*, also went into production, providing some work, creating rain, snow and mist. As in the previous couple of years, commercials filled in the gaps for me. Usually these entailed odd days shooting around Dublin or Wicklow, with the occasional trip 'down the country'. But a biscuit commercial was, for reasons best known to the production executives, filmed in south Wales. The evening before my departure, I had been asked by the production secretary to pick up a package from the production office in Dublin and take it with me to Wales. As we were setting up equipment and preparing for the shoot, by the harbour in Swansea, the following day, the production manager was standing by the guard rails and, as he walked back towards the crew, his jeans caught on a spike and a package dropped from his back pocket into the water. I recognised it as the package I had been asked to deliver the previous day, and which I had carried safely all the way from Dublin. I ran to the edge of the harbour wall and watched the package bobbing about. I spotted a rowboat moored at the slipway, ran down, untied it and cast off, rowed the eighty feet or so to the package – which was by now half-submerged – and grabbed it. The crew's wages were saved!

After three days in Wales, I returned home to a catastrophe. One of the Spanish students who was renting the apartment at the back of the house had left a tap running. The ceiling in my downstairs office was on the floor! While repairing my office, I got a call about a third feature film. The movie was yet another set against the background of the Troubles in Northern Ireland. Cal, a young IRA man, falls in love with Marcella, a Catholic woman who was married to a Protestant policeman. (Her husband was killed by the IRA.) During pre-production, the director, Pat O'Connor, and the casting director had been auditioning children for the part of Lucy, the young daughter of Marcella, played by Helen Mirren. I happened to be in the production office and had Audrey with me. Pat spotted her and asked who she was.

'This is my daughter Audrey,' I told him.

'Hi'ya, Audrey,' he said. 'It's nice to meet you.'

Audrey smiled shyly and shook his hand.

Pat turned to me, beaming. 'She's our Lucy!' he said.

'No, no, she's too young,' I said, and the subject was dropped.

Cal: Audrey, as 'Lucy', with Helen Mirren

The effects shots on *Cal* included a house on fire, rain, and an 'exploding' cow in a field! I began preparations. Then Peter Dawson phoned.

'We've got a picture in Iraq,' he announced.

'Iraq? But isn't there a war going on there?' I said.

'Nah, don't worry, mate. We're working for the bladdy government. We'll be aw'right, mate!'

Six months' work on a feature film sounded a better proposition that a few days here and there working on *Cal*.

'I'll call you back, Peter,' I said.

The Iraq war had been news headlines for almost two years, but to me Iraq was just another exotic location – and a lucrative project to help with the house repairs! When family and friends heard I was going there, however, they said it was risky. I called the Irish embassy, who said that they would not advise people to go to Iraq at this time. A subsequent phone conversation with the film's production manager in Pinewood put me at ease. We were working for a British-Iraqi co-production. It all seemed to be very low-key, and the 'war' had nothing to do with us. I called Johnny Evans, another colleague and supervisor from the UK, and asked him to take over the effects on *Cal*. Following clearance from Terry Clegg, the producer, I packed my bags.

At Pinewood, the atmosphere among the rest of the crew was jovial, and any remaining fears I had about our destination were quickly forgotten. The night before my departure from London, I made a quick call home before settling down to sleep.

'I'll phone when I get to Iraq,' I told Georgina.

16

CREATING WAR IN IRAQ

At Baghdad Airport, a couple of military personnel called us from the queue at Immigration and whisked us through Customs: no delays, no baggage or passport checks – and no questions. Plain sailing! Ross McKenzie, the film's production manager, met us in Arrivals. A team of army guys loaded our bags and gear into a minibus. We passed the time on the drive into the city with chit-chat. Through the gathering darkness, I could make out flat-roofed houses. The highway had no lighting, and there seemed to be a lot of open, barren land on either side of it. Then we were in the city, where, as the U2 song says, 'the streets have no name': I couldn't see any street signs anywhere! On the third floor of our hotel, we emerged from the lift – into a cacophony of chanting. A wedding party milled about, sounding like a gaggle of geese! We caught sight of the bride and groom at the centre of the crowd. He must have been well into his sixties; the bride looked about twelve!

'My God, she's a child!' I said.

'Aw, that's the way it is 'ere, mate,' Peter said, laughing. 'She's probably about his tenth missus!'

Showered and changed, we made our way to the restaurant – a huge mezzanine, surrounded by glass walls, on the third floor. We looked down on a spectacular indoor plaza, complete with trees, rocks and a water fountain – and home to a variety of cats, which scampered around like monkeys and swung about in the trees. At dinner, most of us ordered chicken. When the meal arrived, it looked odd. The meat looked darker than the chicken I was used to. Even the bones seemed different. I took a mouthful; it didn't taste like chicken! I studied the meat. I looked at the cats and back to my plate.

'I'd like to order something else,' I said to Ross.

Next morning, the crew moved to another, French-owned hotel, with a more 'European' atmosphere. Then it was down to business.

In an enormous, high-rise building in the centre of town, we were unpacking some of our equipment, which had been stored in the basement, when Peter and I were summoned by an officer and taken into a ground-floor room, where we met some more military-types, including the liaison officer between the production and the Iraqi government. His name was Talaal. From there, we were taken upstairs; in a large conference-type room on the top floor, a distinguished-looking individual, wearing glasses, introduced himself as Tariq Aziz, the Iraqi foreign minister. He wished us 'a successful film' and said he hoped we would enjoy our stay. Downstairs again, a production meeting began. At lunchtime, we emerged into the noonday heat. Walking along the pavement, I noticed a tank, hidden behind trees, by the side of the building, which I had now discovered was our production headquarters , and to the far side of the building, another tank, again camouflaged by trees. Some yards further along the street, I looked back towards our HQ and spotted anti-aircraft guns on the roof – yet another reminder that we were in a war zone. I learned that this imposing building was also the television centre. Immediately, I felt uneasy, for the first time since my arrival, having heard, somewhere, that when hostilities break out, communications facilities are usually the first targets!

Flaming Borders: Peter Dawson (on extreme left), Kenny Gittens (back row, right) and me with PM Ross McKenzie and the Iraqi production crew on location in Iraq

At the weekend, one of my own technicians, Jim Brady, arrived. Jim had worked with me on several films in the past, going back to *The Red Baron*; I welcomed the presence of someone from home. Back at our hotel, still wary of the chicken on offer around these parts, I ordered cheese sandwiches and Cokes. Off to one side of the lounge, I spotted a group of Europeans and overheard snippets of a conversation in a language that was not English yet sounded vaguely familiar. I looked over, and one of the group smiled and waved. I sauntered across to them.

'*Conas atá tú?*' I asked. 'Gearóid MacEoin . . . '

They were all Irish, working with a medical agency, employed on contract at the hospital.

'We don't speak European languages among ourselves,' one of the girls said. 'We can chat away in Irish and no one knows what we're talking about!'

'What's it like working here?' I asked.

'Ah, you can only take it for a while. The money's great, but you get sick of seeing maimed bodies every day. It's so sad.'

Talk of maimed bodies was another reminder that war was close, but being used to the Northern Ireland conflict, I guessed that it was just another set of 'troubles' that spilled over, now and then, into ordinary life.

It had been two weeks since I had first tried to telephone home, and since then, booking a call through an operator, I had always encountered a long delay. I could not understand why, in the midst of such opulence and diamond-class service, the telephone service was still in the Dark Ages! The postal service wasn't much better. When I finally got to speak to Georgina, I learned that she had sent letters but that they hadn't arrived. When they did eventually arrive, in dribs and drabs, it was clear that they had toured the world! 'Try Australia' or 'Try Iraq' had been scrawled on the envelopes, which had been opened and resealed! I also heard something else – a tapping noise on the phone line – and guessed that calls were being monitored! And too late I learned that, after I had left home, Pat O'Connor had shown up at the house and persuaded Georgina to allow him to cast Audrey as Lucy in *Cal!*

The Iran-Iraq war, or the Persian Gulf war, as it was known, had been simmering away since 1980, when Iraq invaded Iran. The reason given for the invasion was an alleged Iranian assassination attempt on

Iraq's foreign minister, Tariq Aziz. However, Iraqi president Saddam Hussein was also said to have been keen to make Iraq the dominant power in the Persian Gulf region and to strengthen the country's lucrative oil trade. As part of his propaganda campaign, Saddam had decided to make a film about the war and the glorious Iraqi 'victories' along the border; it would be our job to recreate these battles on screen. I did not know who was involved on the British side of the production, nor had I met any British film personnel, other than the production manager. I just knew that, by default, we were part of the war effort! The film was called *Flaming Borders*.

At a disused military base outside town, we were introduced to a local 'special effects technician', dressed in fatigues: a bombastic individual who told us he was in the army. I asked him if he had any explosives materials. He led me across the yard to an ancient, open-back truck, covered with a tarpaulin. He lifted the tarp to reveal a slatted timber container. I climbed up and peered over the edge. It looked as if a JCB had scraped up the leftovers of a military arsenal and dumped the entire load – mortars, shells, and an assortment of other explosives – into the back of the truck. Sorting out what we needed would take a day, at least! Here, we did not need paperwork; the pyrotechnic requirements for the film materialised almost immediately.

Finally, the film began, on a location about an hours drive from Baghdad. In this desolate landscape, I never knew whether we were north, south, east or west. Wrecked cars, buses and trucks along the roadside turned out to be the results of collisions, and not the war. I wondered why they had not been towed away. The road through the desert had a hump along the centre, and sloped away on either side. Vehicles approaching from opposite directions didn't give way. Instead, clinging to the centre of the road, they drove straight at each other, each of the drivers hoping that the other would veer off at the last minute! I was petrified, and wondered whether our minibus would be the next casualty! But our only 'casualty' was the schedule, which was delayed by days of sandstorms. Separated from the rest of the film unit, the effects department worked in isolation, creating the battle scenes: blowing up tanks and aircraft, mutilating dummies, firing off rounds of gunfire. During a test and rehearsal, I asked the 'technician' if he could supply blank ammunition.

'Sure,' he said.

Within an hour, he arrived back with a collection of automatic weapons, lined up two of his guys, and began firing at them. The ground opened, and two barrels that were used for rubbish were riddled. Live ammo!

'No, no, no! Stop! We need blanks,' I said.

'Why you need blanks?' he said.

'This is dangerous!' I explained.

Peter stood there, aghast. The 'technician' just shrugged. From then on, *we* provided the effects; for all we know, other scenes might have been shot elsewhere, using the real thing!

A few weeks into the shoot, we were preparing for our next location – Mosul, to the north – when Talaal, our military liaison officer appeared, in civvies, at our hotel.

'You are on holiday today,' he announced. 'Later, I will take you out.'

Peter and I wandered around Baghdad, looking around shops and rooting through market stalls. Just before sundown, we joined Ross at the hotel, from where we were collected by minibus and whisked off into the Baghdad twilight. We arrived in an open plaza, much like London's Piccadilly Circus. I remarked on how fast the traffic was passing by. No one commented. The plaza was dominated by a palatial building; we drove through barriers that were attended by armed guards and flanked by two manned guns, mounted on pillars. In the massive entrance hall, two guards clicked their heels and saluted, then led the way into a large reception room, where a tall, dark-haired, moustached man, in uniform, stood between two more guards. He took a step forward and held out his hand. One shake of each hand, along the line – his face a mask. Afterwards, he stood and delivered a short speech. One of his officers interpreted. We were welcomed to the country and encouraged to 'do a good job' on the film. He nodded to the guards who had led us in. In unison, they clicked their heels, saluted and marched us outside. I gathered that we had just met someone of importance. I didn't realise that the dignitary we had met was President Saddam Hussein himself! On our way back across the plaza, our liaison officer told us that, a few months earlier, a carload of Swedish tourists had driven into the plaza, stopped and done a U-turn. The gunners had opened fire on the car, and two of the occupants had been killed.

From the palace, we were taken to a nightspot called the 'Moulin Rouge'. About seven 'men in black' checked our passports at the door and then ushered us through – into a vast, dimly lit lounge, with stages, one of which was about eighty feet long. Tables were arranged in clusters around the perimeter. Large bottles of Scotch, brandy, champagne, gin and vodka sat on each table. To the left was a fifty-foot-long cocktail bar, and two waiters worked the floor. Music started, and three bejewelled belly dancers took to the stage. We ordered beers and watched the show; all I could think of was *Ali Baba and the Forty Thieves!* Our only other evening out in Baghdad was a dinner at the director's house. After a lavish meal, the men took themselves on to the veranda, where 'hubbly-bubbly' pipes came out: glass pipes containing water, through which the user inhaled hashish. Sahib Haddad, the director of the film, introduced his wife, his family and a host of friends. The men shook hands and embraced us. The women just nodded. At some point, I found myself seated next to someone's wife and struck up conversation, but after a few minutes I realised that she wasn't responding! The director sauntered up to us.

'She cannot speak until her husband says so,' he told me.

So I joined the men on the patio, and the rest of the evening passed in a convivial blur.

Next morning, we boarded our bus for Mosul and met our fellow passengers – all different nationalities and part of the film unit – for the first time. On the journey, we passed through desert, with the odd tent, herds of goats and the now-familiar wrecks: crashed or broken-down trucks and buses. Traffic consisted mainly of low-loaders carrying armoured tanks, and trucks carrying heavy weaponry. Eventually, we crawled into Mosul. The city had some modern buildings – hotels, mostly – but it was mainly run-down. We arrived at our hotel, tired and dusty, and trooped into the large lobby, which had a bar in one corner. We expected an early start the next morning and fell into bed shortly before midnight.

After breakfast and a two-hour wait in the lobby for our lift to the location, a ramshackle minibus arrived. After a day spent dehydrating in boiling heat, on yet another army wasteland, we were glad to see the decrepit city again! Next morning, we resumed our waiting position in the lobby – and played cards until 11 AM. I tried to phone the PM but had no luck. Eventually, we got a call saying that we weren't needed that day! Not two hundred yards from our hotel, fighter jets roared into and out of a military airport throughout the night. Most of us had now taken to wearing earplugs, but then there was the danger that we wouldn't hear our alarm calls. We needn't have worried! Days passed as we played cards in the hotel lobby, waiting for the call to work!

Five days into our stay, I was jerked awake by a cock crowing! I looked at my watch: 4 AM. The cock crowed again! I dragged myself to the window and opened the curtains. Daylight had broken, and below, within feet of the runway, a cluster of tents had appeared! People in long robes were milling about, goats were tethered to tent-posts, and chickens ran about pecking at handfuls of meal – among them a large cockerel, crowing his lungs out! A MiG fighter roared its way down the runway, its nose lifting; the tents on the ground billowed in the down-draft. I watched the 'village life' unfold for a while before crawling back to bed to catch a few hours' sleep. A short time later, I was awoken again, this time by a voice over a public-address system, intoning prayers!

After breakfast, we assembled once more in the lobby and waited. A tanker pulled up outside the main entrance and a couple of guys in overalls began hauling hoses inside. One of them prised open a man-hole cover in the floor. Immediately, a stench wafted into the air. A suction hose was lowered and a pump revved into action – emptying a sewage tank right in front of the bar! Holding our noses, we hurried outside: the rising temperature was somewhat more tolerable than the rising stink! Then we heard we had another involuntary day off, but by noon, we learned that we were heading back to Baghdad, and then on to Basra.

In Baghdad, the hotel was swarming with press people. Journalists were talking about the fighting in Basra. The television news showed the carnage, including footage of hundreds of kids with guns, wiped out by mustard gas. This time, even Peter was uneasy. We wandered around the city, and in one square we came upon a parked truck loaded with Iranian prisoners of war, who were dehydrated, bruised and bleeding. The local people spat at them, shouted abuse, and threw rocks at them. To the Iraqis, Iranians were 'mules'. Meanwhile, Saddam's regime carried out public floggings and amputations of fingers, hands and even limbs for petty crimes – many of the incidents filmed, to instil fear among ordinary Iraqis. Peasants willingly trekked in from the desert to offer their gold for the war effort. Alongside the torture and extortion, young people were encouraged to go to foreign universities and learn about new technology and other cultures! Many students had returned, having discarded the burqa, the veil and the long robes, and paraded about in Western dress. In the bookstores, English classics and books about technology were devoured by the locals. It was said that, before its demise, Beirut had been the entertainment capital of the Middle East. Now, Saddam was keen to have this title bestowed on Baghdad. But petrol was rationed, and the side streets were a shambles: a warren of tatty stalls selling musk, fruit, spices and misshapen and out-of-date clothing – all smothered in dust and fumes from the passing array of clapped-out transport. I'd had my fill of Iraq and looked forward to leaving it behind. But the film was not yet finished and our hosts insisted on showing us the sights, as if the war was happening somewhere else – as if we were on a 'state visit'!

Our next tour took us to one of the Seven Wonders of the World. Although not entirely relishing the thought of another stifling drive, we were glad of a day out of the confines of the hotel and the mind-sapping atmosphere of the city. The Hanging Gardens of Babylon must indeed have been a wonder, particularly in a vast desert country. The gardens were supposed to have been suspended 'above the heads of spectators', supported on stone columns, with plants cultivated above ground level, the roots of the trees embedded in an upper terrace rather than in the earth. Right now, we were wandering around the ruins of an ancient city. I soon gathered that we were being shown another of the president's projects: the rebuilding of a city on top of the old ruins of Babylon, 'to glorify Iraq'. It was all so pleasant and civilised, but in Baghdad, the TV news, the sight of tortured prisoners locked in the back of a cattle wagon in the street, the constant stream of tanks and artillery on the road, and the distant drone of fighter aircraft brought us back to reality.

I had become friends with some local people who worked on the film. Some of them worked as part of my crew, and one of them was a keen fan of James Joyce! I could never remember their names, but I have often wondered how they fared, and whether they survived the war. Meanwhile, we were looking forward to going home for Christmas. However, each time we mentioned home and Christmas, Talaal would ask us to stay.

'You are our friends,' he told us. 'You are our guests.'

I talked with some of the Iraqi crew, who told me that if we owed money to hotels, shops or to individuals, we could be prevented from leaving the country. I immediately approached each of the UK crew and asked them to make sure that any 'tabs' they had run up were paid in full. I then went to see Talaal and informed them we were going home.

'But you will be back?' he asked.

'Yeah, sure,' I lied.

'Good. We have another film, involving submarines, starting in the Gulf.'

Afterwards, I asked the production manager to book our flights. When I collected our flight tickets, I gladly packed my belongings and souvenirs, but I didn't relax until the plane left the ground, bound for London.

In the event, I never saw *Flaming Borders*, which was underwritten by the Iraqi government. It's a story about a young soldier who is forced to leave his sweetheart behind to go off to fight for his country. I've also been told that the combat scenes are meticulously realistic – and horrifying – but I'm not sure how much of our work ended up in the film, as a large Iraqi unit worked independently of us, at other locations. Peter returned to Iraq after Christmas and Alan Whibly travelled with him, taking my place. Peter told me there is a cameo appearance in the film by Saddam Hussein.

In advance of our homecoming, Georgina and Peter's wife, Audrey, had arranged a Christmas shopping spree. They met us at Heathrow. Over dinner, at the Tara Hotel in Kensington, they told us that they had spent most of the day at Harrods.

'So what did that cost me, then?' Peter jibed, winking at me.

Before anyone could answer, there was an announcement over the public-address system. 'Will everyone please make their way to the front exit – *immediately*! We may have a bomb in the building!'

People rose as one. We followed the crowd towards the exits. The police had erected crash barriers along the pavement.

'Bladdy hell!' Peter whined. 'We've just left a bladdy war zone and we have to come back to London for a bomb scare!'

A British army bomb squad searched the building. Outside, the crowd remained good-humoured, despite the inconvenience, and after about half an hour we were told to return to the hotel, where a fresh meal was served, accompanied by champagne!

After Christmas, I caught up on the film scene in Ireland. Ardmore had closed down and once again, the place was a ghost town. By this time, a deal between Mary Tyler Moore Enterprises and the liquidator had collapsed, and Ardmore was again on the market. A stream of potential buyers had come to inspect the facilities. I was accustomed to seeing groups of 'suits' wandering around and was not surprised when a man with an American accent appeared at my workshop, asking questions about the studios. He said that he was from California and that he was interested in buying the studios.

'You seem to know how this place operates,' he said. 'I could do with your technical knowledge, so let's meet up, shall we?'

A few days later, we met in the Berkeley Court Hotel in Ballsbridge. We were joined by a prominent young Dublin lawyer, who had, it seemed, been called at short notice. He was dressed in a tracksuit and appeared to have just been out jogging. He seemed to be well acquainted with the American, whose name I cannot remember.

'I'm just waiting for the money to come through,' the American told us. 'When it does, I will submit the capital to the liquidator.'

Another three days passed before he called again. This time, I was in for a bit of a surprise.

'I'm still waiting for the money to come through,' he said. 'Could you loan me some money?'

Hesitantly, I wrote a cheque for £300, made out to cash. The following day, the lawyer and I accompanied him to the High Court in Dublin. I had been invited in case the judge needed to know something of a technical nature that our American couldn't answer. I waited outside the courtroom. Soon, the doors opened, and the American and the lawyer filed out, looking crestfallen. The judge had apparently asked to see the bidders' money. The American said that he needed another week, whereupon the judgement was made, approving the sale of Ardmore to a consortium of Mary Tyler Moore Enterprises, Morgan O'Sullivan's company Tara Productions, and the National Development Corporation. (A deposit had already been paid by the National Development Corporation.) We had wasted our time. I never saw the American – or my £300 – again!

MTM and Tara resumed shooting the *Remington Steele* episodes for television, and I was on my way to another exotic location: Cannes. Suddenly, I found myself with a lot of work on hand, and I was stretched even more when I was approached by the stunt co-ordinator to make up stunt rigs. But I was looking forward to being on the shores of the Mediterranean. This time, Georgina and Audrey would be coming to join me. To me, Cannes was the world capital of cinema, the city of the rich and famous, yachts, glitter and stars – and of course the famous film festival, and its red carpets and flashing cameras. It was everything I had expected: the beautiful, glistening bay, with its white, sandy beaches, set against the hills; the bright buildings reflecting the sunlight; the promontory overlooking the beach; the two islands hugging and protecting the coast.

Remington Steele is a romantic detective series in which Pierce Brosnan plays the handsome, debonair and mysterious thief-turned-investigator, opposite Stephanie Zimbalist as Laura Holt, an attractive, independent private detective. Throughout the series, the two have an on-off romantic relationship. One of the scenes involved Pierce and Stephanie cycling around on a tandem. This was where the rig I made

Remington Steele: I blow up a model boat in Malta.

up for the stunt co-ordinator came into play. The rig was attached to the tracking vehicle, from which the camera operated. I also produced bullet hits in water and smoke, and when the unit moved to Malta I had the job of blowing up a fifteen-foot-long model of a luxury yacht. I was kept busy!

Since *Manions of America*, Brosnan was still getting mileage out of 'the most spectacular explosion on television'! His wife Cassie and Georgina hit it off. During filming, they would go off shopping, and on a number of occasions the four of us had dinner together after work. Derek flew out to join us and spent a few days swimming with his mother and Cassie and seeing the sights. It was shaping up to be a pleasant shoot – until the production decided to change the schedule. Suddenly, we were working longer hours for the same pay, and it was decided to form a second unit to work nights. As the days and nights dragged on, the crew became tired and agitated. After a few days of bitter complaining, a meeting with the production team was called. Three of the producers sat at a table. Various departments voiced their dissatisfaction with the long hours, for which they were not being paid. The producers conferred and then asked if anyone wanted to add anything further. One person from our ranks stood up and said: 'I'm not at all happy.'

'Well, if you're not happy, you can go home!' came the reply. 'Anybody else?' His dismissal changed everyone's tune, and we were back where we started. We plodded on with the shoot and then dragged ourselves home.

Back in Ireland, debts of about £2 million, incurred by Ardmore, had been paid off by the Department of Industry and Commerce. The land surrounding the studio had been zoned for film-making purposes until 1987. But film-making was not happening, and the future looked bleak. By now, I was eighteen years in the business, and apart from a few 'valleys' – and despite the endless question marks hanging over what should have been the hub of the Irish film industry – I had forged a niche for myself. I considered myself a 'film person', and despite my unspectacular academic performance I now had a career as a well-established, skilled professional, proving to my father that I could make it after all.

Ever since Uncle Frank's death, my father had seemed to be fading away. Shortly after Christmas, he took a 'turn', and the doctor was called.

'A bad case of indigestion!' the doctor declared, and left.

Looking at him, slouched in a chair, one leg twisted underneath the other and unable to speak, my mother suspected something more serious. She called her neighbour Nancy, who was a nurse. Nancy took one look at him and called an ambulance. I was in my workshop at Ardmore when I got the call. I dropped everything and rushed to the house.

'Your father's had a stroke,' Nancy told me, matter-of-factly.

Within half an hour, he was in St Vincent's Hospital, where tests confirmed Nancy's diagnosis. He recovered sufficiently to be allowed home, but as spring came and went, he still needed the aid of a walking stick, and his activities were severely curtailed. He became cantankerous and difficult for my mother to handle. Then, one morning in early June, while negotiating the last step on the stairs, he lost his balance. My mother tried to steady him as he toppled, but they both fell back on the floor, and my mother broke her arm. For the next six weeks, their roles were reversed, as he helped her, but now they were both partially incapacitated. Georgina and I, and my brother Terry, dropped by every day, did the shopping and the laundry, and brought meals and helped with the cooking.

In July, I learned that Ardmore had changed hands again: it had been sold to the Pakistani-born, American-based film-maker Mahmond Sipra. Several feature films were reported to be coming on stream. While waiting to see if any of them brought me work, I took the family to Spain for two weeks. When we returned, I was told that my father had suffered another 'turn' and had been in hospital.

In November, Father was admitted to St Luke's Hospital in the city, where he underwent a battery of tests. From there, he was transferred to St Michael's in Dun Laoghaire. Upstairs, in a dismal, olive-green room in Intensive Care, I found him with an oxygen mask and a saline drip. Over the next week, with the oxygen removed, we tried, in vain, to persuade him to eat.

'I don't want anything,' he told us.

'He's lost the will to live,' the doctor said.

Terry and I visited every day and I spent an hour with him on the evening of 11 December. He was very uncomfortable and asked me to turn him, but I was afraid to touch anything; I was spooked by the array of tubes and machines to which he was connected. Just then, a nurse appeared and asked me to leave. It was just after 3 AM on 12 December when I got the call to summon the family. My father had been transferred to a small room on the ground floor of St Michael's. We gathered round his bed, my mother in floods of tears, and later went home to get some sleep. Just after 11 AM, we were called to the hospital once more. Terry and I arrived at the same time. The rest of the family were already in the room, my mother in floods of tears. A nurse joined us at my father's bedside.

'Your father has just died. We'll say the Rosary,' the nurse said.

Up the street, the town hall clock chimed; it was noon. Two days later, on a dark December day in 1984 in Deansgrange Cemetery, we laid him to rest.

With varying degrees of bad weather and only a few hours of daylight, December is a gloomy month at the best of times. Christmas was particularly difficult. My father and mother had always made a fuss over the children. Now, the excitement of 'going to Grandad's' on Christmas Day had gone. Mother was inconsolable. Georgina and I tried to make small talk with her and carry on as normal. In the weeks that followed, my mother began calling at all hours of the day and night, saying that she 'could hear something – a noise, downstairs' or 'a noise outside the window'. The 'noises' turned out to be heating pipes expanding and contracting, and birds pecking at the putty around the windows! Living alone now, she became hyper-conscious of every sound. She said that she wanted to come and live with us. My mind flew back to my childhood, when I was about ten years old and my Grandmother Johnston came to live with the family in Williamstown. A formidable woman, six feet tall, who had raised my father and his two brothers and run a dairy business single-handedly in Blackrock, my Grandmother Johnston liked to be in charge. 'Don't talk to my son like that!' she'd snap at my mother. (My father was always 'her son'; never my mother's husband!). My grandmother's presence added to an already highly charged atmosphere – which I had no wish to re-create in my own home! I made some excuse to the effect that I would be away and that Georgina would be out a lot.

In the film world, Mahmond Sipra's company had been in trouble since September, and the studio was again on the market. The hoped-for feature films never materialised. When Peter Dawson phoned to tell me about a film being shot in Africa, I was delighted to have the reprieve from guilt and domestic complications.

'It's a big picture but I can't do it, mate,' he said. 'I'll give you a number in South Africa and you can talk to the PM.'

I phoned straight away.

'Yes, it's a big picture,' John Stodel said. 'We already have an effects crew here. We just need a supervisor and your first-choice technician. But we can't afford the UK rate. Can you drop?'

'I'll call you back,' I told him.

Georgina and I talked it over. She was not terribly excited by the prospect of my absence for three months, but although rumours of a few things that might or might not be happening on the home front were circulating around the studios, there was nothing definite on the horizon. I worked out a deal for the African picture and submitted myself to the obligatory inoculations. I called Jim Brady, and a month later we were both on a flight to London, where we stayed overnight and collected our work permits. The next day, we were on an Air Zimbabwe flight to Harare. A long twelve-hour journey lay ahead of us: time for me to let the trying events and the sadness of the last few months fade. Once again, I was glad to be leaving the winter behind. But as I headed for Africa, changes were afoot in Ireland. New, independent, indigenous production companies were hatching. Boosted by the success of Neil Jordan's film *Angel*, others were negotiating deals on the far side of the Atlantic. The Irish film industry was about to soar.

17

INTO AFRICA

We were staying at the Holiday Inn, a brand-new multi-storey hotel dominating an otherwise unremarkable area close to the centre of Harare. The hotel was a symbol of Zimbabwe's aspirations as a tourist destination. Robert Mugabe's government had been in power since 1980, and on the surface the city looked like a burgeoning, bustling capital, much like any other in the developed world. But the government faced a wide variety of economic problems as it tried to develop a market-oriented economy. We, as film-makers, were welcome: we were 'big spenders' and prospective – if temporary – employers. The rest of the crew came from all over the world: Israel, Italy, South Africa, Australia, New Zealand, the US, Canada and the UK. I had a tight budget, and my mind was occupied with finding materials and equipment. Rory Killalea, the location manager – and the only other Irish member of the unit – gave me a map and a list of local suppliers. After dinner, I took myself to bed clutching a new script. The picture was *Allan Quatermain and the Lost City of Gold*, a sequel to *King Solomon's Mines*, which had just finished shooting elsewhere in Zimbabwe. The next day, Jim and I collected our transport. Mine was a Peugeot 303 saloon, and Jim's a 4x4 pick-up. When exchanged in the banks for the 'Zim dollar', our sterling currency was worth twice the dollar and ensured excellent deals on initial tools and equipment.

I discovered that I would need a considerable amount of specially built working machinery: fans of varying sizes, machines for firing liquid 'gold', as well as welding equipment and so on. I had been told of an engineering plant, somewhere in the countryside, which had been engaged to make armour for *King Solomon's Mines*, but when I contacted the owners, they said that they hadn't been paid. I invited them for a drink to talk it over. They finally agreed that if I paid in advance, they would build what I needed, but I would still have to source many components in South Africa.

'We have a buyer down there,' the PM said. 'He can pick up what you'll need and send it up.'

I phoned the buyer.

'No problem. Just tell me what you need,' he said.

I relaxed, my mind at rest.

By the weekend, I had met most of the unit, including two white Zimbabweans working with Locations, who offered to take me to a wildlife park. The park stretched away for miles, into thick under-growth. As we drove in, I noticed signs warning visitors to stay in their vehicles and not to open their car windows. The driver parked the jeep at the foot of a hill bordered by trees. I was hesitant about getting out, but concluded that these guys knew what they were doing. We wan-dered about, trying to catch sight of a giraffe or a zebra. We had walked about a hundred yards from the jeep down an incline, and came upon a huge, empty animal cage. I suddenly felt uneasy and turned around. Then I saw the lions – about seven or eight of them – on the embankment above us! On impulse, I ran for the cage. My mates followed, pulling the gate shut behind them. The pride ambled towards us and began sniffing through the bars! Eventually, they lay down on the grass. I prayed: 'Please God, somebody come!' Two hours passed, the lions snoozed, stretched, yawned and rolled over. Inside the cage, we sat in silence and waited. Finally, a sound: an engine! Up on the ridge, a ranger's 4x4 pick-up trundled into view. It looked as if it would keep going, but then the driver spotted our jeep and stopped. A pair of binoculars scanned the area, eventually coming to rest on the cage. The jeep reversed. A shot was fired into the air and the lions scattered. As the jeep came towards us, we could see two war-dens in the cab.

'Get in the back!' one of them shouted.

We scrambled out of our 'prison' and into the back of the pick-up. The driver sped away and dropped us to our vehicle.

'Follow me!' he shouted.

In the office, the head ranger read us the 'riot act' and told us about a local man who, some time previously, had left his car to pho-tograph the lions and been attacked. He didn't survive. We returned to the city, duly chastened.

Despite daily telephone contact with the South African buyer, I still hadn't received as much as a nut or a bolt! I had a meeting with John Stodel, the PM.

'OK, maybe you should fly down there,' he said.

I was now on my way to Johannesburg, where I was taken to the studios and introduced to the effects crew, all white South Africans. They had worked on the previous production, *King Solomon's Mines* and would relocate to Zimbabwe to work with me on *Allan Quatermain*. I phoned my buyer and told him that I was on my way to see him. The drive to the Transvaal was interrupted by roadblocks: there were army personnel and police at almost every shanty village. Eventually, we arrived at an impressive entrance to a property, miles from anywhere. The high-security gates opened, and we cruised up a long driveway towards a rambling, Spanish-style mansion. I rang the bell and waited. A black manservant opened the door and led us into an enormous room with a carved wooden table – which could have sat about thirty people – in the centre. 'Wait here,' the manservant said, and disappeared through a heavy door at the far end of the room. I occupied myself by viewing the endless display of stuffed animal heads mounted on the walls. Lions, leopards, buffalo, impala . . . they were all there, practically every animal native to Africa.

Finally, a small white South African man entered. He was holding a chain leash, and tethered to it was the biggest lion I had ever seen! I glanced over at my driver. He was rooted to the spot, eyes wide open, looking as if rigor mortis had set in. I was sweating, the memory of my narrow escape at the wildlife park fresh in my mind.

'Hi, Gerry,' the little man said, strolling forward, the lion padding along beside him. 'Would ya care for a beer?'

I backed away. 'Sorry, I'm not comfortable with that lion here.'

'Oh. OK, mate,' he said, and handed the leash to his manservant. 'Here, take him outside.'

He then called for another servant. Instantly, a woman appeared.

'Get us two beers,' he snapped, then, turning to me, said, 'Let's go and sit outside.'

Out on the terrace, I glanced around for any sign of the lion, but all was quiet. Sensing my unease, my host said, 'He's my guard dog. Sleeps in my room at night.'

After a couple of cool beers and some snacks, my host took me on a tour of his property. Just beyond a vast lawn and through a garden fence, there was a corral, inside which about five or six lionesses romped about.

'These are my other pets,' my host informed me. It was all a bit unnerving. I wondered where my components were!

'Aw, we can get all that,' he reassured me. 'I have some stuff. Tell you what, mate, why don't I take the stuff up to Harare myself?'

We agreed that that would be the best thing to do.

Back in Harare, the South African effects crew had already arrived, but we were also in need of some casual help. I hired about twenty black Zimbabweans, plus a few white Zimbabweans – and the white South Africans duly went on a 'go slow'!

'We don't work with scum!' they informed me.

I'd heard about apartheid, but I hadn't seen it in practice! I pleaded, begged and offered bribes – and told the PM. He reiterated to me that there wasn't enough money to bring in a UK crew, so I'd have to manage. I took Jim off buying detail and, together with our unskilled local labourers, we worked round the clock to prepare for the shoot. For the next three weeks, I managed between three and four hours' sleep a night, at most, and I ate on the run.

At last, we were travelling north to the location at Victoria Falls. I was travelling by air, along with the director, First AD and other department heads. The remainder of the unit would be travelling in convoy, by road – under armed guard. We were told that white tourists had been abducted or hacked to death by rival tribesmen. Until a few

Allan Quatermain and the Lost City of Gold:
With Jim Brady shortly after arrival in Victoria Falls, Zimbabwe

weeks previously, I couldn't understand why this was happening, as the country was now independent and presumably the population had got what it wanted: freedom from white rule. However, when I saw how black Africans were still being treated, the attacks began to make sense. We were now heading out of the capital into the bush and I was already trying to formulate a plan for my survival! I would probably need a gun!

On board the aircraft, still feeling apprehensive, I glanced out the window as the engines started, and noticed green-coloured liquid spewing out of the wing! I called a stewardess and pointed this out to her.

'Oh, it's just water,' she said.

'It's green!' I said. 'It looks like fuel. Tell the pilot!'

The stewardess stared for a few seconds and then ran to the cockpit. The pilot appeared and took a look.

'Crikey!' he said, and rushed back to the cockpit.

'Ladies and gentlemen, we have a technical problem.'

Two hours later, we were trooping on to another plane. Another pilot took his position at the controls. We began to taxi, gathering speed. Suddenly, we were thrown about, as the plane swerved! On the turn, I spotted a herd of elephant scattering off the runway, away to our left! We waited until they had ambled away to a safe distance and then finally took off. I glanced down at the shrinking landscape and the elephant herd, now like ants moving across the plain. Ironically, we were heading for Elephant Hills, near Victoria Falls.

Flying north, the temperature rose a degree or two, and as we gradually dropped towards land again, I noticed a swathe of thick vegetation below us. Ahead, columns of spray rose into the air, like steam from a gigantic pot. For the next six weeks, I would live listening to the hiss and rumble that created the vast clouds billowing from the seething cauldron that is Victoria Falls! The pilot took his time, responding to the 'Oohs' and 'Aahs' from the cabin, allowing everyone a few minutes to take in the view. After touchdown, a ripple of excitement swept through the group as we prepared to disembark.

I was not prepared for the little town's opulence: Victoria Falls had hotels with swimming pools and all the trappings of a modern-day resort. The Makaza Sun was ultra-modern and had a casino. Just up the road, the Victoria Falls Hotel, said to have been a former governor's residence, was also the film's local production office. At the Makaza Sun, I had a room on the second floor. Looking out the window on my first evening, I spotted more lions – three of them – lounging against the wall. I was instantly relieved that I was not on the ground floor! The following evening, buffalo and monkeys wandered about, almost within touching distance of the entrance to the hotel. Every day, I was treated to a gathering of wild animals, and each night I dropped off to sleep to the racket of crickets. But I was constantly on my guard. Just like in India, snakes were everywhere! The Zambezi held another terror: crocodiles, some of them the size of a small elephant! The local people called them 'flat dogs'. I was in 'wildlife country'; I wondered how much the animal population would encroach on our work!

My first task was to suss out the locations. I would need manpower to string cables across the river to manoeuvre a pontoon with actors aboard. I put notices up in the hotel – and in the local shops – looking for workers, and the next morning about a hundred and fifty men were queuing outside the hotel! The Zambezi, so beautiful and harmless-looking from the air, was a mixture of raging torrent and whirlpools, with the ever-present crocs and hippo. The white South African effects crew had no objection to the hiring of the black Africans for work in the river: this was dangerous work and the blacks were 'dispensible'. The scenes involved the two leading actors, Richard Chamberlain and Sharon Stone, crossing the river aboard a raft. We constructed a pontoon: a wooden raft on barrels, with a handrail. It was manoeuvred by winches and cables, laid across the river, and anchored to trees on an island about half-way across. At my request, the production had hired armed wardens, from among military personnel and police – from all over Zimbabwe – to patrol the river bank. I was led to believe that if a croc or hippo attacked one of my crew, the animal – and possibly the man – would be shot! I was wound up with worry. Workshops and storage huts had been erected close by, and some of the local crew stayed behind in the evening, along with a handful of wardens to guard the equipment.

One evening, as I drove back to the hotel, I suddenly remembered something I'd left behind. Turning the car, I came face to face with a giant elephant! He had appeared out of nowhere and stood stock still, thirty feet tall if he was an inch, in the middle of the dirt track. Without warning, his ears went back, a huge foreleg lifted, and in a flash he was charging towards me! I shoved the car into reverse and put my foot to the floor. I found a clearing, where I spun around, as the elephant's massive trunk hit the rear wing! Speeding away, I could

see him through the rear-view mirror, still bearing down on me. I barely made it to the main road and safety. Later, I was told by my interpreter that 'my' elephant had stepped on a landmine during the civil
war and been injured. Since then, 'Big Daddy', as he was known locally, was not pleased to see people.

The threat from the river was constantly on my mind. I had heard
that a year earlier, during filming of the previous movie, a croc had
capsized a boat and an assistant had disappeared! On one trip up river,
on our movie, I noticed Sharon Stone dangling her feet in the water.

'Ah, isn't it wonderful,' she said.

'Tell her that's a bit dangerous,' I said to her partner, Mike
Greenburg, who was also the producer of the film.

'You tell her,' he said.

'Sharon, it's not safe to have your feet in the water,' I said.

She just looked at me and scowled. I must have looked extremely
concerned. Pouting, she withdrew her feet.

'Spoilsport!' she whined. 'Happy now?'

I was already exhausted, supervising an uncooperative crew, on
nights as well as days. I certainly didn't relish the thought of a big
Hollywood actress having her legs amputated – at least not on my
watch!

Because of the South Africans' 'go-slow', I had lost three weeks'
sleep and had barely eaten. By now, my nerves were on edge, and there
was still a lot of work ahead. The 'lost city of gold' had been constructed in the ruin of a hotel which had been bombed on the eve of
its grand opening during the war, in the early 1980s. Since then, it had
been boarded up, and it was infested with bats, snakes and a variety of
other wildlife. My department was responsible for the 'gold': gallons
of gold liquid that spews from gargoyles around the cavernous interi-
or. Flaming spears, fires, dry-ice effects, bullet hits, fire burning on the
surface of the water, and prosthetics were also on the agenda, and a
second unit had been detailed to shoot at night. The 'buyer' from
South Africa eventually showed up with a few machines for making
blank ammunition and then high-tailed it. Fortunately, the engineering
company in Harare came up with supplies and equipment, which had
to be shipped to Victoria Falls. Among the consignment were some
industrial pumps and hundreds of feet of nine-inch fire-hosing to
carry water from the Zambezi into a man-made lake, which was under
construction at a location half a mile from the river. On our first day's
shooting, we were setting up when someone shouted 'There's some-

thing in the water!' The 'something' was either a croc or a hippo, but no one could be sure which. At any rate, ripples could be seen moving on the surface, and occasionally there was a dark shadow under the water. I put a small arsenal of explosives together, laid a few charges around the perimeter, and set them off. Shock waves rippled across the lake, and then at the far side something moved.

Allan Quatermain and the Lost City of Gold:
Crocodiles were a constant threat in the Zambezi.

'He's out!' someone shouted. 'It's a croc! He's huge!'

Fearing that there might be more of them, I set off a couple more explosives, and waited. Nothing.

Nearby, the construction department was busy erecting a timber walled-in platform on stilts, built to replicate the site of an earthquake. About two hundred feet across and rising more than thirty feet off the ground, it looked like a giant rectangular box, on top of a pile of matchsticks. I feared that even one elephant, scratching his rear end against it, would topple it! Sure enough, during the night, it was almost levelled by a passing herd. Next morning, the construction crew arrived to find a day's repairs ahead of them – and a pride of lions in residence! Even after the repairs had been carried out, the platform seemed unstable. While preparing my 'earthquake' – cutting out my crevices on the floor that would slide on rollers underneath the wall, simulating the ground cracking open – the set dressers festooned the inside of the walls with trailing vines. As we moved about, the whole structure wobbled and swayed precariously. Its stability was further compromised by a family of baboons, drawn by the smell of cooking as the locals prepared their dinner. Our 'earthquake' set had become an animal playground!

While I fretted that the set would not support a whole crew and actors, along with heavy lighting, camera and effects equipment, Ms Stone had another problem. In the scene where she slips and falls through a crack in the splitting ground, Richard Chamberlain grabs her and she hangs on, dangling in mid-air for several minutes. But her costume was a skin-tight leather ensemble, and she would not hear of wearing a harness.

'I'm not even wearing underwear!' she said. 'I don't want any lines showing!'

Already having too much wire work and not enough crew, I called Kevin Matthews, a wire specialist from the UK. When he arrived on the picture, I was more than happy to let him take over that particular situation.

Although my energy was deserting me, I joined the rest of the unit after dinner, in the casino, as often as my work schedule allowed. I was afraid to lie down, in case I would never wake up again! I fell into the 'work hard, play hard' routine. But the demands of work increased, and I needed an experienced crew. All I had was the local labour, who tried to make up for their lack of expertise through their willingness to work hard, and their goodwill. Even the women, some with infants strapped to their backs, appeared in droves looking for work. I hired some of them to do some laundry for my crew, make tea and clean up. I discovered that many of them also did intricate needlework: they made some pretty tablecloths for me to take home. I was told women walked everywhere in groups because women walking alone had been attacked by baboons. Nevertheless, they seemed to co-exist happily with the wild animals on their doorstep. I, on the other hand, was terrified of the animals. There aren't too many man-eaters roaming the streets of Dublin! One morning, I heard shouting outside the workshop. I ran out to see what the commotion was, and discovered my workforce gathered around, pointing and talking excitedly, their eyes fixed on the ground. A swirling mass of black mambas had taken up residence in a pit behind a truck. Two of the huge snakes rose, coiling and uncoiling together in a 'dance'. I could have happily watched the display on TV, but there was no way I could continue working with a colony of snakes for neighbours, so I fitted a charge to the end of a fifteen-foot pole and set it off on the edge of the pit. The mambas slithered away into the bush.

The next day, one of my African workmen was missing. Upon

enquiring as to his whereabouts, I was told that he was sick. I found him sitting by the 'snake-pit', shivering. I sent for the doctor, who arrived, took one look at him and said he would be 'OK'.

'Aren't you going to examine him?' I asked.

'He'll be fine,' he declared, and instructed the patient to go home! I'm not sure if the man was ill from infection, or if he had the DTs from drinking 'moonshine'; either way, the doctor seemed reluctant to touch him! Another commotion arose a few days later – again behind a truck. This time it was one of my women 'domestics' – giving birth! No doctor, no midwife, no hospital equipment. The mother delivered her child, with the help of the women who surrounded her; they then wrapped the baby in a blanket and walked her home. Natural childbirth, outdoors, in the wild, was something I had never heard of!

That night, as I began putting away my gear in the old ruined hotel, my thoughts went back to home. Outside, I sat down on a rickety chair by a makeshift workbench on the grass. Beside the workbench, a single timber stake had been fixed in the ground; running up along it was a length of cable, attached to a solitary light bulb. I decided to take ten minutes to put some space between me and the day, before heading back to 'civilisation', dinner and a few drinks with the crew. I sighed, stretched back and gazed up at the stars. What had once been the garden of the hotel had gone back to nature: the long driveway was now a partially overgrown dirt track. Soaking in the silence, I surveyed the vegetation, which was now silhouetted against the darkening African sky. About thirty yards away, a security hut sat in the shadow of a small grove of trees. I guessed that the two guards were sleeping. Then, in the dim light from the single bulb, I spotted a telephone sitting on the workbench – looking bizarrely out of place! But it had a cable attached, and the cable ran back inside the old hotel. I lifted the receiver and heard a dial tone! I called home. The number was ringing, and then Derek's voice answered.

'Dad! It's you!' He sounded so excited to hear my voice. 'What are you doing, Dad?'

'I'm sitting here in the darkness, looking up at the stars on Elephant Hill and . . . ' My voice trailed off. Below me on the dirt road, an elephant's back appeared - caught in the light of the rising moon . . . then another, and another! The leader stopped and his trunk shot up.

'Dad?'

'Can't talk,' I whispered – and waited, holding my breath. Eventually, the herd padded on, the largest one bringing up the rear.

'They're gone,' I said.

'Who's gone?' Derek asked.

'The elephants.'

'What elephants?'

'A whole herd of elephants has just passed by and . . . '

'You're joking!'

I had caught sight of something else. A baboon had bounded out of the shadows! He was joined by more, all bounding along, stopping and bounding off again in the wake of the disappearing elephant! Minutes dragged by.

'Dad? Are you there?'

'Baboons,' I whispered.

Derek was in a fit, laughing. I imagined that the whole jungle could hear him!

'Shh . . . ' I whispered.

Finally, the baboons disappeared and I breathed again.

'What was all that about?' Derek asked.

'I don't believe it,' I said. 'There was a herd of elephants, and then about twenty baboons, all walking by, just about a hundred feet away . . . '

My words stuck in my throat. Another movement – and from behind the trees and on to the track strolled . . . a lion! Another lion slinked into view. My legs went weak.

'There's a lion,' I croaked.

Derek just laughed.

The security hut remained closed and silent. For a moment, I thought of making a run for a shed situated off to my right, halfway between me and the guards' hut. But I knew that the shed was locked. If I ran back into the old hotel, I would be trapped. By now, a whole pride of lions was wandering about on the track. I wished I had my gun with me, but it was in the car, parked in the car park, some three or four hundred yards away at the bottom of the hill. I prayed. The lions began to amble on.

'Gotta go,' I whispered into the handset. 'I'll ring tomorrow.'

I got up and crept towards the shed, inched my way along beside it, and then on to the security hut. I burst in and found the two guards asleep. They jumped awake as I entered.

'You!' I said to one of them. 'Take me to my car – and bring your gun!' Walking to the car park, I glued myself to the man, ready to snatch his Kalashnikov at the slightest movement. Once in the car, I revved the engine and sped away, sweating, my eyes peeled for any more wild animals on the prowl.

But it was in the human world that trouble was brewing. I had checked my bank account and discovered that my weekly pay cheque hadn't been deposited. In fact, two weeks had passed and I hadn't been paid. I talked with some of the other crew and discovered that they hadn't been paid either, so I waited another week. Still no money. Three of us went to Production and asked the PM if he knew what was happening.

'You'll have to speak to the line producer,' he told us.

So off we went to see the line producer.

'Don't worry,' he said, 'you'll get your money. You should have it next week.'

But at the end of that week, we still hadn't been paid. We returned to the office and informed the line producer that we were downing tools. He explained that the money was coming from Los Angeles.

'So does it have to travel via Bangkok, India, Pakistan and China – by rowboat?' I asked.

'It will definitely be here next week,' he snapped.

A week later, our money arrived. But two weeks after that, it dried up once more, and another two weeks passed before our wages materialised again and we were back to regular weekly pay.

Meanwhile, the effects department was swamped with requests from other departments to make up props and other equipment. Wheels for a chariot for a scene in the film were now needed by the art department; this meant days of intensive engineering. I began to suffer blinding headaches, and I had obviously lost weight; my clothes felt loose on me. I had thought it odd that other members of the unit were asking me, on and off, if I was OK. But I was engrossed in the work – and still livid with my South African crew, who were to be found every day sitting around the hotel pool, having a long lunch!

A glimmer of excitement came in the form of a message for me – through the production office – from a producer in the UK. I phoned him. The picture was called *Jakespeed*, and the producers wanted to shoot it in Africa. Shortly afterwards, I received a script. Before travelling to Victoria Falls, part of my sightseeing had included a visit to a 'witch doctor'. I was intrigued – if a little disappointed – with the strange and mysterious old man in rags who sat before me, shuffling a handful of bones. I wondered, for a second, if they were human. Through an interpreter, he told me that I had two children, that I travelled the world, and that I would be back in Africa. Maybe he could see me on *Jakespeed?* But within a couple of weeks, I learned that the UK producer was no longer involved in the film and that the film had been taken over by an American company, who would bring in their own crew.

By now, I was cracking at the seams: I suffered frequent bouts of dizziness and was having problems with my eyesight. I went to a local doctor, who referred me to a specialist in Harare.

'You're overworked and suffering from severe stress,' the doctor in Harare said. 'I'm sending you home!'

'I can't leave the picture,' I told him.

'Have you taken a good look at yourself in the mirror lately?' he asked.

I didn't want to leave – I had work to do – but my body wasn't co-operating. I didn't have a choice. I flew back to Victoria Falls and packed my bags. Back in Harare for the last time, I rested for two days and, when my final week's wages came through, I embarked on the remainder of my journey home. In London, I felt compelled to tell the production office there what I thought of the whole debacle. I needn't have wasted my breath. After *Excalibur*, I should have been accustomed to indifference. I wasn't sure what lay ahead, but I vowed I would never set foot in Africa again!

Allan Quatermain and the Lost City of Gold: The earthquake set that became an animal playground! By now, I'd lost a lot of weight.

18

BACK TO AFRICA

It was springtime in Dublin, my favourite time of year, and although I was feeling the cold, I was beginning to get my strength back. 'Rest' constituted fishing with Derek at weekends. At nineteen, Derek was still in college and spending the rest of his free time with his friends, clubbing and dating. My mind was on filming, and almost as soon as I was given the all-clear by my doctor, a call came in offering me work. TV personality Mike Murphy had raised most of the £1.8 million budget, through his newly formed company New Irish Film Productions, for *The Fantasist*, a thriller about a woman who starts getting seductive calls from a stranger. It was a violent film, requiring a lot of effects. An Irish production team – and locations around Dublin – meant that I was close to home, and I looked forward to working with all my old colleagues. I would also be working with an English prosthetics-effects specialist, whom I would assist in taking a body cast of a young model. The resulting dummy would be a cadaver in the film. I had helped make up prosthetics in Zimbabwe, but I was still relatively new to the craft, and eager to learn as much as possible.

Taking casts and making up latex moulds was one thing, but this time the director wanted realistic-looking skin – with lots of blood – for a stabbing scene, to be shot in close-up. Pigskin was the nearest thing to human skin, and so I took myself around to Hicks' butchers in Dun Laoghaire. Fred Hick was married to my mother's niece. He had been in the pork-butchering business for many years, and Hicks' sausages and bacon were renowned throughout Dublin. But Fred had never been asked to supply an entire pigskin to the movie business! This time, I didn't get strange looks from the butcher: Fred knew about my business. Many times he'd sat in my house as I talked about my adventures in film-making; he would gaze at pictures I'd brought back from my travels, more interested in hearing about activities behind the scenes than in the films themselves. He loved to know the secrets of how we made things happen.

'I'll never be able to watch a film now without wondering about all the action behind the camera! And now I'll be watching something with one of my porkers in it!' he said, laughing.

I watched him place the skin on a machine that shaved off every scrap of hair. Back at my workshop, I set about rigging a pair of two-foot-by-two-foot pigskins with the fat left on, inserting lengths of medical tubing between fat and skin, using syringes to fill it with fake blood, then making a pocket, or reservoir, being careful not to damage the skin or the fat. When punctured with the knife, blood would ooze out. But the flow had to be controlled. Making up blood and rigging the skins was two days' work; blood ended up everywhere. Stabbings, throat-slittings, bullet wounds, amputations and grotesque maimings: real-life horrors are all replicated in the world of make-believe, and make us a living. *The Fantasist*'s director, Robin Hardy, was duly impressed with my work on Hicks' porker, but there was also smoke, wind and rain on my agenda – to create the right atmosphere. Shooting lasted until the end of the summer of 1985. *The Fantasist*, was aimed at the modern-day thriller audience, but it failed to live up to the producers' expectations and was slated by the critics.

Almost immediately after *The Fantasist*, I got another call, this time for eight weeks' work on a movie called *Rawhead Rex*, to be shot

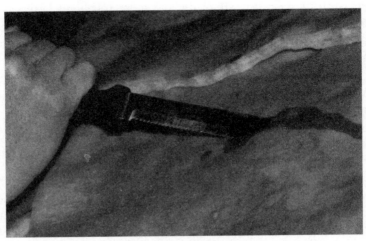

The Fantasist: Testing the 'blood' flow on Hicks' pigskin

around Wicklow and in the Dublin Mountains: familiar territory for me. 'Rex', a particularly nasty demon, is released from his grave – his 'underground prison' – by an unwitting farmer. The film follows the eight-foot-tall Rex's cross-country rampage.

'We just need a bit of smoke and rain,' Al Burgess told me. 'And maybe a car crash. That's about it for you, Gerry – all well within your repertoire!'

I had worked with Al on *The First Great Train Robbery* back in 1978, when he was the PM.

'I'm coming over as producer on this one,' he said.

When I got the script, I knew I would need extra crew. I called Al.

'Bit more on this one than I thought, Al,' I said. 'I'll need a couple of extra hands.'

The 'bit of smoke and rain' was well camouflaged in a screenplay that was full of effects, including a scene in which Rex rises through the granite slab covering his grave, a church altar bursts into flames – which then travel down the centre aisle – candles extinguish themselves, and a stained-glass window blows out. In another scene, the monster grabs the door of a passing car, causing it to crash and burst into flames. I called in Terry Glass, a colleague from the UK; my assistants, including John Doyle, a mechanic living locally, would work on the preparation of the car. The live Rex was played by an actor in costume, and an animatronics double was the work of the prosthetic-effects department, headed by two effects designers from the BBC, George Dugdale and Peter Litton.

Up in the Pine forest in the Dublin Mountains, we had rigged a caravan to blow up. In the scene, Rex smashes a skylight in the caravan and pulls a girl through a window. A ranger fires at the monster and misses, hitting a gas bottle. The caravan explodes. A police car chase, with petrol escaping from a car, leads to another fire. Inside a church, a fuse box sizzles and ignites. To add to the fun, most of these scenes, at different locations, were shot at night. I had everything on location bar the kitchen sink: wind machines, a fire tender and rain equipment, and smoke machines and gas piping, with smoke running constantly. By now, I had my own gleaming red fire tender, driven by an eight-cylinder Rolls Royce engine: a classic that carried about four hundred gallons of water for our rain supply – and fire cover. But style was no match for winter in the mountains. Water froze in the delivery hoses, resulting in a scramble to defrost them and get the

Rawhead Rex: Georgina meets the animatronic 'Rex',
as Audrey looks on.

water through! We were permanently on the go, with 'all hands on deck'.

I had lately acquired a new aircraft engine and manufactured a big wind machine for stormy rain scenes. The de Havilland Gipsy Major is a four-cylinder, air-cooled, inline engine that was used in a variety of light aircraft in the 1930s, including the famous Tiger Moth biplane. For years, these old engines have been used by effects people to create strong winds. For my wind machine, I had modified the prop and built a cage around the unit, and mounted it on a two-wheel trailer that I could tow behind a jeep or a big car. In the hustle and bustle of a particularly busy evening in the Pine Forest, an aircraft mechanic, whom I had hired to be in charge of my precious Gipsy Major, forgot my instruction to hitch it to the truck. I heard the engine running as he tuned it up, and then someone yelled 'Look!' I turned, to see the unhitched Gipsy careering downhill, prop rotating, gathering speed! Travelling at about twenty miles an hour, it hit a tree, rolled over and crashed into a ditch. The prop tore through the cage. The crew gathered round the wreckage and carefully hauled it upright; a flat-bed recovery truck transported it back to the studios. It was a sorry sight, but fortunately the engine suffered no damage, and two days later, thanks to my mechanics and technicians, the cage was repaired, and my Gipsy was back in action, as good as new.

Apart from a few weeks' shooting left on *Rawhead*, my work for the year was at an end. At Christmas, my mother joined us for a party at the house, helping Georgina with the preparations. It had been a trying year for her since my father had passed away, but she was in good spirits and somewhat more secure. Derek stayed with her for a while after my father's death and later my brother Terry had moved in to live with her. Looking to the next year, and with an ever-watchful eye on Ardmore, I was eager for more work. But apart from the usual rumours and a couple of shoestring-budget arthouse films, all was

The runaway Gipsy Major – restored again, good as new

quiet. (The Film Board was busy funding a slew of these productions, which did the rounds of festivals in London, Edinburgh and Cork – making little, if any, revenue.) It was rumoured that John Boorman was taking his next film to the UK; once again, the sound-stages and workshops at Ardmore remained locked up. By the end of February, with *Rawhead* done and dusted, the diary for 1985 was empty.

A company called City Vision had teamed up with two other production companies, Euston Films and Palace Pictures, to make a feature film called *The Courier*, with Gabriel Byrne. I was asked to do the effects. The effects scenes involved bullet hits on actors, on cars and on walls. Rain, wet-downs, smoke and fire were also in the script. A smash-and-grab at a jeweller's called for breakaway glass and a wax light bulb – to simulate the real thing, used in a torture scene. The film is about a motorcycle courier who stumbles across a pile of money. He becomes suspicious and, after some personal investigation, finds out that the company is a front for a drug business. A reformed drug user himself, he sets out to destroy the business. I enjoyed working with Gabriel again and was thrilled to see him do so well in later years in Hollywood.

On a windy night in March, I was less than an hour in bed, having just come home from a split day on *The Courier*, when the telephone rang. Georgina answered it.

'OK, Terry, I'll tell him,' she said.

'It's your mother, she's not well. Terry's waiting for the doctor to come.' Georgina offered to go over to the house, and I fell into a fitful sleep. A couple of hours later, she returned and told me that my mother had been taken to the Adelaide Hospital. A short time later, the phone rang again. I took the call this time.

'Can you get in here?' Terry asked. Georgina and I sped into the city in the early, grey dawn, not knowing that my mother had slipped quietly from the world. We were told that the nurse had just left the room to make her a cup of tea and, on her return, found that she had died. When we arrived at the hospital, it was just a matter of taking a last look. Terry made the arrangements and I went home, to deal with an empty feeling inside.

It had been a year and three months since we buried my father, but this time it was somehow different. This time, I grappled with unfamiliar feelings I could not name. As my mother was buried in Deansgrange Cemetery with my father, it seemed as though a door had closed. It only hit me then that I would never see them again. While Terry and Cormac and my sister Barbara raked over the events of the past few days, I wanted to be somewhere else. Derek was bravely trying to hold back tears. He would miss his 'Nanny Johnston' terribly. Audrey, at aged six, was still too young to understand. I prayed for work. I heard that Pierce Brosnan was in Ireland, working on a 'big film'. I pitched for the effects, but nothing happened. Then I got a call from a TV director in the UK – and with it came the fulfilment of the Zimbabwean witch doctor's prediction: I was on my way back to Africa!

The director in London told me that he would be directing a TV series in Nigeria and asked if I would be interested in working on it. The remainder of the funding was being negotiated, he said. A script was mailed to me. I could see that I would need a floor supervisor. I called Peter Dawson, who agreed to stand by. When I got the go-ahead, I took myself off to the Nigerian embassy in Dublin to obtain a work permit. It took two weeks to process my application; when I glanced through my permit, my name was spelled incorrectly – without the 't'. This was a common mistake, and while it irritated me – and even got me arrested in my own house on one occasion! – I often let it go. But having the correct spelling on an official document was crucial. I pointed out the error to the embassy official. He said that it could take another two weeks to rectify it. I was already behind time; I should have left more than a week ago. The official suggested that I take the document to the Nigerian embassy in London – en route to Nigeria.

When Peter and I presented ourselves at the London embassy, there seemed to be a somewhat more efficient system in operation, and we were told to come back in two days. On our return, a smiling official duly laid the permit, along with my passport, on the desk and said: 'That will be two hundred and fifty pounds, please!'

'I already paid in Dublin,' I told him.

'The documents needed to be sanctioned by *this* office,' he replied.

'I want to see your supervisor,' I said.

'He is not here, sir. If you want your visas, you must pay.'

And there and then, I handed over £250 for the piece of paper that would allow me to work in his country – and another £250 for Peter's.

'Corrupt bastards!' the production manager said, when I phoned him with the news. 'We'll reimburse you. Just get your ass down to Shepperton!'

He told me that corruption and mismanagement were rife in Nigeria; it was said that millions in 'petroleum dollars' were stashed in overseas accounts. To me, Nigeria was just another remote, underdeveloped country. I knew little of Nigeria's politics, nor was I interested in it. Besides, nothing could beat Iraq! But I wasn't taking any chances with my own money. This time, with the problems I had encountered in Zimbabwe still fresh in my mind, I felt that I needed to be paid my wages in advance. After a few phone calls, the production office agreed, and both Peter and I had our wages deposited in our bank accounts. That settled, we set about buying some effects materials to take with us. We had a limited budget and, from experience, decided to go prepared rather than try to find supplies in Africa. A few days later, we were on a flight to Lagos.

While queuing to clear Customs at Lagos, we were surprised to hear our names being called. Two men in light-blue shirts were scanning the lines of passengers, calling 'Johnston!', 'Dawson!' – a replay of our arrival in Iraq! One of the men was holding a clipboard. Peter and I exchanged glances. We were among a small number of Europeans who had travelled on the British Midland flight from Heathrow, and no one else seemed to be called 'Johnston' or 'Dawson'. I stepped forward.

'My name's Johnston,' I said.

'Ah, Mr Johnston, can we have your passport please?'

I immediately handed him my passport.

'And yours, Mr Dawson?' he asked.

Peter duly handed him his passport, and the two men left us. Minutes passed, but there was no sign of them coming back! The queue shuffled on towards the Customs desk.

'Passport, please,' the Nigerian Customs Officer intoned.

'We've already given our passports to some officials,' I told him.

'What officials?' he asked.

'They were here about ten minutes ago and they took our passports and . . . '

'Step to one side, please,' he said.

We waited, watching the last of the passengers go through, wondering what would happen next.

About half an hour later, three military-type men marched towards us. One of them appeared to be in charge; he carried a baton, tucked under his arm.

'Good evening, gentlemen,' he said. 'What is the problem?'

I explained that we had been approached by two official-looking guys, who seemed to know who we were, and who had asked us for our passports.

'You silly people!' he barked. 'What were these men like?'

'Medium build, about five foot eight or five-nine . . . '

'Sit down over there,' he ordered, indicating a row of seats. Fifteen minutes later, he and his companions were back – with our two blue-shirted individuals in tow!

'Are these the men?' he asked.

'That's them!' I said.

He struck one of them a blow on the head. Then he produced two passports.

'Are these your passports?' he demanded.

We duly checked our passports and told him that they were indeed ours. The 'sergeant major' then ushered us towards the Customs desk. A Customs official was called and, with our precious passports stamped, we were escorted to the Arrivals hall.

'Hold on to your passports at all times,' the 'sergeant-major' called, as he turned and left us.

At Arrivals, I noticed a hatch, over which hung a large banner, which read: 'ALL FOREIGNERS MUST EXCHANGE £100 OR US$100 FOR LOCAL CURRENCY'! Peter and I resigned ourselves to this situation and made the exchange. After what seemed like days, we collected our gear, which consisted of fifteen large boxes, containing our equipment and some camera gear that Production had asked us to carry. We loaded it on to trolleys and made for the exit. The exit was barred by a long trestle table, where two hefty-looking uniformed men were sitting, waiting. What *now*?

'Passports, please,' one of them growled.

'I want to shoot those bastards!' Peter mumbled.

I handed over my passport. The 'growler' flicked through the pages, closed the passport and pushed it back towards me, but kept his hand on it. I got the message. I extracted a £20 note and slid it into the passport. He pulled it off the surface of the table, leaned back in his chair and leafed through the pages, leaned forward again, thumped the passport with another stamp and returned it to me. The £20 note was gone. This performance was repeated with Peter's passport.

Outside, a large estate car stood waiting. The driver rushed forward to greet us.

'Ah, Mr Gerry, Mr Peter!'

We began loading our bags and equipment into the car.

'My God, the hassle we had . . . ' I began.

I was cut short by a sudden commotion. Two policemen were now beside us!

'Take your things out!' one of them ordered.

I stood there rooted to the spot, my mouth open.

'Take your things *out*!' he said again.

Peter and I jumped to the task, and the two policemen pushed the driver aside. He jumped into the car and sped away. Another taxi was hailed.

'That was a bogus taxi', the policeman said, as he hailed another cab. 'You have to be careful of bogus taxis. You could have been robbed – and killed! Where are you going?'

I handed him my piece of paper, with the address. He scanned it as the taxi drew alongside. He then spoke to the driver in his own language. The driver came around and helped us load our luggage, and we finally pulled away. We guessed that the two 'blue-shirts' who had taken our passports had given our details to an accomplice outside, who was waiting at the taxi-rank to accost us. The consequences didn't bear thinking about!

On our way to the city, we passed factories and shanty towns, and a gigantic oil pipeline running alongside the road. As darkness fell, we pulled up outside an apartment building. I checked the number on my piece of paper and rang the doorbell. The door was immediately opened by a grey-haired Indian gentleman, dressed in a casual shirt and trousers, and dripping with jewellery.

'Hi, my name's Gerry Johnston. I'm with the film company,' I said.

'Ah, yes. Please, come in,' he said, holding the door open. 'You must have a drink . . . '

He led us into a luxurious suite, crowded with people. Over drinks and spicy snacks, I learned that he was one of the executive producers. After a few hours, our host called a manservant and we were escorted back to the car, where our taxi driver was waiting patiently to take us to our hotel.

By 5.30 the next morning, Peter and I were on our way back to the airport again, headed for Jos, in central Nigeria. A Nigerian production assistant met us at the airport in Jos, but before I would trust him to take us anywhere, I quizzed him about the production and asked him to tell me the names of the DOP and the production manager. After our near-abduction the previous day, I was taking no chances! After he rattled off a few names I was familiar with, I relaxed. At the travel lodge, which also housed the production office, we met the production team. Filming had got under way, and I was anxious to make up for lost time and get started. At the location, a black man, wearing a blue robe and a turban, emerged from a tent. At around six foot five, he towered over us.

'I am Sunday,' he said, in a deep voice. 'Sunday' was our driver.

'You guys go and settle in,' the PM said. 'We'll catch up with you later.'

Sunday took us back to our hotel. Our rooms were situated across a courtyard. I opened the door into a room with cream-coloured walls – which were splattered with blood!

'That's from dead mozzies!' Peter laughed.

'Is your room the same?' I asked him.

'Yeah,' he drawled.

I noticed a gap of about two inches under the door, big enough for snakes and rodents to slither through! But I couldn't worry about that right now: I had to go in search of some extra supplies. After lunch, Sunday took us to a large house, out of town, surrounded by tin sheds, from where a lot of hammering and machinery noises emanated. Another tall Indian man in his fifties came out to greet us. He was a military type, dressed in civvies.

'I am in charge,' he said. 'Just tell me what you need – ammunition, explosives, army participation . . . '

We returned to the hotel to unpack. Peter and I headed across to our rooms. In the long corridor, clouds of mosquitoes swarmed around the fluorescent lights overhead. I dashed into my room and shut the door, but the room was already occupied – by thousands more of them! I had no choice but to begin swatting, adding to the mess around the walls! I unpacked some fresh clothes and dived into the shower. Washed and changed, I marched into the production office.

'I'm not staying here!' I told the co-ordinator. 'Find me another hotel, please!'

'I'm sorry,' he said. 'This is the only hotel available. All the crew are here.'

In the lobby, I found Sunday and, through an interpreter, asked him to take me to another hotel. Ten minutes' drive away, I found a luxury establishment, with security guards outside and a traffic barrier across the entrance. At reception, I asked if there was accommodation available. I produced some £20 notes. The receptionist's eyes lit up.

'Yes, sir,' he gushed. 'I will ask someone to show you.'

It was a dream: a double suite, with dividing doors between the bedrooms, and a balcony overlooking the lush garden, complete with fountains. We did a deal and I headed back to 'Mosquitoville' to collect our things. Production whined about paying for the upgrade, but Peter and I had nothing to lose. Our wages were already paid, and we could have hopped on the first plane for London then and there. After some to-ing and fro-ing in the office, we were packed and on the move – to our new abode. We said goodnight to Sunday, and asked him to pick us up at 6 AM.

After breakfast, we sat in the lobby and waited. Sunday arrived at 7.30. The next morning, his arrival time was 8 AM, then on the third

Soweto: With Peter Dawson and one of our local crew in Nigeria,
in front of one of our burning wrecks

morning, 9 AM. It was Iraq all over again. I asked for another driver
from among the ranks of 'Monday', 'Tuesday', 'Wednesday',
'Thursday' and 'Friday'. Sunday pleaded to be retained.

'What's his problem?' I asked the interpreter.

Following the ensuing conversation between Sunday and the interpreter, I was informed that Sunday had six wives and that he travelled
over 150 kilometres, several times a week, to visit them all – and his
twenty-five children.

'Tell him he's fired!' I shouted.

A look of horror appeared on Sunday's face. 'No! No! No! Please,
master, I will come,' he pleaded.

I glared at him. But with no guarantee that the other 'Days of the
Week' would be any better, I gave Sunday one more chance to redeem
himself. If he showed up late again, I vowed that he would be fired.
Right now, a day's work lay ahead of us.

The series was called *Soweto*, but the content has long since faded
from my memory. It did involve conflict and violence – which is why
we were there. At the front of a ten-storey college campus, we would
blow up a truck and stage several riot scenes. I arranged for an ambulance and a fire tender to be on standby, and set off, shopping. It was
another day's work trying to explain to Sunday what I needed: I ended
up in all sorts of back alleys and tin sheds trying to buy materials.
Added to this, every supplier of everything from pumps and piping to
electrics seemed to pluck prices out of thin air – and the prices were

far too high. I didn't have time to haggle, but haggling seemed to be what they wanted to do! Each transaction took forever, because I had to use Sunday as a buyer, and questions and answers had to be repeated over and over. When I reported this to my Indian 'money man', he said: 'You don't need a buyer.' From then on, initially with the help of an interpreter – I managed to get deals in the stores around town. After about three days, I was summoned to the production office, where the PM informed me that from now on, I would do my own buying, with the help of an interpreter; the production was saving money!

Evening entertainment in Jos consisted of bars and clubs, frequented by well-off locals and international visitors. At one of these clubs, Peter and I were invited to join a group of three Americans, surrounded by about a dozen black women, all in animated conversation. Their table was laden with an array of food and bottles of champagne. During the next few hours, we learned that these men had set up home here and had hitched up with local women, who were their 'wives'. They all had children; each family lived in a large bungalow. The men earned enough money, in the oil business, to support two families – one in Nigeria and another back home in the United States!

'It's a good life here,' they said. They laughed when we told them what we were earning.

'We'd spend that in one night! Why don't you come and work with us?' they said.

A couple of months' drilling for oil was a tempting proposition, but I was not enamoured by what I'd seen of the country. For one thing, human lives were cheap, and while bars and clubs might have benefited from the 'petroleum dollars', road infrastructure and buildings were sadly neglected. Many of the streets were unpaved, with a large drop onto the street from some of the footpaths.

It had been just over a month since we'd landed. Two weeks' preparation had passed, and we had four weeks' shooting left. The rest of the series would be filmed in South Africa. I was already looking forward to going home. But a last-minute change of schedule meant an extra shoot day. The production office had changed our flight tickets, and when we arrived back in Lagos we learned that our departure wouldn't be for another four to five days! Our Indian producer located an apartment for us while we waited, and walked the streets, for the next two days. Poverty was everywhere; cars, with balding tyres, were held together with chewing gum; truck exhausts spewed smoke that caught in our throats. On the third day, we stayed in the relative luxury of our fourth-floor apartment and played cards. On the fourth day, our flight tickets were delivered.

At the airport, wads of cash were again handed over at the check-in desk. The flight was delayed for an hour, and we wondered if we would ever get home. Finally, on board, I held my breath. Peter and I didn't speak a word until we were airborne.

'Drink, sir?' a stewardess asked.

'Double Scotch and ginger,' we said, in unison – then burst out laughing, flooded with relief.

While I was in Nigeria, Pierce Brosnan's film *Taffin* went into pre-production in Dublin. Supervisor Kit West and a crew from the UK were providing the special effects. I had missed out on an opportunity to work with Pierce again. Worse, on returning to Ardmore, I found that my fledgling business – along with my hopes of continuing to work in Ireland – was under threat.

19

MYSTERY AT ARDMORE, A TRICKY WATER SYMPHONY
AND A SOCIETY WEDDING

Mahmond Sipra's company had collapsed in 1984, and Ardmore had closed down. Then, with the acquisition of the studios by MTM and Tara Productions, activity had once again resumed. Arriving back from Nigeria, I headed out to my workshop, swung round the bend at the top of the avenue, and stopped. Ahead of me, a gigantic new building stood encased in scaffolding, dwarfing my little 'cowshed', not a hundred feet away. Workmen were all over the place. The big wrought-iron gates were gone; so was my 'Secret Garden'. I was now staring at an expanse of mud that stretched to the high stone walls around the perimeter. I stood, silently lamenting the disappearance of the apple and pear trees that had dropped their bounty each year on to the roof and down into my yard.

A foreman told me that the building would be the new 'D Stage'. The addition of a large sound-stage could only mean more work coming in. Feeling rather elated, I walked across, through the weeds, to my workshop. About to put my key in the lock, I noticed the stump of a heavy-duty cable protruding from the ground, beneath the solitary little window. It took a minute or so for my brain to compute the fact that the stump was all that remained of the three-phase cable that was my power supply! I unlocked the door and stepped inside. Out of habit, I flicked the light switch. No power. I walked into the workshop, gazed about me in the semi-darkness, picked up the kettle, and turned on the water tap. A splutter of muddy water shot out, then a trickle, then nothing. By the front gable, I found the severed water pipe. What the hell was going on? Back at D Stage, I consulted the site foreman.

He knew nothing. I strode up to the offices. Management knew nothing! I drove home and tried to think of a solution.

Over the next three months, efforts to have the electricity and water supply reconnected fell on deaf ears. I gave up trying and, instead, bought a small diesel generator to run equipment. Every day, I fetched water from the sink in the gents toilet beyond D Stage. Then, through a series of missed telephone messages from home and missed work opportunities, I learned that the studio receptionist had been instructed to tell callers that I 'was not on the premises'! To verify the allegation, I asked Georgina to call the studios, ask for me and record the conversation. That evening, she played the conversation back for me, and I heard the receptionist's response for myself. I had obviously incurred someone's wrath, but no one was talking! Georgina was worried. I vowed to keep going, no matter what.

Barry Blackmore had been wanting to talk to me about a TV production. 'It's a period thing,' he said, when he finally reached me at home. 'We're using an old castle in Sligo. We want it to burn down, but we don't want any damage!'

'Well, at least we're not blowing it up!' I said.

'God, no! It won't be *The Manions* again!' Barry laughed.

Troubles is the story of two women caught up in a dangerous political situation that is about to boil over. It was a TV drama from the producers of the hit mini-series *The Irish RM*. Barry was co-producer.

'Thanks for the call, Barry,' I said. 'I'll have a chat with the DOP and the director.'

I duly had a meeting with Kevan Barker, the PM, Bruno de Kaiser, the DOP, and John Lucas, the production designer, but the director did not attend, and several subsequent attempts to meet with him failed. Halfway through rigging the castle, I was still asking for a meeting. I soon discovered that the rest of the crew was just as frustrated as I was; no two people seemed to be 'on the same page'! Schedules were out the window, and on a particularly busy day during the rig, as I hung precariously from a girder about seventy feet up on the roof of the crumbling castle, I heard someone shout my name. I climbed down and was told that the director was shooting in Killala, in Mayo, and wanted bullet hits – now!

'Are you sure?' I asked.

'Yep, you're to go straight away!'

There were no effects listed on the call sheet that day – nor was I requested to have a technician on standby.

In the 1980s, Irish country roads were renowned for their potholes, and Killala was a good hour's drive away – along some of the worst roads in the country. But the director wanted bullet hits, and that was that. Fortunately I knew the road, from my stint on *The Year of the French*, and made it in good time. When I reached the set, I found a very tall man, with a strong military presence, standing in the middle of the floor. Someone said: 'Gerry's here.'

'Ah, welcome to the set,' he boomed.

The hits were on a window pane.

'How long will this take to set up?' he asked.

'About twenty minutes,' I told him.

He looked at his watch.

'The clock is ticking,' he barked, and marched off.

Fifteen minutes later, the window was rigged.

'Tell the director I'm ready,' I told an assistant.

The camera rolled, and I fired the hits.

'Mmm . . . Good,' the director said. 'I think we'll go again, just to be sure.'

I de-rigged, and another window was set in place. This time, I had it rigged in half the time. The camera rolled again and the window smashed.

'Excellent!' the director declared. 'You can go now.'

'We need to talk . . . ' I began.

'I'm too busy,' he said. 'Go!'

I was on my way back to Sligo, as frustrated as ever, still not knowing the director's requirements for the fire scene.

At the old castle, my crew, augmented by local labour, was turning the sod and running in the gas piping just under the turf. Through the piping, gas would be fed from two twenty-ton liquid-gas tankers, which had just arrived on site. In the building, we had miles of piping, running from the ground up to feed gas to various areas where the fire would appear, including a tower that Construction had built, rising forty feet from the roof. Digging, fetching and carrying, pipe-fitting, shinning up and down scaffolding: all hard graft, with only a day or two left before the big fire. But before we could finish the job, the director wanted something that I hoped I would never have to repeat. We now had to plumb the building again: not for gas, but for water! More piping, drilled this time: hundreds of holes in dozens of pipes,

Troubles: The tower and false roof, built by Construction
on the castle at Sligo

suspended from the ceiling and criss-crossed, like a spider's web. Water manifolds and pumps went in to pump water through the pipes, which would drip – in time to music!

At rehearsal, the director stood twiddling his moustache in the middle of the old banqueting hall, listening and watching.

'No, there are two drips out of time!' he barked.

We went again. This time, one drip was out of time. Next time, there was still another one out of time.

'I think it's close enough,' Bruno said.

Then Barry intervened. 'Can we not live with it?'

'Let me know when it's working. If it's not right, you're off the picture!' the director huffed – and pranced away. Another day of pipe-drilling and re-drilling, fitting and dismantling, getting drips of water to synchronise with the music – at which stage my crew and I were about to sign ourselves into the nearest mental institution! On the afternoon of the second day, we heard the First AD say the immortal words: 'OK, boys, we got it!'

In the grounds, Construction had erected a massive plaster statue of Queen Victoria, on horseback and my job was to blow it off its pedestal. This procedure involved using lifters inside the hollow plinth and the strategic positioning and camouflaging of explosive charges around the outside. In a room off the conservatory, false tree roots were laid in. Effects would wriggle the roots up through the floor, for a scene in which the roots burst up through the floor tiles. Of course, this called for more rigging – all behind schedule now because of the 'water symphony'. On the final night of shooting – with two fire tenders, extension platforms, and fifteen fire-crew members in attendance – we turned on the gas, and flames crept up along the interior, finally licking up the tower on the roof. The old castle roared and hissed as the fire took hold. Sparks floated into the night sky, as actors and crew looked on in silence. Later, I would be told that the fire could be seen for miles around. Many people thought that the castle was in fact burning to the ground! Finally, the First AD called 'Cut'. As soon as the cameras had been checked, the fire crew set to work, extinguishing the flaming tower. We carried out our usual checks, and wrapped. Almost a week of de-rigging lay ahead of us. The two bulk gas tankers were towed away, and when the last of the film unit had left the site, the building resumed its previous forlorn and dilapidated appearance, preserved for future developers. Today, it is a fine hotel.

After *Troubles*, I did some work on *The Dawning* (based on the book by Jennifer Johnston), another TV drama, starring Anthony Hopkins and a very young Hugh Grant. (In later years, I would be consoled by the fact that 'Sir Philip Anthony Hopkins' also had an 'unproductive' school history, preferring to draw and paint, or play the piano, rather than studying!) Like *Troubles*, *The Dawning* is set in 1920s Ireland. It is the story of a young woman in her late teens caught up in the political unrest. She is talked into delivering a message to Dublin. Only when she witnesses the shooting of twelve British officers does she realise the content of the lethal message. The 'shootings' were my department, along with the usual fare of smoke and rain. Near the Sally Gap in the Wicklow Mountains, a truck carrying 'Black-and-Tans' blows up. We used a real vintage army lorry – which required several days to rig with charges – with dressed dummies on board. *The Dawning* also took me to Mallow in County Cork, to film a scene at a racetrack – the shooting of a 'British officer'. On the day, as my assistant and I rehearsed with the actor, I heard my name called. I looked around. Then I heard it again: a woman's voice. I saw a hand waving from among the 'spectators' – extras in costume – packed into the stands. I didn't recognise the woman. I walked towards the stand to get a closer look. She leaned forward against the rail.

'It's me, Geraldine . . . Your cousin!'

It had been a number of years since I'd seen any of Uncle Frank's daughters, and Geraldine and I had a lot of catching up to do, but time allowed for only brief exchanges of news about the family.

Unlike *Troubles*, *The Dawning* was a cakewalk, and the rest of the locations were close to home. At the end of the shoot, I got a call to do some minor effects on *Lamb*, starring Liam Neeson in the role of a priest at a reform school for boys. Elsewhere, Neil Jordan was notching up credits with *High Spirits*, starring Peter O'Toole, Daryl Hannah and Liam Neeson. *High Spirits* was followed by *We're No Angels*, starring Robert de Niro, Sean Penn and Demi Moore. The talk around Ardmore centred on the recent axing of the Film Board; while some film-makers condemned the move, others cared less. By this time, I was thinking about going into film production, but with no hope of assistance from Irish backers, I began exploring the availability of international funding. I had been approached by a couple of budding screenwriters and I was quite taken by some of their work and ideas. But more opportunities for effects work suddenly became available. With Ardmore now in the hands of MTM, the industry in Ireland looked like it had been given a new injection of life!

As 1987 drew to a close, a theatre director and a writer were working on a script based on an autobiography by a Dublin man crippled by muscular dystrophy. Although severely disabled, Christy Brown could write and paint with his left foot. *My Left Foot* went into production and was shot in seven weeks, around Bray and in Dublin, and at Ardmore Studios. It was my first time working with Daniel Day-Lewis,

My Left Foot: The stunt crew checks out the rig for
Daniel Day-Lewis in Dublin.

My Left Foot: I'm in here somewhere, among the cast and crew!

who plays Christy, and my first time to observe an actor who remained in character, even when not acting! Daniel was never Daniel – even in the restaurant! He was 'Christy', the disabled character – complete with speech impediment – who had to be spoon-fed and helped into and out of his chair, throughout the production. Few people, even seasoned film crew, had ever seen such a performance! Some scenes involved his wheelchair whizzing down a steep cobbled street in old Dublin – ending at a busy intersection! I had to make up a rig for the chair with cables and pulleys, and remove one side of a Citroën car, including the doors and the seating, leaving only the driver's seat. But I could never discuss the logistics with Daniel because I couldn't understand him, and wild horses wouldn't make him drop the speech impediment! I had to go ahead and rehearse and perform tests with the stunt double, and hope that Daniel wouldn't actually end up in a wheelchair! I had to obtain permission from Dublin City Council to drill steel fixtures into the cobbles on the street to anchor the cables for steering the chair and controlling the speed. I needed to acquaint Daniel with much of this. While he seemed to take it all on board, I couldn't be absolutely sure!

My Left Foot was directed by Jim Sheridan. Sheridan had never directed a film before, but the producer, Noel Pearson, is said to have had enough confidence to put Sheridan at the helm. Pearson told me that he had hauled the script around Dublin looking for investment and had been laughed at. Those he approached must have been sorely aggrieved when the film picked up twelve Oscar nominations and won in two categories: Best Supporting Actress (Brenda Fricker) and Best Actor (Day-Lewis).

In early March 1988, I heard a rumour that John Boorman was making a new movie. I enquired at Ardmore, where the receptionist said that she'd heard that the film was in pre-production.

'I think he's set up a production office at his house in Annamoe,' she told me.

My daughter Audrey was approaching her ninth birthday and had just been diagnosed with diabetes. Georgina was distraught. As far as we knew, there was no history of diabetes on either side of the family, and yet Audrey was the second of our children to have developed the disease. Despite years of caring for Derek, during which Georgina had become an expert in the management of the illness, Audrey's diagnosis was a blow. But we were both determined that life would carry on as normal, and on Audrey's birthday we took her out for the day. After lunch, we took a drive in the countryside. Late afternoon found us in Wicklow, and I decided to detour to Boorman's house, on the off chance that I could enquire about work on his film. But he was not at home. His private secretary informed us that he was abroad and would not be back until the end of the month.

'I suggest you write him a letter,' she said.

On the drive home, I pondered my next move, not relishing the thought of a long summer with no work. That night, Georgina typed up a letter. Towards the end of the month, I heard that Michael Dryhurst had returned to Ireland with his wife Anna. Mike was the PM and Anna the make-up artist, and it looked like work had begun on the film. But several phone calls to the office elicited very little information. During one conversation with Dryhurst, I learnt that Boorman also had another project on hand: his daughter's wedding!

'It's on June twenty-fifth. I think it's shaping up to be his biggest production ever!' Mike laughed.

I was in Ardmore when a truck pulled up outside the construction workshop. Several massive canvases were unloaded: vivid paintings, which were stacked inside against the wall.

'They're for the Boorman film,' one of the carpenters remarked.

'When's it starting?' I asked him.

'Don't know,' he said. 'There's talk of problems. It's always the same story with Boorman.'

Feeling despondent, I was barely listening as he rattled on.

'Are you going to the big weddin'?' he asked. 'Boorman's daughter. I thought you and he were great buddies!'

I laughed.

'I hear the world and its mother's goin'. Big celebrities and all . . . Big PR company handlin' the whole thing . . . '

'No, I'm taking a holiday,' I said.

But holiday plans were soon scuttled.

'Gerry Johnston?' the woman's voice asked.

'Speaking.'

'Do you do fireworks displays?'

It was mid-May, and Katrine Boorman wanted a fireworks display at her wedding. In order to obtain a permit to import materials, a month's notice, in writing, was required by the Department of Justice in Dublin. I had three weeks! I was well acquainted with the civil servant in charge of the department, but when I explained my case, she wouldn't budge!

'The Department must have thirty days' notice, in writing.'

It was like a mantra! I got the paperwork together – regardless – drove to the office on St Stephen's Green and plonked it on her desk.

'This is very unorthodox practice,' she said.

'This is an emergency!' I replied.

Back at my workshop in Ardmore, I mustered a crew and began work. For the next two weeks, we worked all hours to manufacture mortar pots and procure other equipment. Every other day, I harangued the Department. No one had looked at my application! I lost sleep but ploughed on, hoping against hope for a miracle. It came two days before the wedding!

The materials were shipped in at the eleventh hour, and for the next thirty-six hours straight, we travelled back and forth to Annamoe, setting up our pyrotechnics in a field behind the Boorman residence. The place was hopping! Security guards and Gardaí swarmed the estate and surrounding neighbourhood. The secretary and household staff were tight-lipped about the guest-list, and the air was filled with the sound of crackling walkie-talkies, hammering, and cars, trucks and vans coming and going as two huge marquees were erected, wired for lighting and sound, furnished and decorated. On the day of the wedding, the combined populations of two villages turned out at the church to catch a glimpse of the celebs – and the fashions. They were not disappointed! The sun shone from a clear sky as my former neighbour, Bob Geldof, and his wife, Paula Yates, along with Mick Jagger, Jerry Hall and a host of people from the film and entertainment worlds, as well as heads of major retail chains – and even royals – stepped, in their colourful finery, from a fleet of limos and minibuses, to the strains of an Irish harp.

At the house, we scuttled about behind the trees and hedgerows, putting the finishing touches to our work. Underfoot, the grass crackled, even in the shade. Weeks of dry weather had left the village with a rationed water supply. Acres of land separated us from the river. The swimming pool had been filled, over several days, from a deep spring well nearby. It looked like our most convenient water supply, for fire cover. One of my crew had uncoiled the fire hoses and attached submersible pumps, concealing the hoses in the shrubbery. But John's wife was having none of it.

'Take them away, at once!' she told him. 'They are so unsightly!'

'But what happens if there's a fire, ma'am?' he said.

'You call the fire brigade!'

The guests arrived back from the ceremony to the strains of Strauss, Beethoven and Bach, played by a string quartet by the pool. At around 6 PM, a helicopter was due, carrying another film director and his wife. Early that morning, a track had been cut through the tall meadows leading to another field where a circle, with a large 'X' painted in white on the ground, had been cut, indicating the landing spot for the chopper. The chopper arrived, the couple alighted, and a car took them back along the track through the meadow to the champagne reception by the pool. Dinner was served at 7.30, with the music provided by the Chieftains. The reception went on till midnight.

Under cover of darkness, we ran the fire hoses back to the pool, and I did final checks. I handed ear protectors to the crew and the security guards. A Garda sergeant stood nearby with his arms folded, the ear muffs dangling from his fingers. I fired the first rocket. Out of the darkness, an object hit me on the shoulder – part of the cardboard packaging from one of the rockets. It almost knocked me off my feet. From the corner of my eye, I saw the Garda sergeant hit the ground! I paused, gripping my throbbing shoulder. He rolled over, with his hands covering his ears.

'You OK?' I asked him.

'Jesus!' he said, as he picked himself up and shook his head. 'I'm outa here!'

Georgina and Derek join the crew as we set up the fireworks for Katrine Boorman's wedding at Annamoe, County Wicklow.

As the crowd, still applauding the display, moved back inside the marquee, we stashed our equipment away and joined the party. A seven-piece band was now on stage, and the dancing went on until dawn. We slipped away at about 3 AM.

My role in John Boorman's 'biggest production' had come about because a friend of the bride and groom in London – who, according to one source, was a chef who 'dabbled in fireworks' – had withdrawn his pyrotechnics services at the last minute! My letter to Boorman, written in April, was on company headed paper, which bore a list of services, including 'Fireworks'. The secretary had spotted it, the PR company had been informed, and I had been contacted – as a last resort!

Behind the glitzy wedding, Boorman had been trying to bring his movie to Ireland, but the financial backers had insisted that the film be made in the US. John finally managed to get them to agree to shoot *Where the Heart Is* in Toronto. The film is about a real-estate mogul called McBain who earns his living blowing up old buildings in order to erect new ones. A group of protesters object to the destruction of one lonely old building, called the Dutch House. A television crew is sent to the scene of the protest, and an unyielding McBain appears on TV. His laissez-faire children ridicule him, and in response he drops them off at the Dutch House with $750 apiece and tells them they're on their own. They must find jobs if they expect to survive. The children adapt to their new lifestyle, meeting new friends and inviting all sorts of people into their new home, including a decrepit bum. The story was originally set in London, but much of the script had to be rewritten to suit the American setting. Had it been made in Ireland, it would have been right up my street!

As an early-morning mist crept through the Annamoe valley and mingled with the dying embers of the midsummer wedding, many changes were already afoot – both in Boorman's life and in mine. In the months following the wedding, Georgina discovered a lump in her breast. Tests revealed a malignancy, and she underwent surgery to remove the lump, as well as the lymph glands under her left arm. About six weeks later, a check-up gave her the all-clear; she was overjoyed. Then, early in 1991, she was diagnosed with multiple sclerosis. Later that year, the cancer reappeared. It was the beginning of a ten-year spiral into disability.

Derek finally moved to live and work in the UK, and Audrey struggled through her teenage years, trying unsuccessfully to come to terms with her mother's illness. I was proud that, despite the ongoing battles between mother and daughter, Audrey did extremely well in secondary school. But on obtaining her Leaving Cert, she had no idea what she wanted to do. She drifted into an early marriage and had two children. Derek married too, and within a few years, Georgina and I were grandparents. For the next ten years, I would juggle work and caring for an invalid wife, making the most of every day – and every opportunity – in a business that still fascinated and excited me as much as it had the day I began work on *The Blue Max* in 1965.

By now, another company had been established to provide effects services to the Irish film industry. As several Irish technicians had trained and worked with me, in effects, it was only a matter of time before some of them would follow our British counterparts into freelance work. Competition was a good thing, and on the face of it growing numbers of skilled technicians would give effects a stronger presence in the industry, provide producers with more choice, and keep the work at home. That would have been the ideal, but the reality was something else.

Although a film and video section had been established within the Irish trade union SIPTU, special effects did not have its own department listing and, unlike other departments, there was no grading system. Supervisors, technicians and trainees were all lumped in together, under the heading: 'Special Effects'. This meant that producers and directors didn't know who was who, whereas in BECTU in the UK, different rates of pay accompanied different grades, enabling a producer or production manager to tailor their budget accordingly. Not surprisingly, producers – even Irish producers – generally opted for teams from the UK. I felt out on a limb. While I loved foreign travel and working abroad, there were times when it would have been better for me and my family if more work was available at home. Now there were Irish freelancers touting for business in the small Irish market. So whenever work in Ireland came my way, I was more than grateful.

20

Near-abduction in Israel

Just as I was beginning to think that the film work had dried up again, Colonel O'Kelly called with news of another picture.

'It's a film about Belfast,' he told me. 'The director is a man called George Schaefer.'

'Where are we shooting?' I asked him.

'All around Dublin. I'll fax over the locations now, and I'll get a script to you tomorrow.'

Children in the Crossfire is the story of four children, from both sides of the religious divide, who travel to host families in the US so that they will have the chance to meet, away from their hate-filled world in Northern Ireland. As usual, my job entailed recreating the 'hate-filled' world of Belfast, with its relentless rioting, bombing, tortures and killings. This meant setting armoured cars ('pigs') and trucks on fire, creating petrol bombs, sniper fire, buildings on fire, rubber bullets, CS gas, creating rain and 'wetting down' the ground, which created a sheen for night shots. Derek, on holidays from college, was eager to give me a hand, and with technicians Jim Brady and Ted Castells, we 'battled' our way around Guinness's Brewery and Ringsend, beginning each morning with tea and toast 'drummed up' in my truck! The director, George Shaefer, was a gem; despite the theme of the film, *Crossfire* turned out to be one of the most relaxed and happy pictures I'd worked on in a long time.

Then I got a call from George Dugdale in London. I had met with and worked with George Dugdale and Peter Litten on *Rawhead Rex*. The two were now working on a new project and wanted me to join the crew. The effects workshop was located in a small building close to Wormwood Scrubs prison and the locations also included the prison hospital. I worked on making up bodies and doing bullet hits on heads, and blood coming from limbs. The picture was called *Living Doll*, directed by George Dugdale, Peter Litten and Peter MacKenzie-Litten. I also met a writer who hailed from Dublin. Johnny Byrne was working with George and Peter on a fascinating project and I was blown away by the sophisticated storyboard for *Dr. Who: The Movie*. Chatting with Johnny and browsing through the storyboard fuelled my dream to create a project of my own, in the same genre. I would meet Johnny again at his home in Norfolk, when I began trawling the marketplaces, hoping to break into film production.

In 1989, Jim Sheridan and Noel Pearson teamed up again on a new Irish production. This time it was an adaptation of County Kerry playwright and novelist John B. Keane's play *The Field*, about the confrontation over the possession of a field, between 'the Bull McCabe', played by Richard Harris, and 'the American', played by Tom Berenger. At the end of the shoot, cameraman Jack Conroy called me to discuss pick-up shots – extra scenes that the director had asked for – and I got a few days' work here and there with a second unit, providing wind and rain. Although set in Kerry, the film was shot in County Galway in the late winter. The pick-ups were shot near Glendalough in the Wicklow Mountains and in Dun Laoghaire harbour. Just as I was wearying of Irish weather – and of 'creating' Irish weather – I got a call. Director Roger Corman's brother, the producer Gene Corman, was about to go into production on a World War II movie, and in late spring I was on my way to the desert!

As was often the case, The journey began with a call from Peter Dawson.

'We got a picture in Israel. Can we go and do this, mate?'

'What's it about?' I asked.

'Oh, bladdy war, mate. What d'you think? You know, the usual shit: tanks blowing up, bullet hits, explosions . . . '

'Sure,' I said. 'Let's go for it!'

'It's a man called Sarge,' Peter said.

'What is?'

'The bladdy picture, mate! The name of it's *A Man Called Sarge!*'

A production office had already been set up in Israel, and within days of Peter's call I was on my way to Pinewood, where Peter had already started prepping. The Victorian mansion that was once Heatherden Hall still stood amid the crowded sound-stages. As I walked between the buildings, I remembered my 'brush with royalty' in the restaurant: my fleeting handshake with the Queen. But there wasn't time for trips down memory lane. In the weeks leading up to our departure for Tel Aviv, Peter and I had plenty to occupy us.

The Hilton in Tel Aviv was luxurious, overlooking the beach, with lush gardens and a ritzy restaurant. Our suites each sported a bar and a balcony. We were on the fourteenth floor, with a panoramic view of the bay. Emerging from the shower, I was almost deafened by the sound of a helicopter; it sounded as though it was actually in my room! Looking out, I saw a large 'gunner' chopper sweep out over the beach. I would discover that a couple of these choppers patrolled all day long, over and back, along the border with Lebanon. Again, we were close to a war zone. I would also learn that airline staff, both pilots and crew, were all ex-military personnel or military 'off call', who worked in civilian-type jobs when they were not on active military duty, and many of them would work with us on the film. On the one hand, I was comforted that we were accompanied by Israeli military personnel; on the other, I'd heard that foreigners were fair game: valuable as hostages, to be 'traded' for rebels held in Israeli prisons!

Gene Corman remembered me from *The Red Baron*. We caught up over drinks in the hotel bar, before heading to a restaurant said to be run by Christine Keeler, of the famous (or infamous) 'Profumo Affair', the political scandal that rocked the UK in 1963, named after the then Secretary of State for War, John Profumo. The restaurant was lavishly decorated in a sort of 'bordello' style. A piano player entertained the customers, and the food was excellent. Outside on the seafront, beautiful supermodel-types paraded up and down, in miniskirts and high boots.

'Hi,' one of them drawled, as Gene, Peter and I made our way back towards our hotel.

Gene nodded and smiled, and we kept on walking. I guessed that they were 'working girls', touting for business.

'They're girlie boys,' Gene said.

It seemed that there was a lot I didn't know!

Next day, our gear arrived from Pinewood. A local effects buyer took us to the studios near Jerusalem, an hour's drive through villages, along good roads packed with traffic. Here, we would have a storage facility and workshop. The approach to the studios was an uphill drive, through forests on either side. On the approach, our guide pulled into a forecourt and coffee house.

'You must see this place,' he told us. 'It is very popular with tourists.'

Rock 'n' roll music filled the hot, late-morning air. Inside, the whole place was a shrine – to Elvis Presley! Every inch of space, from floor to ceiling, was filled with Elvis photographs and memorabilia. Elvis records were on sale, along with postcards, T-shirts and key rings. We took it all in over coffee, and then proceeded to the studios. The place was run-down, with rusted trucks and a scattered assortment of leftover equipment from other films. We looked at some well-used wind machines, having to dust the sand off them first. There was no activity in the place, giving it an eerie, forgotten atmosphere. We picked out the best of whatever we could find and headed back to Tel Aviv to begin buying. Filming started two weeks later.

A Man Called Sarge is about a group of American soldiers – led by a sergeant who is only slightly smarter than his men – doing battle with the Germans in North Africa. Our first day's shooting consisted of a street gun battle with the Germans: a full day of creating ricochet bullet-hits on buildings. We had packed watermelon, oranges and an assortment of vegetables with squibs and arranged them on stalls. We then sent the fruit and vegetables flying in all directions, as if they were being shot up by gunfire.

Back in Ireland, it was the eve of the national holiday. I had forgotten about St Patrick's Day, but the production office had done its homework. That evening, we were handed call sheets edged in green, bearing the instruction that the next day, everyone had to wear something green! On the bottom was the message: 'We Wish Gerry a Happy St Patrick's Day!' Next morning, sporting a pair of green shorts, I was met by people all wearing green T-shirts – or green kerchiefs, green ribbons or green baseball caps. Everyone had made an effort on behalf of the 'Paddy', as Peter jokingly referred to me, the only Irish member of the unit.

But the bonhomie was short-lived. After four weeks, we hadn't been paid – another replay of Zimbabwe. I approached Production and was told that the money had been paid into my bank account. I checked with my bank. No money. Back to Production.

'I want proof,' I said.

'Well, it should be in on Friday,' I was told.

Friday came, but still no money.

'I'm not coming to work tomorrow, and I'm not coming to work again until I have my money,' I said.

Saturday found me lounging at the hotel pool, soaking up the sun, reading a brochure about the tourist sites in Israel.

'Gerry!' It was Gene Corman. 'Can I join you?'

'Sure,' I said.

'Look, I'll give you a personal cheque. The director and Peter and the First AD are really strapped without you.'

'Thanks, Gene,' I said, 'but I couldn't take your cheque on principle. The production company needs to be held responsible. I've experienced this racket – with this company – before and if it's not sorted by next week, I'm going home.'

It was Peter's picture, and I felt guilty about letting him down but, on principle, I stayed by the pool, in my robe and swimming trunks, determined not to replicate the Zimbabwe situation and run myself into the ground.

On Tuesday, I got a phone call. It was Stuart Gillard, the director. 'Gerry, can you please come to the set. We need you.'

'Sorry, Stuart,' I said. 'I haven't been paid for nearly five weeks.'

'I know, but we'll sort something out. We just need you, right now!'

On the set, work had slowed down but I wanted some sort of concrete reassurance before I lifted a finger. Gene appeared at my side.

'We really appreciate your coming, Gerry,' he said.

'Well, I'm here, but I'm not doing anything until I have my money.'

He pulled a chequebook and pen from his pocket.

'I'm going to write you that personal cheque now,' he said. 'If your money is not through by the weekend, feel free to lodge this.'

Reluctantly, I accepted the cheque – as security – and got back to work.

'Jeez, mate, you had me worried. I thought you were never coming back!' Peter whispered.

I held on to Gene's cheque for another week. At the end of week six, our payroll arrived. We continued to re-enact the battle between Sarge's platoon and the Germans. We blew up tanks, shot up cars and people, threw hand grenades, created sandstorms, started fires in the street, and set buildings on fire: all in all, pretty much the usual routine for a war movie.

In this film, Sarge and his platoon also blow up a fuel dump. The 'fuel dump' was built by Construction. It consisted of thirty-foot-high poles, arranged in a circle; between the poles, sheets of black plastic were tacked up. From a distance, it looked like a gigantic black steel tank. Three of these 'tanks' were erected to replicate three huge oil tanks. The location was somewhere near the town of Jaffa, on a strip of barren land overlooking a beautiful cove that reminded me of

Killiney bay. One of the cameras was positioned across the bay to film the effect of the burning 'tanks' reflected in the water. Inside each tank we had our collection of forty-five-gallon drums: thousands of gallons of kerosene and petrol, with our mortar charges set to lift the fuel and create the flash. As usual, the authorities were informed well in advance and the area was secured for days beforehand. And, as usual, it was a night shot, not just in keeping with the original story, but because explosions and fire look a lot more dramatic in darkness. I had one concern: the safety of the ancient artefacts contained in the site on which we were creating a massive explosion! The cameras rolled, we counted down, and up it went: bits of flying black plastic looking like strips of torn metal. The ensuing fires gave off heat that could be felt by the camera crew across the bay! Just before daybreak, we disconnected our batteries and cables and began our safety checks as the rest of the crew wrapped for the night. A few days later, I was told by the military on site that the explosion had been picked up by an Israeli AWACS E 3 plane flying over North Africa! And I believe that during World War II, a fuel dump in Tobruk had been blown up and its destruction had a huge impact on the tank war in the region.

We worked six days a week, with Saturday, the Jewish Sabbath, as our rest day. Nightlife in Israel centred on the family, and most of the entertainment was in people's homes. Come sundown on Friday, Peter and I were generally guests of the Israeli production crew. Around the dinner table, I was hearing a lot about the Dead Sea, our next location. But before we left, there were certain security measures to be taken. Peter and I were issued with guns. Our colleagues, all ex-military guys, were armed with sub-machine guns and ammunition. I didn't ask any questions. We piled into our hired minibus in the late afternoon and, within an hour or so, darkness fell. I was driving.

Beginning a steep climb, someone shouted: 'Slow down!' I looked in the rear-view mirror. One of my passengers was leaning forward, gun at the ready. I slowed down.

'Stop here,' he said.

I stopped, switched off the engine and dipped the lights. He got out and stood for several minutes looking into the darkness and listening, then climbed back in.

'Drive on,' he said.

Occasional glances through my driving mirror told me that all five of the Israeli crew were squinting through the windows, on constant alert. A few miles further on, I was again asked to slow down. An armoured personnel carrier was parked in a lay-by up ahead. I pulled in behind it. A couple of my passengers got out and approached the vehicle. Other armed figures appeared, and our crew joined them. After about five minutes, my passengers returned, and we drove on. We came upon a second carrier, and again we stopped, and the crew disembarked and 'visited' with the occupants. I wondered if we would ever reach our destination! A little further on, I noticed that the road was dipping, and soon we were careening down a steep incline; the road weaving and twisting. After what seemed like hours, I saw a few faint lights ahead. A badly lit petrol station appeared on our left and, just beyond it, a few houses and then the entrance to a hotel.

Daylight brought the first chance to take in my surroundings. Scanning the view, my gaze came to rest on a mountain looming above the valley. A ribbon of road cascaded down the mountainside, winding and twisting, with no guard rail. I had come down that road the previous night, in a left-hand-drive minibus with six passengers on board, in inky darkness, illuminated by candle-power headlights at about sixty miles an hour! Later that day, I would see some of the wrecks that had come off that road – buses, cars, trucks – probably thousands of feet, in deep ravines. I wondered how rescuers had managed to reach them.

We were here to shoot scenes involving 'troop movement' through the desert. The effects department would be creating 'sandstorms'. Some of the shots were close-ups of the actors' faces being buffeted by the storm. For these shots, our wind machines were mounted on camera-tracking vehicles and we had to order tons of Bentonite, used in the manufacture of soaps and cosmetics – and rather less abrasive to actors' skin than desert sand. We used coloured art powder for various explosion effects; for others we used spices – swelling the coffers of the local spice markets, whose owners were not to know that their produce would be added to high explosives rather than food! *A Man Called Sarge* was a spoof/comedy and in the middle of all the usual war effects, we found ourselves shooting an Indian reservation! The director wanted 'smoke signals': smoke 'rings', about twenty feet in diameter, rising from behind the hills! Creating such so-called 'simple' effects is often more challenging than creating battle mayhem, and this was one of the most tedious jobs on the film. Peter was exasperated.

'Tell him I can do the bladdy rings with a cigarette and he can shoot it in close-up!'

A Man Called Sarge:
Dropping the jeep on to the
'German' tent in the
Valley of the Dead Sea

The Dead Sea area has become a major health-treatment centre. The sea itself is the saltiest body of water on earth and the mineral content of the waters is said to have many health benefits. The reduced ultraviolet solar radiation allows sufferers of the skin disorder psoriasis sunbathe in the area for long periods. Four years later, when I was plagued by psoriasis, I would have welcomed the opportunity to return!

Our last sequence in the valley of the Dead Sea involved all sorts of unlikely shenanigans. One shot involved a truck – with a driver asleep at the wheel – dropping by parachute from a Globemaster plane. A small fleet of wind machines was used to open the parachute, and we used a crane to drop the truck, with a dummy at the wheel, from 150 feet, right into a German tent. Then it was back to the German tent and the battle that ensues, following the descent of the truck from mid-air. Another scene involved a checkpoint, at which a jeep was riddled with bullets. Others involved armoured tanks coming under – and returning – fire, and soldiers being shot during exchange of gunfire. This was all 'par for the course', all part of what we do. It was a lot of fun, but hard work.

My worries about security had faded and I had become friendly with the military personnel and the locals. At the same time, the real, present-day business of war with Lebanon lay just beneath the surface.

A Man Called Sarge: One of the tanks that would come under fire
in the Valley of the Dead Sea

We were very close to the border and the watchful eyes of the oppos-
ing forces, on both sides, missed nothing! Reconnaissance aircraft
were a frequent sight; on our second or third day in the desert, we were
setting up our equipment when we were almost lifted off our feet by
the backdraft from three jets that we hadn't even heard approaching!
They couldn't have been more than 300 feet off the ground. When
they had passed over, however, my ears nearly exploded! A few days
later, I spotted them again, just a split second before they zoomed over
my head. These F16 jets were flown by pilots who were training to fly
below radar. Day or night, aircraft of some sort filled the sky.

We travelled to other locations: Nathariyya, Haifa and Har Meron,
to the north along the Mediterranean, to film yet more scenes involving bullet hits and minor explosions. Following a day's filming at Har
Meron, Peter and I were driving back to Tel Aviv. It was after dark, and
this time we were unaccompanied. All around us, the desert scrubland
stretched to the horizon, with not a signpost anywhere. Suddenly, the
car was lit up, and there was a deafening noise from overhead.

'What the hell?' Peter shouted.

Another flash, and a pink hue lit up an area off to our right. A helicopter was firing what looked like flares into the surrounding countryside. A second chopper appeared and began dropping more flares;
the glow, as they hit the ground, was much like an explosion. This display lasted for about fifteen minutes. Sure that we would be hit at any
second, I kept my foot to the floor until we were again motoring along

in quiet darkness. Days later, I looked at a map and discovered we had driven miles out of our way, along the Golan Heights and the West Bank, the areas that made it into the news headlines on a regular basis, on account of the continuous fighting.

Back in Tel Aviv, our final week was spent at a military airport, simulating clouds floating past the windows of a Globemaster, as the plane is taxiing before take-off. Then the unit returned to Jerusalem. Our hotel was a sort of headquarters for journalists and TV reporters. On our first afternoon, I set out on foot to explore the Old City. At a checkpoint, a guard asked me about my visit and where I was staying. He cautioned me not to wander off too far, as the gates would close at 4 PM. I meandered along old, narrow streets, where most of the shops were closed, due to a curfew; any passing trade was left to the street vendors. From these humble scenes, I wandered on to more upmarket areas, all the while unaware that the city was enclosed by walls. At a second checkpoint, I was quizzed by another guard and again told about the closing time. I wandered through more streets and alleyways, taking in the sights and the smells, then came upon a third guard and finally a fourth, before exiting through another gate, somewhere miles from where I had started. Just then a car approached, and stopped beside me.

'Taxi?' I asked.

The driver nodded and, just as I was about to climb in, a jeep came roaring to a halt, amid much shouting from the occupants: four soldiers, armed to the teeth! The driver of the car was pulled out and pushed to the ground and interrogated, before being allowed back into his car and, as far as I could make out, told to get lost! I was questioned, and when the army sergeant discovered where I was staying, he bundled me into the open-sided jeep and we sped away. 'You were in danger of being abducted!' he told me. 'We are taking a risk, driving you back to your hotel, but it seems that we have no choice!' The driver then said something, indicating to his sergeant that a vehicle was approaching from behind. I was pushed to the floor and told to stay down, out of sight. A black limo, with flags waving on the bonnet, sped past.

'That was our general,' the sergeant told me. 'If he had seen you, we would have been in trouble'.

'You bladdy idiot!' Peter said, when I was safely deposited back at the hotel. 'You couldn't wait to go to the city with the rest of us tomorrow! You could have been taken hostage, you know!'

The following day was devoted to our official tour of Jerusalem. Just inside the gates, we were each given a skullcap. At the famous 'Wailing Wall', we watched the faithful – mostly bearded men, wearing black hats or skullcaps – standing by the wall in prayer. Off to one side, clusters of black-clad men and women stuck folded pieces of paper into the crevices in the wall. I was told that these were their prayer requests. Our guide led us across a courtyard and round to an even older portion, to an opening which led into an almost pitch-dark passageway, and then underground. Two more levels down, we reached a chamber with mud walls: it was airless and eerie; our guides carrying torches to light our way around. It was a quick visit, a special 'concession' for us. Apparently, the public never sees this place! But neither Peter nor I were familiar with the history. We just knew that we were in the Holy Land. I felt like an explorer! Back at ground level, we emerged into the sunlight. We returned our skullcaps to the baskets on the tables inside the gates, left the past behind and returned to the comforts of our hotel. Despite the comforts, however, there was an air of anxiety, as there had been in Iraq and Africa – as if people were waiting for something to happen. Although I enjoyed my stay, for the most part, I was glad to be going home.

21

'MAKING UP A FEW BOMBS'!

Early in 1990, Irish eyes were on Hollywood. *My Left Foot* rose to expectations, bringing Oscars to Dublin in March. In September, *The Field* broke box-office records at Irish cinemas, and the 1991 Oscars saw Richard Harris receiving a nomination for his portrayal of the Bull McCabe. Neil Jordan's *The Miracle* created excitement among the townspeople in Bray, where the seafront was transformed into an early-tourist-season carnival, complete with circus lions and elephants on the promenade. In Dublin, Roddy Doyle, a schoolteacher and little-known novelist, suddenly rose to fame when a film, based on his novel *The Commitments*, went into production. It went on to win four BAFTA awards and also broke home box-office records. Both *The Miracle* and *The Commitments* employed a sizeable number of Irish crew, but I was not among them.

I had been thinking a lot about film production, and I had formed a production company, Legend Productions, with a view to producing or directing – or both – one or more of a small 'slate' of projects by various writers and artists. I approached the Irish Trade Board (now Enterprise Ireland) for funding to travel to the trade fairs and festivals. One of these was MIP (now MIPCOM), an audiovisual-content market held each year in Cannes. MIP offered what the organisers called 'key market knowledge and access to the right companies and people'. In 1990, I hoped to find someone from among these companies who would be interested in looking at one or more of my projects and taking it into development.

Over the five days of the festival in Cannes, I met a few of these company representatives, left several packages – containing story-outlines, scripts, budgets and press-packs – with them, and came home with a couple of promising leads. One of these packages contained a script entitled *My Friends, My Enemies*, with a budget of £10 million Irish. It was originally called *The Big Fella*, written by Rosemary Ann Sisson, who had been a staff writer in several episodes of the TV drama series *Upstairs Downstairs* and had written *The Manions of America*. Rosemary had spent a considerable amount of time in Ireland with the Collins family, descendants of Michael Collins. I met Rosemary in her home in London on a few occasions and talked about the story of Michael Collins and his part in the War of Independence and the foundation of the Irish Free State. British Screen, a UK financing body, had been negotiating the rights to the screenplay, which were now held by an individual whom, I was told, had taken himself off to Tibet to become a monk! Months passed while British Screen tried to track him down. Finally, the call came. He was willing to sell the rights, and I took the option to develop Rosemary's script.

On my first visit to MIP, I moved around from meeting to meeting, and at one of these I was approached by a woman who had spotted the artwork on the cover of my Collins script. This woman, whose name I have long forgotten, told me that her father, who was proud to be of Irish descent, negotiated finance packages with companies in the US. She seemed very interested in *My Friends, My Enemies* and took my script, with a promise to call me within forty-eight hours. True to her word, she did call, and told me that she'd had a telephone conference with her father and a company called Carlton, in the States, who would put up £5 million towards the production costs! I returned to Ireland with high hopes, and trawled the banks in Dublin for the remaining £5 million. I couldn't raise a penny.

I spent the next two years lugging my scripts around to people who were 'in the know', following every lead that came my way, knocking on doors, making calls and travelling – back to Cannes, and then to the film festival in Toronto. I had heard that Liam Neeson was staying in a nearby hotel, and I asked the Trade Board office to connect me. Liam answered the phone, and I asked him if he would be interested in looking at *My Friends, My Enemies*.

'Sure,' he said.

The film was to be set in 1920s Dublin, Cork and London. It was a strong story, and I figured that Neeson would be ideal as the strong, charismatic Collins. But I left Toronto, having had no further response from him.

I met an Irish writer and former TV presenter, who seemed very interested in the script. After he read it, he suggested a few changes.

My Friends, My Enemies:
This script cover caught the eye
of a potential investor in Cannes.

Photo: Derek Nolan

We teamed up and amended the script to include updated information from historical records, and together we continued our search for finance. A year passed and, with no joy on the Collins front, I turned my attention to a short story. It was down time in the industry, and with no work on hand, my colleagues from among the film fraternity rallied round for the shooting of the project, adapted from a full-length feature script that had already done the rounds of the trade fairs. A former seminary at Glencree in the Wicklow Mountains, now in disrepair, would be the location. We arrived to find the location covered in a blanket of snow and had to postpone shooting for the day. However, over the next three weeks, we managed to get what looked like a nice little twenty-minute 'short', shot on 35mm film, with the Irish stage and TV actor, Jim Bartley, playing the lead role. When filming was over, I was pleased with what we'd done, but when the material was edited I realised that it was still incomplete. I decided to do some further pick-ups during the summer. Then, effects work took over, and the cans were packed away.

A few days' work on *Fatal Inheritance*, a thriller starring David McCallum and shot in Rush in north County Dublin and in Meath, called for bullet hits on a van and bullets on some buildings, as well as rain and wind. Dubbed 'Fatal Distraction' by the crew, the film faded into obscurity. It was quickly followed by a rather more decent stint in the tiny village of Redhills, in County Cavan. The film, *The Playboys*, brought me together with the veteran Irish actor Milo O'Shea, whom I hadn't seen since *Strumpet City*, back in the 1970s. The film also

The Playboys: With Milo O'Shea

starred British actor Albert Finney, as Constable Hegarty. Robin Wright played Tara Maguire and between scenes also had her young infant to feed, off the set. One of my first tasks was to purchase a transformer, to enable Ms Wright to operate a breast pump! Her suitor, Tom Casey, one of the travelling players who perform in a tent in the village, was played by a young Aidan Quinn, with whom I would work again – rather sooner than expected, in fact. Rain scenes, smoke, small explosions in a river and the burning of a barn caused considerable excitement among the locals. A travelling theatre had been set up on the village green but, after a week or so, people became so accustomed to the activity, with colourful tents, gypsy caravans and an assortment of trucks and equipment coming and going, that they hardly noticed it. Local businesses, needless to say, gained much from our presence, with hotels and guesthouses booked out and hardware stores and petrol stations staying open long after their usual hours.

The Playboys even caught the attention of the president. On a sunny Sunday afternoon, Mary Robinson's entourage glided into the village, amid cheering crowds, flashing cameras, waving flags and a brass band. The president, accompanied by her husband Nick and a few security staff, viewed the set, chatted with the cast and walked the length of the street, shaking hands with the crowds of people who had come out to greet her. The geographical border with Northern Ireland weaved through the village green; Mrs Robinson's fans included villagers who lived 'in the North'! Throughout the shooting of *The Playboys*, as we went about our daily business, we encountered border patrols, but these didn't hamper the constant traffic to the North, made up of people availing of cheaper petrol and diesel!

Meanwhile, there was a new buzz in the industry, sparked by the arrival of another film. While I worked on the modest-budget *Playboys* in Cavan, my old haunt in the far south in Dingle was a hive of activity. For the second time, film construction crews built a village above Dunquin, on the Dingle peninsula. This time, the film was the $20 million extravaganza *Far and Away*, starring Tom Cruise and Nicole Kidman. The film provided Dingle with yet another few months' excitement – not to mention Hollywood revenue. John Richardson, a supervisor and colleague from the UK, was in charge of *Far and Away*. He had asked me to work with him but because I was already engaged on *Playboys*, I had to decline.

The Playboys was a significant film for me. It was the last picture on which my good friend Peter Dawson and I worked together. A few years later, a horrific accident while he was working with a gas-operated machine on a movie at Pinewood, left Peter with severe injuries and brought his career, as one of the top and most dearly loved effects professionals in the British industry, to an abrupt end. Happily, Peter recovered, but he remains in retirement to this day. I visit him as often as I can, but I miss working with him.

As the excitement died down in Dingle, I followed work in the northwest. *The Railway Station Man*, based on the novel of the same name by Jennifer Johnston, provided me with a few days' work in

The Playboys: With Albert Finney in Redhills, County Cavan

Donegal. Alan Whibley, from the UK, with whom I had last worked on *Excalibur*, was the supervisor; as the production wanted someone with additional health-and-safety expertise, Alan called me.

My first task was to organise a consignment of pyrotechnic materials. As usual, I would require a Garda escort while transporting them. I was assigned a plain-clothes detective from the station nearest the location in Donegal. On the appointed day, a tall man, in his late forties and dressed in shabby tweeds, arrived at my workshop at Ardmore and produced his ID. Parked behind him was a rather tired-looking Hillman Avenger, with two hubcaps missing. I packed my firing boxes into my own car and set out, closely followed by the Avenger. Two hours later, we picked up the consignment of materials from the supplier and headed north, the Avenger following at a discreet distance, until, along a straight stretch of road, an Audi shot past, doing at least 80 miles an hour! In a flash, the Avenger crunched through a gear change and roared past me in a cloud of exhaust fumes! I drove a further twenty minutes, unescorted, before catching up with him again. He had pulled over and was standing, arms folded, against the Avenger. He flagged me down. I thought that the car had conked out, but the detective was grinning from ear to ear. He sauntered around to my side of the car and declared: 'Caught the bastard! Contraband!'

Three hours later, we pulled into the location, where Alan directed me to the storage facility. Back in the effects truck, my escort remained with me as I set about putting the pyros together. As the day wore on, he became restless.

'Can I do anything?' he asked.

I set him some simple tasks, cutting tape, unpacking materials. Below the tailgate of the truck, a shadow fell across the ground.

'Ah, Mick,' my detective said. 'How's it goin'?'

'Game ball,' 'Mick' replied, in a Scottish accent. 'What'ye at?'

'Ach, sure, we're just making up a few bombs!'

'Is that so?' Mick asked, with a laugh. 'Why don't I give ye a hand.'

Now I had two 'assistants', busying themselves beside me at the benches. We worked until seven o'clock that evening, breaking only for a quick coffee and a sandwich. By the time the unit wrapped, we were ready to load the finished arsenal and store it until it was needed.

'I'll be off now,' 'Mick' said. 'Enjoyed that . . . See ya 'round . . . '

'Friend of yours?' I asked, after he'd left.

'Ach, he's one of the local IRA lads. He's just back from Scotland.'

I felt weak.

'Jesus! Now they know we have stuff and where it is,' I began.

'Ach, y'ere all right,' the detective drawled. 'They wouldn't do anythin'. We're makin' a fillum here, ye know!'

The 'fillum' was the story of Julie, a widow who has come to live in a little Irish village. She takes up painting as a hobby and meets with a restorer, who's working on the local railway station building, and they fall in love. Julie Christie played Julie, the widow, and Donald Sutherland played Roger Hawthorne, the restorer. Sutherland's contract stipulated 'no smoking on set'. I sauntered up to Bruno de Kaiser, the DOP, who was brandishing a fat cigar. Bruno was always in a jovial mood.

'You'll have to put that out,' I said, and winked.

'There's nothing in *my* contract saying *I* can't smoke on set!' he said, laughing.

With *The Railway Station Man* safely in the can, I returned home, to learn that director Mike Newell had gone into production with another potential award-winning film written by Jim Sheridan. *Into the West* tells the story of two young traveller boys whose grandfather gives them a white horse called 'Tír na nÓg'. This is a magical horse, and the boys adore him. Their father, 'Papa Riley', recently widowed, has given up the life of a traveller and opted to join the settled community, and the family lives in a tower block in the city. Then Tír na nÓg is stolen by a rich, unscrupulous stud owner. The boys steal him back and run away – into the west.

The script called for continuous atmospheric effects: snow, rain, fire and wind. In one scene, the horse's hind legs had to crash through an interior wall of the apartment. I found myself again in an abattoir, acquiring another animal skin; this time it was the entire skin of a horse. This poor departed animal had obviously been quite old. His body parts would never be dedicated to science, but at least his skin would make it onto the big screen! Days of engineering went into constructing movable steel bones, to fit inside the hind quarters, which then had to be stuffed and stitched. We hadn't bargained for one side effect of the job: a vile stink, rising from the untreated skin, which filled the workshop for days! We also replicated a waterfall, behind which the boys, astride the horse, hide from their pursuers. Part of the Powerscourt demesne, Ireland's highest waterfall at over 360 feet, has been used in countless films. From a distance, it's quite plausible to imagine the possibility of the boys and their horse hiding behind the

Into the West: The cast and crew. I'm second from the right in the fourth row. Derek is standing, arms folded, at the extreme left of the second row.

cascading waters, particularly close to the base of the fall. But, in reality, gigantic slippery rocks, and the pools and rivulets flowing on down through the valley prevent access, and this is no place for a horse and two young children. So we built a waterfall – twenty feet wide and ten feet high, constructed on the back lot at Ardmore. We pumped the water, taken from the River Dargle, through two thousand feet of fire hose into a collection of tanks, then into twenty or so elevated manifolds, from which the water cascaded on to and over a massive awning, built by Construction. It was a night shoot, and although it was late summer, we were cold – partly because we were covered in mud and soaked, despite our waterproof apparel. By three or four in the morning, blood-sugar levels drop, as tiredness kicks in.

The film, shot over ten weeks in Counties Offaly, Wicklow and Galway, provided me with another brief chopper ride involving aerial shots of the horse, with the children on board, fleeing through a forest. Barry Blackmore asked me to accompany the cameraman, Tom Sigel aboard the helicopter, with a list of shots. Up we went. Below us, the horse and riders galloped, appearing and disappearing among the thick canopy of oak, ash, and sycamore that is Childers' Wood. After about half an hour, Barry's voice came through my headphones.

'You can come down now, guys,' he said.

I motioned to the pilot to land, but Tom shouted 'No'. I told Barry: 'Yeah, we'll be down in a few minutes.'

Another ten minutes passed, as we continued to track the white horse zig-zagging through the trees. By now, we had more shots than the list required.

'Come down, guys,' Barry's voice called.

'We have to go down,' I told Tom.

'I'm not going down yet. Give me another five minutes,' he hollered.

'What are you doing?', Barry shouted into my ear.

'Ahm, we're just getting the last one, Barry,' I said.

Another ten minutes and then Tom nodded. The pilot swung the chopper around and headed back towards the field. I caught sight of the director, Mike Newell, running towards us, in his green wellie boots, waving a script in the air. He kicked open a gate, leading into the field and the script fell from his hand, pages scattering into the mud. I was sure we were in for a telling-off.

'Did you get all the shots?' he shouted, as we cleared the whirring chopper blades.

'Yes, we got some fantastic footage,' I said.

'Bloody marvellous!' he screamed, jumping up and down.

Newell's enthusiasm surfaced again when we had to burn a gypsy caravan on B Stage at Ardmore. It was a tricky procedure, given that B Stage has a timber floor and this fire would not be contained in a fireplace, nor could the fire be turned on and off. We positioned our steel plates, layers of protective sand, fire troughs and the set was dressed with grass, to make it look like an outdoor location. The stage lights were switched off and as the cameras rolled, the fire took off. The crew donned surgical masks, as smoke built up and I watched for the red light on the fire alarm, in the roof.

'Tell me when, Gerry,' Newell said.

'We've only a few minutes to do this,' I told him.

Newell eked out every ounce of the inferno and the minutes rolled by. The stage was now thick with smoke.

'Okay, cut the fire!' I called.

'No, no, I need a few more minutes,' Newell shouted.

The extractor vents were not designed for this type of operation and I watched in trepidation as the swirling smoke began to change colour. The heat from the burning caravan was now practically unbearable.

'Cut! Everyone out – now!' I shouted and flung open the nearest door. The crew toppled outside, whipping off their masks, gasping for air. I have no doubt that another twenty or thirty seconds and the smoke would have reached flash-point and the stage would have exploded.

Into the West starred Gabriel Byrne as 'Papa Riley', the boys' father; David Kelly, with whom I'd worked on *Strumpet City*, as their grandfather; and Ellen Barkin and Colm Meaney, as their traveller friends. It was an instant success in Ireland.

The only other big movie talked about in film-making circles in 1991 was Neil Jordan's *The Crying Game*, most of which was shot in England, where Peter Hutchinson was in charge of effects. Neil Jordan told me later that, like Noel Pearson, he had tried in vain to raise funds for the film in Ireland, and my mind went back to my own attempts to get development funding. The people Jordan approached for funding in Ireland must have been kicking themselves when *The Crying Game* went on to pick up six Academy Award nominations, and Jordan won an Oscar for best original screenplay. The film netted more than $62 million at the box office.

The new year began with some hopeful rumours and kicked off with *The Snapper*, which provided a number of weeks' work, both around Dublin and in the studios. Starring Colm Meaney, it was a hilarious and poignant story adapted from the novel by Roddy Doyle. It was part of a trilogy of novels: *The Commitments, The Snapper* and *The Van*, all of which made it to the screen.

Meanwhile, I had struck some good fortune, in the form of 5,000 ECU (then the new currency in mainland Europe) in development funding from an organisation called 'Cartoon' in France. I had submitted a project dealing with an Irish legend, in animation form, and the award was just the motivation I needed. I knew Jimmy Murakami, who had been the art director on *The Red Baron* back in 1970; he had recently opened an animation studio in Dublin. I went to see Jimmy and his crew, and the work on my project began. In the days before sophisticated computer animation, all of the work was by hand: this was a lengthy and expensive procedure, and pretty soon the funding had expired. I re-submitted the project to Cartoon a couple of years later, but it got nowhere. I approached the Irish Film Board for funding for another couple of projects, including *My Friends, My Enemies*, without success. A year or so later, I had to abandon these projects yet again. I had over-extended my own finances and needed to get work. It was back to effects: my bread and butter. But the idea of film production wouldn't go away, and with the tax incentives introduced by Section 35 of the Finance Act in 1983, I felt sure that something would come

In the Name of the Father. Daniel Day-Lewis chats to the crew, in the snowed-up exercise yard at St Patrick's Institution in Dublin.

along. But it looked like I was destined to stay with effects. I still loved my job; the only problem was getting enough work to pay the bills.

Thankfully, Jim Sheridan came up trumps again, and *In The Name of the Father* went into production in Dublin. The effects department was headed by Joss Williams and Peter Dawson's son, Michael, both English colleagues who had a crew of four or five technicians on board before the production came to Dublin. Joss called me and asked me to join the department, with my crew. Dublin's inner city was again transformed into the twin war-torn cities of Derry and Belfast. Against the backdrop of a block of flats in the inner city, we burned buses, petrol-bombed armoured cars, and bombarded the place with rubber bullets.

The script also included a snow scene, created in the exercise yard at St Patrick's Institution, a prison for juvenile offenders, next door to the high-security Mountjoy Prison, on Dublin's north side. We 'hitched our wagons' in the prison compounds, for almost two weeks, which included a week of night shooting. St Pat's looked even more forbidding at night. Every barred window was lit up by glaring strip lighting and, from within, shouts and screams filled the night air as inmates argued and fought, and those on the upper floors dropped mysterious items on lengths of string to the windows below. Hands protruded through the bars and broken glass, and groped about, trying to retrieve the dangling object and pull it inside. The word around the set was that the kids 'inside' were dealing in drugs.

In the Name of the Father is based on the book *Proved Innocent* by Gerry Conlon, one of the men accused of the pub bombings in Guildford in England in 1975. Conlon is played by Daniel Day-Lewis, who again poured himself into the part, even submitting himself to twelve hours' interrogation by a team of real detectives! His northern Irish accent was flawless but, unlike in *My Left Foot*, at least I could understand him this time! Daniel's mother was not faring as well, however. During their telephone conversations home, she was unable to understand him, and she called my childhood friend Louis O'Connor, who was Daniel's driver, and asked him to 'fill in the blanks'! Filming lasted a couple of months. Once again, having been caught up on several occasions in the fallout from the Troubles, I was now helping to recreate them! *In the Name of the Father* cleaned up at the box office and received seven Oscar nominations.

Section 35 became 'Section 481', under new management, in the Dublin government. The Department of Arts, Culture and the Gaeltacht was set up under the leadership of Minister Michael D. Higgins, and an all-out effort was launched at government level to generate incentives for both Irish and foreign producers to film in Ireland. In the absence of effects work, apart from a few days here and there on TV commercials, I began my search once again for film funding. I had the makings of a short film in the can, and a slate of varied and interesting projects just waiting to see the light of day. I engaged a writer to polish up a great story about inner-city Dublin that would make a really good drama documentary. Instead, he came back with about ten pages of a synopsis – of fiction! I had meetings with people in TV, writers, and people in finance and distribution, none of whom would bite. Towards the end of 1993, I returned to revamping my effects business and, for the first time, I began advertising my business in earnest. I would take anything that came my way in the line of work: theatre, commercials, promos and events.

In response to Section 481 tax incentives, one production, *An*

Awfully Big Adventure – a British film set in Liverpool in the 1950s and starring Hugh Grant – came to Ireland. The main locations were the Olympia Theatre and Henrietta Street in Dublin, and a football pitch in Bray. It brought me a small amount of work, adapting a prosthetic leg, and doing rain and wet-downs for lighting. *An Awfully Big Adventure* was followed by *A Man of No Importance*, about a middle-aged, closeted-gay bus conductor in Dublin in 1963. His sister is always trying to find him 'the right girl', but his passion is Oscar Wilde, and his hobby is putting on amateur theatre productions in the local church hall. It's a quiet film, with few effects, other than smoke and rain. It featured the British actor Albert Finney – as Alfie Byrne, the Dublin bus-driver-cum-poet-cum-playwright – whom I had first met while working on *The Playboys* in Redhills.

Back at Ardmore, I was operating with a new diesel generator and a mobile phone, one of the early models, with hit-and-miss reception. Crew who had worked with me through the years helped me repair the roof of an outhouse in the yard, clear out the cramped workshop and fit out a new office. In February, they and a number of my friends in the business threw a party for my fifty-first birthday, with braziers burning in the yard, food and drink, and even taped music! It was a complete surprise, and I was deeply touched. That night, we vowed to redouble our efforts to obtain work. Foreign producers were familiar with the work and status of the UK effects department. Living in Ireland, we were out of the loop, relying on overseas producers and supervisors to put work our way. With a growing number of talented technicians and trainees now based in Ireland, it was time to take action.

Derek and crew had kitted this truck out
as my second mobile workshop.

A month later, we drew up a list of technicians, set out a proper grading system and called a meeting with our SIPTU union representative. Promises were made, but the union administration either lost or ignored our meticulous grading paperwork. Several subsequent meetings proved fruitless and, to this day, there is no effects grading system in place within the Irish union. I contacted BECTU and it was agreed that my crew could join, as the British union had now established Ireland among the 'regions' and appointed a regional representative. We had made a timely decision. The newly registered Irish crew's first 'big one' was just around the corner!

In January 1994, Sean Corcoran and I were sitting in my office. Across the yard, the 12KVA diesel generator rumbled so loudly that I sometimes had to turn it off to get some peace and quiet. Lately, it had been acting up, and I had tremendous difficulties trying to start it in the mornings. I began many a day treated to a liberal spray of diesel!

'There's a big one coming in, Gerry,' Sean told me. 'Better get prepared!'

'How many times have we heard that, Sean?' I asked.

'Honest to God,' he replied. 'There's important meetings going on in town and there's a big period drama on the way.'

The money from the 'big one' would buy me a new generator. But one of my staff had other ideas. A few days later, he was in the workshop when the genny died.

'That's it!' he said. 'We can't work like this. It's ridiculous! Let's get the power in!'

I explained that my supply had been cut off since the 1980s and I had been unable to get it restored.

'What's to stop you getting an independent supply?' he asked.

I wasn't sure.

'Ask a solicitor,' he said.

I immediately sought legal advice and then contacted the Electricity Supply Board. Within a few weeks, a cable had been run in, power connected and I could walk in, flick a switch, and hey presto!

'What about a telephone line?' I asked my solicitor.

'What about it?' he quipped.

And so the telephone company soon had a new customer, and I had the luxury of direct-dial telephone and three-phase, as well as single-phase, power supply – enough to run a factory! Newly confident, I was also able to restore my water supply.

22

THE BIG ONES – AND BECOMING A PRODUCER

I got a call from a special-effects colleague in the UK.

'We're coming over to Ireland,' he said. 'Do you have any qualified technicians?'

'I do.'

'Do you have a workshop we can use?'

'Yes,' I told him, gleefully. 'We have three-phase power supply, water, telephone and fax.'

'Excellent,' Nick said. 'See you in a couple of weeks, then. I'll send you a script.'

Oscar-winner Nick Allder was the effects-department chief; I had worked with him on a smaller film years earlier. This 'big film' unit had already spent a number of weeks shooting in the mountains of Scotland, in severe weather conditions. Vehicles were bogged down, and the unit had even lost equipment. The 'important meetings in town' had taken place between Minister Michael D. Higgins and Mel Gibson, during which about 1,500 members of the Irish army and the FCA were made available. The film was *Braveheart*, the story of Scottish clan leader William Wallace's defiance of England's King Edward in the thirteenth century. Wallace was played by Gibson, who also directed the film. The script was one tremendous battle scene after another: blood, gore, armoury, including long lances and flaming arrows, mechanical horses and air-ram arrow launchers, along with the atmospherics – fire, rain and fog. It was certainly an 'effects picture'. This was more like it!

A ruined castle in Trim, County Meath, and another in Dunsoghly, just north of Dublin Airport, were transformed into thirteenth-century Scottish castles. As Dunsoghly was situated so close to the runway, filming was a pain: every few minutes, a plane approached to land or one took off, and filming had to be suspended. At Trim, part of our job was to run in miles of gas piping, to burn the castle, during an attack by the 'English'. A field near Ballymore Eustace in County Kildare would also become a raging inferno. Preparation included the laborious digging in of gas piping, fed by two bulk tankers of liquid gas. These were augmented by extra manpower, controlling the feed from 75-pound and 104-pound gas bottles, for close-ups of horses rearing at the flames. We were re-enacting a battle at Stirling between Wallace's forces and the English, when the Scots had doused the field with oil and pitch, which they then set alight by bombarding it with flaming arrows. The plains surrounding the Curragh Military Camp in Kildare would become the scene of the earlier Wallace victory over Edward's English.

At both locations, stunt horses and stunt riders from Spain, England and Ireland charged, fell over and reared on cue, and came away unscathed – testimony to the skill of both horses and riders. Irish army riders made up a large part of both Wallace's and Edward's cavalry, while foot soldiers – also from among the ranks of Ireland's defence forces – marched in formation each morning from Wardrobe, Make-Up and Hair to breakfast, in one of two massive marquees, and then trooped back, to be cleaned up after a day of marching and 'fighting', sometimes in hot, sultry weather. One morning, as we nosed through 'the Hollow' at the Curragh, daylight was breaking, and a thick mist meant that we were driving with full headlights. The first effects shot listed on the call sheet was 'early-morning mist'! Nick Allder's wife looked at the call sheet and then, looking about her, declared: 'Done that!' But if it was that simple, we'd be out of a job! By the time the cameras were set up, the mist had evaporated, and we set to work among the bushes, with fans, smoke machines and 'lay-flat' (miles of tubular plastic wrapping, which is perforated by hand and concealed in the undergrowth. Smoke machines and fans attached to it then blow smoke through, the smoke oozing out evenly through the perforations and spreading around through the vegetation.)

From a temporary engineering workshop in Lucan, we supplied steel tracks for the amazingly realistic-looking mechanical horses, which had been delivered to us by a company in the UK. These 'horses', with stunt riders aboard, would be fired down along the tracks and would tumble in among the Scottish 'army'. We made up arrow launchers and moulds and blood-bags for countless 'English' helmets, and took casts and moulded body parts. Soon, the workshop resembled a sort of medical laboratory! Next door, the armoury made the swords and lances. Effects lances, filled with 'blood', were our department. The tips of the lances were made from balsa wood with a hollow centre, which served as a reservoir, filled with blood. On impact, the blood spurted out, simulating a wound.

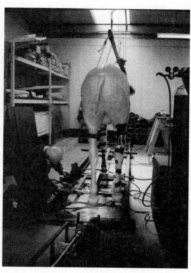

Braveheart: A UK colleague, Bob Bromley, works on the tracking, with a mechanical horse aboard, at our workshop in Lucan, west Dublin.

At the Curragh, a close-up of an arrow piercing Mel Gibson's shield required that I fire an arrow at him from an air gun, from just a few feet away. Forever bantering with fellow actors, army and crew, Mel was laughing, waving his shield about.

'Mel, I need you to be very still,' I said, not wanting to repeat Sean Connery's accidental shooting of John Boorman on *Zardoz*! But it took every ounce of willpower to steady myself and to not laugh. Mel composed himself, his face deadpan, his war paint and mad hair giving him the look of a clown.

At Ballymore Eustace, John Toal, the DOP, took me to a promontory and asked me to fill a vast swathe of forest with 'mist'. This was an unexpected shot, requiring extra manpower and equipment, gathered together in double-quick time — and filled me with added stress. But the stress of work pales next to the stress of no work. Early in the shoot, I was approached by one of the Irish production team.

'You'll have to let your guys go,' she told me.

'Why?' I asked.

'We're just going to have to let some of the crew from the second unit go,' she said, and headed off in the direction of the camera trucks. I waited. After a few minutes, she walked away, and I walked across to the camera crew.

'What's the story, guys?' I asked.

They want to let the Irish crew go,' one said.

'Here we go again,' I said. 'Just like *Excalibur*. So, what now?'

'Nothing,' he said. 'We're not going anywhere. She can get rid of the English instead. It's always the same feckin' story!'

This time, however, after a couple of days' negotiation, the matter was resolved; the second unit was absorbed into the first unit and I breathed again.

But the uncertain nature of work, along with Georgina's ill health, had, it seemed, taken its toll on me. I had been experiencing some chest pain on and off for some time, and during a recce on a location in the mountains near the Wicklow Gap, I suddenly found myself out of breath, with a pain shooting down my left arm. Fortunately, a colleague was with me, and she sat me down and took me through some breathing and relaxation routines until the pain subsided.

'You need to see a doctor straight away,' she said.

'What for?' I asked. 'I'm fine!'

'Get yourself to a doctor – now!' she said.

I arranged an appointment with my GP, who, after examining me, scathingly told me that I was as fit as a fiddle! I insisted on seeing a

Braveheart: With UK supervisor Graham Longhurst at the Curragh, County Kildare. (I don't remember who modelled for this piece of effects anatomy!)

Braveheart: With effects Oscar-winner Nick Allder and some of the Irish and UK effects crew, positioning the tracks for the mechanical horses at the Curragh, County Kildare

specialist – much to his annoyance! A week later, further examinations and a stress test, carried out by a woman who reminded me of something out of *One Flew Over the Cuckoo's Nest*, revealed a 'slight problem', and I was given an appointment for an angiogram, under the care of a top cardiologist. He examined me and studied my stress test while I was prepared for the procedure. A partially blocked artery showed up, and I was prescribed medication. A year later, my GP died in his sleep – from a heart attack!

Shortly after my procedure, my health problems took a different turn: my legs broke out in a raging rash. I was diagnosed with psoriasis. The film-unit nurse procured a cortisone cream, which I had to apply all over my legs each day. Over the ensuing four weeks, this ritual continued, but the rash remained. My colleague, who had tended to me on the day I had almost collapsed in the Wicklow Mountains, told me about a 'quack'. At this stage, I would have flown back to Africa and consulted the witch doctor! Instead, on a fine afternoon in June, I headed off to County Carlow to seek out the quack. On the kitchen table, he laid out a chart of the human anatomy and a long list of foods, soaps, washing agents – and clothing fabrics. He then produced a pendulum which he held over each item on the charts, while he held my non-writing hand in his. The pendulum swung wildly when it 'hit' on something. I had been given a notebook and pen, and each time the pendulum went berserk, I had to make a note of the offending item. I came away with a long list of foods to avoid, including several green vegetables and a few varieties of fish – most of which I loved! However, after a week on my new regime, the rash cleared, and I felt fitter than I had felt in more than a year!

About halfway through *Braveheart*, the Irish soccer team qualified for the World Cup quarter-final: on 24 June, the team would line out against Mexico in Orlando, Florida. Thanks to the benevolence of the production office, we ended the working day at lunchtime and proceeded, in convoy, to Dublin, where every hotel and pub had laid on extra TV sets and big screens. By 4 PM, the nation's roads were practically empty, as the country ground to a halt to watch Ireland's moment of soccer glory.

At the Burlington Hotel in Ballsbridge, hardly anyone expected victory for Ireland, but there was no shortage of cheering for a win for the home squad. In the lobby, I bumped into RTÉ's Pat Kenny, whom I hadn't met since *The Year of the French*, and we chatted briefly about the film, amid the din and excitement of the assembled Irish supporters, swelled by the English and American film crew. Sadly, Jack Charlton's boys were not the victors, which – as with the Scottish defeat during the making of *The First Great Train Robbery* back in 1978 – was probably just as well for Mel Gibson and the remainder of the shoot!

On a quiet, dewy night in Ballymore Eustace, during a break in filming, Mel sauntered into a rebuilt thatched cottage where I was working. He sat down beside me on a wooden crate and started chatting. He said he would love to screen *Braveheart* as a four-hour movie. I asked him if an audience would sit through a four-hour film.

'Of course!' he said. 'Well, I hope so, anyway.'

With shooting almost at an end, Mel was giving an interview on the lawn at Ardmore and wanted some 'weaponry' with which to pose for the American television crew. I dug out a rubber club, some effects lances and a retractable sword, and waited behind the camera. 'What's the budget for *Braveheart*?' a reporter asked.

Quick as a flash, Mel turned to me.

'What's the budget for the film, Gerry?' he asked.

'Eighty million dollars!' I blurted out.

'There, eighty million dollars,' Mel announced.

I've forgotten what the budget was, but the film had a final running time of 2 hours 57 minutes, and received ten Academy nominations and collected a very respectable five Oscars, including Best Film and Best Director for Gibson. The critics fell over themselves in their praise for the film, and the battle scenes were regarded as some of the most realistic and spectacular ever seen on screen.

The months following *Braveheart* were a bit of an anticlimax, with only sporadic jobs coming our way. *Frankie Starlight*, Noel Pearson's next production – a small-budget feature, filmed in Dublin, Cork and Kildare, and based on the book *The Dork of Cork* – required some minor effects and a couple of weeks' work. *Words Upon the Window Pane*, a $3 million production based on W. B. Yeats' short play, had to comply with dictates from its European backers that most of the filming and post-production be done in Europe. Some scenes were shot in Dublin, providing me with only a couple of days' work. Nevertheless, as 1994 came to an end, I rested in the knowledge that I – and my business – would survive for another while, although I grew a little despondent as I watched the all-too-familiar scenario of work going elsewhere. Two small features passed me by, and my workshop remained mostly silent for many months.

At home, sixteen-year-old Audrey was battling her way through teenage-hood, and Georgina's life was punctuated by visits to hospitals, a growing supply of medication and decreased mobility. She began to look at alternatives and thus began a spell of visits to healers, churches and various therapies, including regular treatments in a hydrotherapy unit in County Meath, which seemed to give her relief from pain and lift her spirit. Derek phoned from the UK every day, which also gave her a boost, and she now had a car, which was specially adapted with hand controls, which meant that she could get about, shopping and visiting friends and family.

Back in the film world, the talk of the town was Neil Jordan's success with *Interview with a Vampire*. I still yearned for a shot at production. While working with a second unit on *The Field*, I had shown Jim Sheridan my Collins script and told him that I hoped Liam Neeson would play Collins. He flicked through the pages, and then handed it back to me, with a wry grin.

'The best of luck with it,' he said, and walked away.

I had heard rumours that there were other Collins scripts 'out there'. I knew that Kevin Costner had a script. I didn't know that Neil Jordan had another. In the spring of 1995, I discovered that Jordan was in pre-production with his latest film when I got a phone call.

'We're coming out there to do a picture and we'll need a crew,' Yves de Bono informed me.

Yves was the effects chief this time, and this was another 'big picture'. When the script landed on my desk, I stared at it in astonishment. The picture was *Michael Collins*, and the script, with the exception of the opening scene, was almost a carbon copy of *My Friends, My Enemies* – and Liam Neeson was playing Collins!

Within about ten days, Yves's entourage, including a forty-foot container, cruised into Ardmore. Yves's crew immediately kitted it out as a workshop. *My* workshop and office facilities were also in full operation again, and the studio construction workshops were humming with activity. Nearly four months of intense work, including preparation, lay ahead: this was at least some recompense for my disappointment at having been diddled out of a chance to produce my own Collins story.

The long list of requirements for this version included a planeload of explosives and pyrotechnic materials from a large supplier in the US. I was again doing business with the Irish army, arranging customs clearance, transport escorts and storage. Reams of faxes flew between our office in Ardmore, the US, and the Department of Justice in Dublin. All went well until the eleventh hour, when the Department raised a query about two components in the shipment.

'We can't allow these to come into the country separately,' they said.

'What does that mean?' I asked.

'We can only allow them in if they are already combined.'

'Well, these materials are highly volatile,' I said, 'and if they are already mixed, well . . . Do you want a plane to blow up over the Atlantic?'

'Sorry. If they are combined here, it would constitute manufacturing. It takes three years to obtain a manufacturing licence.' Deadlock. It took three subsequent visits to the Department and a meeting with the Minister's second-in-command to obtain final clearance.

Over the next fourteen weeks, we bombed 'O'Connell Street' – a massive set, built in the grounds of Grangegorman, a former mental hospital on Dublin's north side. We set fire to Dublin Castle, blew up a vintage car carrying British Special Branch personnel at Dublin Castle, and shot up the Carlisle Grounds in Bray, replicating the GAA playing pitch at Croke Park, where the infamous Black and Tans opened fire on the players and spectators in 1921. We rocked the real

Four Courts, on the quays, with smoke and gunfire, and 'shot' British undercover agents in their beds. In quieter moments, we 'rained' on various Dublin and countrywide locations, and covered others in mist and fog.

Michael Collins: The real Four Courts in Dublin takes a hammering, but remains intact.

In the final weeks of shooting for *Collins*, I was driving down along by the Grand Canal, on my way home after a day's shooting, when I spotted an odd-looking character, with a cap, weaving about ahead on a bicycle. Drawing alongside, I discovered it was Neeson, still in his 'Collins' costume, and riding his 'Collins' bike. I lowered the passenger window and called out 'Hello'. He grinned and waved.

'Just goin' down to the hospital,' he said.

His wife, the actress Natasha Richardson, had just given birth to their first child, at Holles Street Maternity Hospital. In 2002, while visiting my daughter in Holles Street, I met the hall porters, who told me that Neeson would arrive, straight from the set, still in costume, to visit his wife and baby. The porters would take the 'Collins' bicycle inside and mind it, while the actor was upstairs, and I'm told that a plaque has been erected on the ward where 'Baby Neeson' made his appearance.

During her stay in Ireland, Julia Roberts, who plays Kitty Kiernan, Collins's fiancée, threw a party for about fifty of the crew in Dublin's Shelbourne Hotel, which had been used for some interior shots in the film. Julia thanked us all, and we raised a glass on the spot where Michael Collins and Kitty Kiernan had observed the comings and goings of British forces along St Stephen's Green in 1921.

Michael Collins: I'm in the centre of the front row with the cast and crew at the 'GPO' – built at Grangegorman, Dublin.

Following the film's Dublin première, the Irish playwright and novelist Hugh Leonard remarked that, as he walked along the quays a day or so later, he was pleasantly surprised to see the Four Courts still standing! *Collins* was nominated for two Oscars: Chris Menges for Best Cinematographer and Elliott Goldenthal for Best Original Dramatic Score. Liam Neeson played a blinder, ably assisted by a cast of mainly Irish actors, including Aidan Quinn.

The appearance of another big-budget production took me back to Ardmore. Alex de Grunwald, the line producer, asked me when I'd be free. D Stage had already been transformed into a massive 'space station'. I left the Ireland of 1921 behind on a Friday evening and on Monday morning walked into sometime in the mid-twenty-second century! The set was built on an elevated platform that took up the entire stage. Underneath, a maze of cables, hoses and piping fed the lights and our equipment. My office and workshop was again taken over by a UK crew, who were happy that they only had to walk a few hundred feet on to the set each morning. Once again, I was happy that I had work for the remainder of the year.

Spacetruckers is a sci-fi comedy in which John Canyon, played by

Dennis Hopper, is an independent space-transport entrepreneur, competing against large corporations. Lean times force him to carry an illegal cargo to Earth. The cargo turns out to be a multitude of unstoppable and deadly killer robots, known as 'BMWs' ('bionic mechanical warriors'). Canyon and his crew are intercepted at a space station by Captain Macanudo, played by Charles Dance (who had also appeared in *Michael Collins*). Battles break out, and the station is riddled with gunfire. For this, we drilled literally thousands of holes in the walls of the set and filled them with charges. We pumped steam up through vents in the sidewalk – and sucked a passenger out of the cabin (using the front half of an old 747) in flight. Our last interior scenes constituted a series of explosions, culminating in an explosion that ripped through the space station's two massive steel doors.

The effects department, physical and pyrotechnic, worked the set, at Ardmore's D Stage, while Brian Johnson set up a green-screen and computer-animation workshop at Sandyford Industrial Estate. Our only exterior-location work took place on Dollymount Strand in Dublin, which doubled as the Mojave Desert, with a parachute landing. Echoes of the World War II sequence in a real desert on *A Man Called Sarge*! With a budget said to be in the region of $27 million, the film was a big disappointment for the punters and, having aired at a few festivals, went straight to DVD. For me, though, the film was a godsend.

Just as I was wondering what would come in next, I received a call from a young first-time director who wanted some effects work done on a movie he had written. Owen McPolin was sparkling with enthusiasm. He had been granted Film Board development finance and had amassed considerable funds from private investors. But his ambitious effects scene – a large-scale explosion – would far exceed his budget. By this time, he was ready to go into production and had a crew and cast lined up to begin filming in London.

Drinking Crude is about a youth, played by Andrew Scott, who is fed up with life in a rural Irish town and heads to London in search of greener pastures. There, he runs into a Scotsman who offers him a job. But the job is back in Ireland, and he finds himself cleaning out giant oil-storage tanks – minutes from his own doorstep! The story hit a spot that brought back memories of my own journey, way back before the start of my film career, and I immediately wanted to help get it off the ground. I offered Owen a deal: I would supply the effects as an investment in the film – and source some extra private investment. In essence, I would become an executive producer. We shook hands. The deal was done – and I fell into a nightmare.

At that time, Irish film-makers were favouring original and more contemporary scripts: crime, comedy, romance, and the lives of the Irish abroad. *Drinking Crude* fell into this mix. I had managed to obtain £3,000 in private investment and felt sure that the film would figure among Irish successes in 1997. I was very excited about co-producing my first feature, but several things took my eye off the ball; one of them was a course set up by BECTU. Delivered by military explosives experts and run over five days at Cranfield University in the UK, the course was mandatory in order for supervisors and senior technicians to retain their tickets and their public-liability insurance cover.

I stayed at the home of an old friend and colleague, John Markwell, and his wife Diane. John had been an aircraft design engineer before training in special effects, and now held a supervisor's ticket. An avid reader, John had already immersed himself in the written material, while I had procrastinated, remembering my difficulties in childhood with reading and written work. I was dreading the prospect of sitting in a classroom and hoped that it would go away. I was also a little peeved that some pompous army sergeant would be telling us how to suck eggs! As it turned out, the classroom was a comfortable lecture theatre and the theory, covering the handling, transportation and use of explosives and the completion of risk assessments, was already familiar. Out on a firing range, we were each assigned a demolition task and had to familiarise ourselves with the defence forces' standard firing mechanisms, as we had no standard equipment in the film industry: we were always designing or adapting our own. Demolition and bomb-disposal experts were intrigued that we could blow up buildings and vehicles, shoot people and set them on fire, and make it all look so realistic – without harming anyone! They listened intently to tales of our adventures and even learned some of our secrets! On our fourth day, we were presented with written examination papers, on which we had to answer about thirty questions. At the end of the week, we were awarded our certificates and returned to our respective lives and the 'real' work.

The next week, I was mustering a crew to work on *A Further Gesture*, a Channel 4-funded thriller about an IRA terrorist, played by Stephen Rea, who travels to New York to escape from the knee-capping, bomb-making and violence in Northern Ireland. However, in New York, he meets a group of Guatemalans who are planning an assassination, and finds himself drawn back into violence. It was a low-budget production but with lots of atmospheric location shooting, bullet hits and mayhem. This was followed by a six-part health-and-safety commercial, ironically in Northern Ireland, necessitating several trips to Belfast and its environs, and introducing me to two young production managers, Vincent Kinaird and Paul Largan.

Several meetings with Owen McPolin, *Crude*'s director, followed. My office went into production, with Vincent Kinnaird as my PM. Jimmy Murakami's description of working with Roger Corman came back to haunt me: I would indeed find myself 'doing everything', from effects supervision to making tea, and everything in between! In London, the *Crude* camera was now rolling. But hiccups had caused delays, one of which had to do with the action car, a vintage Cadillac. The director was assured that the car was in perfect working order, but after the car had been shipped from Ireland to the UK, it died! The schedule had to be changed, and filming of scenes that didn't require the car – interior scenes and street scenes – went ahead.

Back in Ireland, however, a car was required, and I had to buy three second-hand cars, to replace the Cadillac. One of these would run into an oil tanker and blow up. My main task was finding a location for the explosion; after much negotiation and many meetings, it was arranged that the scene would be shot in a local quarry. John Markwell travelled from the UK to help with the pyrotechnics, and Martin Grace came on board to co-ordinate the stunts. I had also engaged Eugene McVeigh, with whom I had worked in Belfast, as second-camera operator, and Owen operated a third camera. The second vehicle involved, a disused oil tanker, was towed from Kerry to the quarry, and we set about rigging. The explosion went like a dream, and I prepared to join the unit and begin shooting the final sequences in the south, including a couple of days' shooting at the oil refinery at Whitegate. I was looking forward to revisiting the refinery, where I had worked in my late teens and where my uncle Frank had worked for many years after he had retired from the British navy.

Vincent Kinnaird had controlled the expenditure from my end. Vincent then had to return to Belfast to take up a prior engagement; Paul Largan was due to arrive in two days to take his place. Then I got a call from the production.

'We need to have a meeting,' Owen said.

It was Sunday, around 10 PM, when I arrived at the hotel after a five-hour drive from Dublin. The production team strolled in.

'We've run out of money,' Owen said. 'And the cameras have to go back to the UK!'

I stared at him.

'Does that mean we have to pull the picture?'

'Yep,' he said sombrely.

'Where has the money gone?' I asked.

A plastic bag full of crumpled receipts was produced, but it was soon evident that it would take more than a cursory rummage to extract the figures. It was now after midnight. A more pressing issue was the camera gear; payment was well overdue.

On Monday, I met briefly with Owen and the co-producer, and we worked out how much money we would need to complete the picture. The amount was £12,000. I got on the blower to my bank. By mid-morning, I was on my way back to Dublin. I had secured a loan, and the paperwork awaited my signature. I picked up my new production manager, who had travelled from Belfast to Dublin by train. On Monday night, I was back in Kerry, having negotiated a 'stay of execution' with the camera company in the UK.

On Tuesday, we resumed filming. Later on Tuesday, I drove to the train station in Tralee to pick up a young actor who was to play a cameo part. Some of his scenes would be filmed that night. He had called to say that he had borrowed the train fare. I told him that he would be reimbursed as soon as he arrived.

'OK, see ya so,' he said. 'How will I know ya?'

'I'll be parked outside the station in a dark-blue Mazda,' I told him.

Six hours later, a dark tousled head appeared at my passenger door.

'Gerry?'

'Yes, that's me.'

'I'm outa fags,' he said, sliding into the passenger seat, 'And I'm starvin'!'

We bought the cigarettes and then had coffee and a sandwich, before joining the rest of the unit. Over the next few days, he took to the small but important role of 'Click' effortlessly and without fuss. He was a natural – and a pro – from the start. We filmed at the oil refinery, where practically all of the management remembered Uncle Frank with great fondness, and I was cordially welcomed. At the week's end, we were headed back to Dublin, where a few more locations had to be nailed down. More meetings.

It had been an ambitious project from the start but both Owen and I believed in it. Without the benefit of a sophisticated publicity machine, we ploughed on, trying to do what we could to get it to the screen. With the film finally in the can, I breathed a sigh of relief and waited for the final edit.

Drinking Crude: Colin Farrell and Eva Birthistle
at Whitegate Oil Refinery in County Cork

Meanwhile, a somewhat more mundane task awaited me. A flat-bed trailer, which had been hired to take the Cadillac from Ireland to the UK and back to Ireland, had broken down. The trailer was sitting, minus a wheel, in the car park at Holyhead in north Wales. I had to take the ferry from Dun Laoghaire, dragging a large trailer wheel in a bag, which I had borrowed from a friend of Georgina's and introduce myself to the port authorities at Holyhead. After much negotiation with a very annoyed port official, I eventually managed to get help from some port workers to change the wheel, and the borrowed bag, now in tatters, was dumped in a bin. I then travelled back home on the evening ferry, hitched up the trailer, and towed it back to Ardmore. A few days later, I had to go shopping for a replacement bag for Georgina's friend.

Paul Largan, my production manager, had to return to Belfast. Owen and the rest of the production team had returned to London – and their day jobs – and I faced a mound of paperwork. A few weeks later, I was on a flight to London to sit in on the editing. When I saw the final cut, I could see the cracks that shouted 'low-budget'. This was a shame, given the calibre of the script and the actors, and the effort we had all put in. Nevertheless, I was confident the film would sell.

Owen entered it in the Dublin Film Festival, where it premiered to an appreciative audience. The media reviews were all favourable. RTÉ screened it, in two late-night slots, during their 'Season of Irish Film'. The viewing ratings were only marginally less than for *In the Name of the Father*, shown at 9.30 PM, just after the news. Months later, the film was picked up by an Australian television network. In the intervening years, it has had possibly two more outings.

Drinking Crude launched the young gent I picked up from the train in Tralee into feature films, and he would soon become one of Hollywood's hottest stars. It would be another year before I would hear the name 'Colin Farrell' again! Andrew Scott has since received awards and appeared on the Broadway stage, and *Crude*'s leading actress, Eva Birthistle, has also become a big name on the international scene. In hindsight, we might have made a killing had the film gone straight to video. But I had exhausted my resources and still had a twelve-grand loan to pay off. Owen was in more or less the same predicament. We went our separate ways: Owen back to camera work and I went back to effects. *Crude* had taught me many lessons, and my 'producing' bug soon gave way to the demands of my bread-and-butter work.

By April 1997, the excitement following the film première in March had died down. Three weeks' set construction had buried my office and workshop – behind a street! A new television production had moved in, and over the next six weeks, a bustling 'London' went about its daily routine, the life of this particular street revolving around 'Mrs Lovett's Pies'. *The Tale of Sweeney Todd* is the story of a murderous nine-teenth-century barber who resorts to dispatching his clients to a cellar beneath his barber shop, from where their corpses are duly collected for Mrs Lovett's kitchen! A cut-throat razor was the murder weapon.

The director, John Schlesinger, wanted to see blood, and so we rigged the razor and tested it on a member of the crew before rehears-al. John Markwell became Sweeney Todd; Andrew, our 'victim', swathed in protective paper towelling, was seated in a chair in the workshop; another assistant videoed the 'murder'.

'OK, camera rolling,' I said. 'On three, John . . . One, two, three and . . . Action!'

John slid the cut-throat across Andrew's exposed Adam's apple. Blood spilled down the paper towelling. Andrew stared patiently at the ceiling. I studied the effect.

'What are yiz waitin' for? Applause?' Andrew quipped!

The Tale of Sweeney Todd: Fire on 'Fleet Street', just a few feet outside my workshop

On the set, Andrew was pressed into commission once more. John Schlesinger and 'Sweeney' (Ben Kingsley) lined up to watch. This time, I 'did the honours' as Sweeney and performed the 'action'.

'Oh my God! Yuck!' Ben Kingsley said. 'Ooh, I'm not sure I can do that!'

So I showed him the secret, complete with medical tubing and a drum of fake blood. Andrew assured him that he had felt nothing, although by now, after several 'takes', some of the blood had found its way beneath the layers of paper towelling, and Andrew looked more like a murder victim than an effects technician! Ben's face was a picture, scrunched up in disgust. 'The missus'll kill me when she sees the state of the clothes!' Andrew declared.

Getting dirty is part and parcel of the job, and *Sweeney Todd* was just another dirty job. By the time we'd run in gas piping, set up our equipment, burned a large section of the street, started a fire in a fabric shop, pumped smoke through street vents, windows and doors, and worked through a night's filming, our work-clothes – even underwear – were probably one more job away from the bin. The burning of the fabric shop had been the most intricate job, involving feeding the gas to flame troughs – hidden behind bales of cloth – and holding our breath, fire hoses and extinguishers at the ready, as the flames rose. When the First AD called 'Cut!' the set had survived. Outside, three or four inches of molasses was used to dress the street, and our rain, pounding on this muck, would leave our clothes in an even worse state, as we squelched around, erecting rain stands, connecting hoses and moving equipment. And it wasn't finished until after we'd struck the set and stored the equipment away.

Starring Ben Kingsley and the delightful Joanna Lumley, as Mrs Lovett, *Sweeney Todd* brought me much-needed work, much laughter, and – carried in on boots and equipment – enough stinking horse, hen and goose shit, mixed with tons of molasses, to fertilise a ten-acre field! Outside the workshop, the London street disappeared into skips; after six weeks, we could park our cars in the forecourt once again.

Hot on the heels of *Sweeney Todd*, I got a call to do a feature. Mark Geraghty was the production designer.

'Not a lot of effects, Gerry,' Mark said, 'just a bit of rain and a couple of wet-downs.'

I'd heard that before, but when I got the script I found that it was indeed a slow-moving drama, with little in the form of effects. Nonetheless, in addition to the rain and wet-downs, there were bonfires and a working forge to prepare for. A few days later, following a production meeting in the big house with Pat O'Connor, the director, and the rest of the HODs, I sat alone at the table making some notes. The door opened and a woman, in old-fashioned apparel, entered.

'Oh, hi,' she said. 'I'm looking for Pat. Has he left?'

'Yeah, they've all gone. Can I help you?' I asked.

'What's your name?' the woman enquired.

'I'm Gerry,' I said.

She strolled in, and we shook hands across the table.

'I'm Meryl Streep.'

I hadn't recognised her. I thought she was an extra, wandering around, trying to find her bearings!

The film was *Dancing at Lughnasa*, based on a Brian Friel play and set in the 1930s, just before the Second World War. It's about the Lundy family: five sisters and a brother, all living together in a cottage in Donegal. Lughnasa is a Celtic harvest festival that died out over the

Dancing at Lughnasa: The cast and crew at the 'Lundy Cottage', home to a colony of bats, in Hollywood, County Wicklow

years. The film would revive the festival – for a short time, at any rate – in the hills of Wicklow.

One of our tasks was to create a 'practical' fire in the kitchen of the Lundy's home. The cottage, in the wilderness near Hollywood in west Wicklow, had not been lived in for quite some time, but after the construction and props departments had got their hands on it, it had been transformed into a habitable-looking, even cosy, little dwelling with an inglenook fireplace, where we would place our plaster logs and turf, simulating a log-and-turf fire using gas flame. This called for a vent to run up the chimney to take out the fumes. I gathered my equipment and materials together and set off on the drive over the Wicklow Gap. Walking across the bridge spanning the King's river, I met Eamonn O'Higgins, the property master, a scowl on his face.

'Gerry, we have a problem,' he said.

'Oh, what's that?'

'We have bats in the roof!'

'What does that mean?' I asked.

He sighed and left down the bag he was carrying.

'Look, the bats go out just after dark and come back in the morning, via the chimney, so they're stuck up inside the bloody roof all day! We have strict instructions from the wildlife people that they're not to be disturbed or endangered in any way!'

'But I have to run an extractor vent up the chimney!' I said.

'I know, Ger. But there's nothin' we can do. The feckin' bats have more rights than we do!'

Inside, carpenters, set-dressers and electricians were busy putting the finishing touches to the kitchen. I crossed to the fireplace and examined the chimney. I found that I could run in the vent – about ten feet of stainless-steel tubing – and anchor it to one side, leaving the bats free access to their home. Next day, we shot the scene and all was well – with not a squeak of protestation from our nocturnal residents in the roof!

23

SAVING PRIVATE RYAN

My next feature film had a bit more meat – literally! I was back in the border counties – the Cavan–Monaghan border, to be precise – back working with director Neil Jordan, and back working with a UK crew, including Peter Dawson's son Michael, under the supervision of Joss Williams. The script for *The Butcher Boy*, the story of a young boy who descends into madness, was littered with blood and gore! But our biggest effects scenes involved covering the village square in Clones, County Monaghan, in snow! Summertime in Clones abruptly turned to winter, and people with cameras were out, recording the phenomenon for posterity. At a fountain on the village green, Francie, 'the butcher boy', and his pal play around, trying to crack the 'ice', courtesy of the effects department – for which we used a combination of ice and wax, with wax icicles, created by dipping slim plastic tubing in hot wax and allowing it to drip-dry, then dipping it again and again until the icicle is formed, much like a candle, dripping as it burns. Dry ice created the fog of a cold winter's day. A big steam machine came into play for the interior of an 'abattoir', and down a back lane we burned a house, from which Francie is rescued by firemen. We also created a blizzard – using cranes and wind machines – blowing the 'snow' on the two young actors as they confabbed in the street. The blizzard scene was shot on our last night in Clones. For the last two hours before departing, we fell to de-rigging, sweeping, shovelling and hosing the streets and the square, so that, come daybreak, the good people of the village could go about their business.

The summer sun was casting a faint glow in the sky as I got into my car to drive the two hours home. Cruising along the seafront in Dun Laoghaire, the sun was well up, and the town had a visitor for the weekend. Celebrating Independence Day, the *JFK*, the largest US aircraft carrier, stood in splendour, dwarfing the passing passenger ferries, like a mammoth rising from the glistening water, about two miles out to sea. To try and get a closer look, I hurried up to Dun Laoghaire Shopping Centre and splashed out on a high-powered telescope. All that weekend, Georgina and I watched from our front window as the little ferries took celebrities and politicians out to visit the ship.

On Monday, I was back at Ardmore for the final scenes on *The Butcher Boy*. D Stage had been transformed into the aftermath of a holocaust, and we enhanced the eerie scene with smoke and fires. Then, a break in film activity gave me an opportunity for a holiday. Georgina was battling health problems. Recent tests had revealed that the cancer had taken a firm hold and was spreading. Her doctors were mystified that she was still alive and active. By now, she was using her wheelchair more frequently, and our holiday activity in Egypt was somewhat curtailed. Although in the company of our friends Joan and Norman, who had travelled from Ireland, she was finding it hard to sit by the pool and watch as I swam or played water polo, and on the day I hired a sailboat and set out on the Nile, I missed having her with me on board. Instead, I took Joan with me. As I struggled to manoeuvre the boat, having had only basic sailing instructions from the locals before casting off, Joan screamed each time the wind took the sail, and I had to abandon the effort about half an hour into the trip!

At night, Georgina was also waking up with cramps or needing to use the bathroom, and needing help. Indeed, the whole holiday was fraught with problems, culminating in a near-disaster at the airport before the journey home. Norman was also confined to a wheelchair. We had been checked in and told to relax; someone would come and take us on board the plane. The rest of the passengers filed through the departure gate. Time passed. I watched from the departure lounge as the passengers boarded the plane, sitting on the tarmac about a quarter of a mile away, and then saw our aircraft doors close!

'Come on!' I said to Joan, and we ran, each of us pushing a wheelchair, out on to the tarmac! I intercepted a vehicle, with a type of hydraulic lift platform, much like a mini car transporter, and asked the driver if we could climb aboard! The scene must have resembled something from *The Keystone Cops*, as we tried to remain upright aboard our unlikely transport as it trundled, with its two wheelchairs and two standing 'passengers', about fifteen feet in the air, towards the aircraft, which was now preparing to take off! We drew alongside, and our driver raised the platform. Frantically, I knocked on the door to the front of the plane. Nothing happened. I then stretched up and hammered on the cockpit window. The pilot went pale. I shouted: 'Let us in!' Suddenly the front door was slid open and the chief stewardess stood there, aghast.

'How could you take off with unaccompanied luggage on board?' I asked her.

She just looked at me, speechless. Finally, gathering her wits, she apologised, and we were helped inside. Cold and traumatised, Georgina's friends would have a trip to remember. Georgina was in tears. On the journey home, I wondered what the future held.

Shortly after our return, I got a call to work on the TV mini-series *Trojan Eddie*, a story about a travelling community. My job involved creating smoke from traveller caravans, along with campfires and rain. It was all pretty low-key work, but it kept the tax man happy. And then I heard that Steven Spielberg, *the* biggest Hollywood director, was in town! The film location was in County Wexford. Supervisor Neil Corbould was in charge of the effects department, and he and a large crew had travelled from the UK for the film. I joined Neil and John Evans, the other supervisor, and, with four of my Irish technicians, we brought the size of the department to more than seventy.

A village of marquees had sprung up beside the beach at Curracloe, one of the most beautiful stretches of beaches along the Wexford coast. Again, the Irish army would help make the battle

Saving Private Ryan: Curracloe Beach in County Wexford
– aka Omaha Beach

scenes look realistic. Before filming began, weeks of training with American Vietnam veterans and stuntmen took place around Curracloe. For nearly three weeks, we prepared for the 'D-Day Landings' at Normandy, beginning each morning with a pep talk from the effects coordinator in the effects marquee. It seemed that the martial modus operandi extended to crew as well as soldiers! However, the focus and discipline paid off: in the weeks that followed, we set mines, shot up landing craft and their occupants, blew up 'bunkers' on the cliff and generally wreaked havoc along a three-mile stretch of the fine sandy beach, which, in the course of each day's filming, we littered with harrowing images of war – dead and mutilated bodies and blown-off body parts.

A flotilla of landing craft ferried the Irish army and their American counterparts out to sea, where they came under fire from our massive artillery. Miles of piping, this time carrying compressed air, ran out from the shore, the compressed-air jets simulating a barrage of mortar fire, creating plumes of spray around the landing craft. Along the beach, actors and stuntmen had to be drilled in avoiding our labyrinth of cables, which were looped back to firing mechanisms feeding the thousands of explosives hidden beneath the sand. More charges, placed up along the dunes and cliffs, had to be negotiated, while the cameras panned along the soldiers' ascent, under fire, into enemy territory. Up on the cliff-top, they met with more 'hazards': explosions and heavy gunfire from the gigantic barrels of big guns protruding ominously from the German bunkers. Here, we set stuntmen – portraying German and American soldiers – on fire as they were thrown forward by the explosions, while out in the fields which looked down on our village of tents, a fleet of open-back 4x4 trucks, each with a fog-maker aboard, combined with large smoke generators on the ground, created mist, flame and black smoke to block out the summer sun.

Runabout boats, with more 'bezzlers' (fog-makers) aboard – burning gallons of oil until it became vapour – created the heavy, white sea fog, which gave an eerie, foreboding feel to the minutes just before the landing craft, filled with quietly praying soldiers, fetched up along the beach. We made up thousands of gallons of blood to pump into the sea; in the bloodied, choppy waters, Spielberg saved the props department the trouble of faking soldiers vomiting: he got the real thing. This was how we passed the seven weeks that turned into the first twenty minutes of *Saving Private Ryan*.

Saving Private Ryan: The atmosphere of war –
black-and-white smoke at Curracloe Beach

Tom Hanks plays Captain Miller, leading his men on a mission to France, behind enemy German lines, to find a missing American soldier whose three brothers have been killed in combat. Matt Damon plays Private Ryan, and Andrew Scott, our leading actor from *Drinking Crude*, 'fought' among the 'soldiers' on the beach. Spielberg marshalled the troops through a loud hailer, and when he called 'Cut' and the cameras were checked, the dead and dying got up and walked. But in the heat of the fighting and mayhem, it was hard to believe that this was not real war. Often, I found myself engulfed in feelings of sadness, and at times I felt I was right there, on Omaha Beach! The feeling of reality even touched the director. Standing on the beach, with his megaphone, he paid tribute to the Irish army and reserves. 'You guys can fight for my country any day!' he declared, the emotion in his voice palpable. The response was a resounding cheer.

On 9 July, at lunchtime in a crowded marquee, a couple of army boots appeared opposite me and a voice asked: 'Mind if I sit here?' I looked up – into the smiling face of Tom Hanks, with a smiling Spielberg at his elbow.

'Sure,' I said.

The atmosphere was particularly jovial, and the reason became obvious when someone broke into the strains of 'Happy Birthday to You'! A giant cake was wheeled in. Tom Hanks was celebrating his forty-first birthday in a tent in County Wexford! Tom introduced me to his wife and, as she watched Tom cut the cake, Spielberg told me that he hoped to come back and film in Ireland again.

Saving Private Ryan was reported to be one of the most critically acclaimed films of 1998. Nominated for eleven Academy Awards, it won five, including an Oscar for Spielberg's direction. It also won a Saturn Award from the Academy of Science Fiction, Fantasy and Horror Films, USA, as well as a BAFTA and other awards for best special effects, cinematography, editing, sound editing and design. The film went on to rake in more than $250 million at the American box office. It became a hit worldwide, and Steven Spielberg notched up another multi-million-dollar credit in his already illustrious directing career.

Towards the end of shooting, I got a call from RTÉ. A drive-time radio programme wanted to include a slot on the making of *Private Ryan* and asked me if I would do an interview. I agreed, and the producer told me to expect a reporter. A couple of days later, a chap, not more than a youth, appeared at the workshop. He had a beaming smile and introduced himself as 'Ryan, from RTÉ'. His energy was infectious and, like a kid in a toy shop, he was intrigued, excited and curious, poring over posters and photographs on the wall, bombarding me with questions and revelling in the 'tricks' I showed him in the workshop. I explained, as best I could, how we created bullet hits, blood and some of the explosions on *Private Ryan*. This 'Ryan' duly examined my hands, to see if I still had all my fingers! The recording finished, we said our goodbyes. But I wasn't finished with him. Not long afterwards, my friend, stunt-co-ordinator Martin Grace, found himself taking the dedicated young broadcaster to Dun Laoghaire, shopping for second-hand clothes. These would dress him for a stunt, in which martin would 'throw' him down the steps of the RTE Radio centre, in Donnybrook and I would set him on fire! The slot aired the following evening, but I didn't hear it, and I forgot about the interview – until I saw a new Saturday-night talk show on RTÉ television, hosted by my interviewer, Ryan Tubridy! Since then, I have followed his progress to national prominence.

Such media exposure can boost one's credibility, but my credibility with my bank had been hanging by a thread. Spielberg's film had just about saved me from bankruptcy. With mounting medical expenses, carers for Georgina, business overheads, and on-going house and workshop maintenance, I needed to keep the work coming in. As my crew and I unloaded and stored away the equipment at Ardmore, I was already chasing another picture.

Following the assassination of Martin Cahill, one of Dublin's most famous criminals, criminal activities in the city were providing the newest material for Irish film-making. Two film companies went into a breakneck chase for the rights to the story of Cahill's life. The journalist Paul Williams had written a book called *The General,* and John Boorman had fallen in love with it. Through his company Merlin Films, he had negotiated the rights to the story. At the same time, Little Bird Films were well advanced on another version of the General's life story. In the end, following much to-ing and fro-ing between lawyers, and a court hearing, two films based around the life of the late Martin Cahill went into production. I was hoping to get work on one or the other. Instead, I would be eking out the year with a few commercials and dealing with a succession of housekeepers at home, as Georgina tried to replace a dear, sweet and loyal woman who had been with the family forever. 'Why can't I find someone like Molly?' she wanted to know, but they didn't come like Molly, who had babysat and read bedtime stories to Audrey, and had been a nanny as well as a housekeeper, until she passed away. In the ensuing parade of domestics, only one managed to hold the position long enough to establish a routine, and some peace of mind for Georgina. In my spare time, I was repairing, refurbishing, cleaning and cooking.

Over the next year, Georgina's mobility decreased, and I had to fit handrails all over the house. A few small-budget productions were added to my film credits: *My Green Freedom* and *The Most Fertile Man in Ireland,* the latter involving a massive loyalist bonfire. The third, *Rebel Heart,* a mini-series set in Northern Ireland from 1916 to 1922, is about Ernie Coyne, a young, idealistic eighteen-year-old from a well-off family who decides to fight for Irish freedom and join the rebels. Dave Beavis, another fellow supervisor from the UK, was in charge of effects, and the sets, costumes and effects were similar to those employed on *Michael Collins* – but on a much smaller scale. Dave's father Arthur, an old friend and mentor, from whom I learned a lot, retired many years ago. It was a great thrill to meet him again, when he and his wife Marie visited Ireland during the making of *Rebel Heart.* Filming lasted seven or eight weeks. In real time, 1999 had just weeks to live. On new year's eve, we welcomed in the new millennium. I would soon have a 'production' of my own on hand – and it had nothing to do with film-making.

24

ENDINGS AND BEGINNINGS

By now, Georgina's main problem was access to the house, both on foot and by car. Manoeuvring her car in and out of the lane, our nearest parking facility, became almost impossible – as was negotiating the steps from the back yard down into the back hallway, and the half-dozen steep stone steps at the front, up to the hall door. Space for the construction of ramps was limited, and putting them in would have been a major hassle. The alternative would be a single-storey residence. With a sheaf of property brochures in hand, we went scouring Dun Laoghaire and its environs for something suitable and affordable. The property market in Ireland was on the upturn – which didn't favour buyers – but we hoped that the sale of Windsor Terrace would provide enough for a smaller house and a nest egg that we could invest for our future. In the end, my brother Terry found a house in Killiney that was well within our price range. Built in the 1950s, it was spacious but lacking in facilities: it had only one bathroom, no shower, a tiny kitchen (with cramped and outdated fixtures) and an inaccessible attic. The pluses were the location – it was situated in a quiet cul-de-sac, with just residential traffic – and a sizeable back garden. By June, we had a buyer for Windsor Terrace, and the builders began tearing our new house at Avondale Crescent asunder!

Georgina's routine included weekly activities at a nearby rehab day centre, where she had learned to paint. Multiple sclerosis had left her without the use of her right arm but, using her non-dominant hand, she had become quite an accomplished artist, and her pictures were among those entered in a competition and exhibited at one of AIB's offices in Dublin. One of her pictures won first prize in the competition, and at an awards ceremony in the Clontarf Castle Hotel, she received the award from none other than Pierce Brosnan. They hadn't met since *Remington Steele* had taken us all to Cannes, back in the 1980s. In the intervening years, Pierce's wife Cassie had passed away, and Pierce had become involved in numerous causes, including research into cancer treatment and prevention, and women's-health issues. It was a poignant moment both for Pierce and for Georgina, who was a great fan of his. After the ceremony, Georgina's award-winning picture was auctioned for the charity. She was approached to sell more pictures, but declined.

While waiting for the building work at our new house to be finished, we rented a holiday house in Wexford. For me, film work arrived, and I spent each week commuting to Ardmore. *The Abduction Club*, a period drama set in the 1700s and shot around Dublin and Wicklow, called for rain, bullet hits, breakaway windows and some rigging for stunts. It provided a number of weeks' work during the autumn, and in late November, we moved into Avondale – just in time to prepare for Christmas and a little house-warming party. In January, *The Abduction Club* took me back to work for a few days, and in early February 2001 we went on holiday to Florida, one of Georgina's dream destinations.

In Orlando, I hired a red Mustang convertible and we set out to explore, feeling like a million dollars! Disney World was a must – particularly the effects! It would have taken a week for us to take it all in, but after two days we were moving on. An hour's drive took us to Key Largo, from where we ventured on a cautious drive through the Everglades, mindful of the croc population living within feet of the roadway. We spent the remainder of the week sightseeing along the Florida Keys, before heading back to Miami, where the highlight of our stay was a visit to the Space Centre. We were fortunate to get a look at the Space Shuttle *Columbia*, sitting on the launch pad, before we travelled back to Orlando and our last evening in Florida. This time, despite her disabilities, Georgina's discomfort was minimal, considering the state of her health, and the holiday was a magical experience for both of us.

In spring and summer, attended by carers, friends and part-time nurses, she delighted in buying seeds and bulbs for planting in the garden, and arranging patio furniture for entertaining outdoors. With all the new comforts and space, and improved ease of movement, it looked, for a time, as if her health might improve. On the work front, I had received calls from colleagues in the UK offering me films abroad, but I couldn't travel very far from home – and Georgina. In Ireland, *The Count of Monte Cristo* and *Bloody Sunday* passed me by.

Then I got a call. A gigantic set was already under construction at the Wicklow Gap, but an outbreak of foot-and-mouth disease halted work, and the unpredictable weather in the Wicklow Mountains result-ed in delays in construction. By May, the giant burnt castle was sur-rounded by vegetation in full bloom – instead of the blackened land-scape called for in the script. However, filming went ahead, the pro-duction team deciding to digitally remove the greenery in post-produc-tion. Two more sets were built: one to replicate a part of London at Ringsend in Dublin, and a massive underground cave on D Stage at Ardmore.

Reign of Fire is about a family of fire-breathing dragons that emerge from underground and begin setting fire to everything in an attempt to establish dominance over the planet. Creating constant fires and fireballs, the effects team numbered about twenty-five, in two units, working at full tilt, and I was happy to be back in the thick of it.

Summer rolled into autumn, and Georgina became increasingly dependent on help with day-to-day tasks like washing and dressing. By Christmas, I was needed at home – full-time – and resigned myself to the role of caregiver, 24/7. Derek and Audrey visited as often as pos-sible, and with the arrival of spring 2002, I planted out gladioli bulbs; Georgina could look forward to the blooms coming out in the sum-mer. As the weather improved, we took regular excursions to visit her family, went for drives in the countryside, or sat in the back garden.

It was on one of those days, in late July, as I looked across to where she was sitting in her wheelchair on the patio, her head forward on her chest, that I tried to come up with an idea for a head support. The local health board had provided a brace, used for car-accident vic-tims, but it had been too uncomfortable for her, and as I sat there, ideas floating around in my head, a huge, dark 'thing' burst out through the hedge and landed on the head of a four-foot stone statue that sat on a ledge over the water feature! All I could do was stare, in dumbfounded silence. Suddenly, massive wings flapped, and the huge bird sprang into the air and soared across the garden. I could make out markings, in varying shades of brown, as it skimmed the tree on the other boundary and flew into the distance. It was as big as an eagle! My heart pounding, I looked at Georgina. She hadn't moved. Despite the heat, I shivered, all thoughts of head supports scattered.

In August, Georgina was extremely unwell. I called her doctor, who explained to me that cancer had spread throughout her body – even to her eyes. He said that he didn't expect her to live more than a week, and advised me to summon the family. Audrey, now expecting her second child, and Derek came back to Killiney. Their arrival seemed to give Georgina a new lease of life and she expressed a wish to take a trip to her birthplace in Athlone, to the Hill of Down, in County Meath, where she had lived for the first ten years of her life and to the pub in Capel Street, from where she went to school at the Holy Faith convent. I wasn't sure if she would be able for the travelling, but finally agreed. The daily trips seemed to revive her and at the

Reign of Fire: Snacking on a sandwich – with director Rob Bowman and unit driver Colie Sharkey

end of the week, Derek and Audrey returned to their respective homes and families in England and Spain. Within weeks of their departure however, Georgina was deemed in need of hospice care. Ten days later, she was admitted to Our Lady's Hospice in Harold's Cross, about a thirty-minute drive from home and my daily routine now involved visits to her bedside.

On the fourth or fifth evening, I sat on the floor of her room at the hospice, talking up to her, as she was unable to lift her head. Early next morning, I got a call. She was in a coma. I asked Derek and Audrey to make their travel arrangements and I returned to her bedside. When they arrived, all three of us sat and kept vigil until Georgina gently faded away. It was 17 September, just over three months before her fifty-ninth birthday. For me, disjointed memories of the remainder of September and October 2002 are all that remain.

Audrey expressed a wish to have her baby in Dublin and after her mother's funeral she stayed with me until her second little girl was born in November, at Holles Street Hospital and mother and child then returned with me to Killiney until after the baby's six-week check-up. After Audrey and the baby returned to Spain, I spent Christmas with Derek, his wife, Nickie and the children in the UK and then returned home to face life alone, as a widower.

In February, my brother, Terry stepped in with what he knows best: administration and over the next eight months, Wills, Probate, financial affairs were all handled. I had said goodbye to my home of thirty-two years and to my wife of thirty-seven years. I didn't know what to do now. I visited my workshop and collected my mail and kept up to date with what was happening in the film industry. It wasn't a lot. Once again, Ardmore was silent. Section 481 was under threat of abolition and, as usual, there were rumours of 'something big coming in'.

Fortunately, Pierce Brosnan came in – with a contemporary comedy, set in New York and Ireland. The film was *Laws of Attraction*, in which Pierce plays a divorce lawyer who falls in love with another attorney, played by Julianne Moore. A lengthy argument between Brosnan and Moore takes place in a downpour and the downpour was our job, along with fog, covering a vast area of the parkland around Powerscourt Demesne. A scene where he falls down a bog-hole: a night's shoot at Powerscourt Waterfall, never made it to the screen. As usual, however, the work was welcome and Pierce was his affable, gentlemanly self and as always, a joy to work with.

Almost immediately following *Laws of Attraction*, I was called to the set of another small-budget feature, shooting in County Kildare. The Irish director, Paddy Breathnach was shooting his fourth film called *Man About Dog*, a comedy set in the world of greyhound racing in Ireland. The film brought a few days work here and there and involved blowing out the back window of a van. The rest involved making rain and doing wet-downs. The Breathnach film was followed by a short stint on *The Blackwater Lightship*, starring Angela Lansbury and shot in Greystones, Enniskerry and Brittas Bay. The film called for a couple of exterior and interior rain scenes and a practical fire in a kitchen stove.

Another lull in filming activity gave me the opportunity to look at a project that had been presented to me in January, one that would require live action as well as considerable digital effects. I was still eager to get into production and, looking back, I now see that I was trying desperately to avoid dealing with the awful feelings that came over me, from time to time, in the months following Georgina's passing. People would ask me how I was 'managing' and I would say, 'I'm not letting it get me down'. And so, I launched myself into this new project with gusto. I had sets built at a disused factory in Dublin, got a small crew together, augmented by a number of film students, one of whom had brought the project to my attention, and bought second-hand computer equipment with a view to completing the project in-house. It was called *Minor Blues*, a short, futuristic fantasy about the aftermath of a nuclear attack, featuring a twenty-something musician and his ten-year-old sister, orphaned by the blast. Completely self-financed, the film was shot, processed and then digitally enhanced and edited, using the equipment at my offices.

Then effects work came in and a small film called *Johnny Was* took me back to Belfast, working with Paul Largan, my erstwhile production manager on *Drinking Crude* – now a producer – and the actor, Vinnie Jones, as an ex criminal who is drawn back into a life of crime, by a former partner, Flynn, played by Patrick Bergin. It was the second project in which I had to create explosions north of the border; the other being a documentary about the death of Lord Louis Mountbatten, in which, in an ironic twist, *I* was blowing up Mountbatten's boat, with the co-operation of high-ranking members of the North's security forces!

By the spring of 2005, *Minor Blues* had been set aside, due to lack of finances and significant life changes were on the horizon. The house – bought, modernised and refurbished to facilitate Georgina – felt empty and with no sign of any substantial film work on the horizon, I also needed funds. The property market had jumped into first position, ahead of blue chip and pharmaceuticals, and was now driving the country's economy. It was a good time to sell. At the beginning of November, I said goodbye to Avondale and took up residence in rented accommodation in the 'sticks', within half-an-hour's drive of Ardmore.

Shortly after Christmas, I got a call to do some rain sequences on a film called *Strength and Honour*, a film about a prize fighter, written and directed by Mark Mahon, that was about to start shooting in Kinsale, in County Cork. American actor Michael Madsen was cast in the lead, as Sean Kelleher and 'Smasher' O'Driscoll was played by Vinnie Jones. My cousin, Geraldine's name popped up again, playing in a cameo part – as Mary Murphy – appearing briefly, opposite

Richard Chamberlain as Denis O'Leary. I wondered if I would meet Chamberlain again, twenty-one years after *Allan Quatermain and the Lost City of Gold*, in Africa, but by the time I was needed in Cork, Chamberlain had finished shooting and returned to the US. At the end of my week in Kinsale, Geraldine and I caught up on family events over drinks in one of the town's new, luxury hotels, and the next day, I left for home. I had a new project in hand - an unlikely undertaking – in many ways, and my most challenging adventure!

Being a slow reader, book-reading has always been a chore for me. I have relied heavily on pictures to tell me a story, which is probably why I became involved in a visual industry and found a place there – creating pictures. Until now, book-writing was the furthest thing from my mind. My late father, a 'pen-pusher', who would never have seen me embrace anything as academic as writing, would be gobsmacked!

It was Sean Corcoran who started it.

'Famous people are always writing books about the film industry and the glamour, but very few people know the hardship and the challenges involved, behind the scenes.'

A spark had been ignited. The more I thought about it, the more I wanted to get my own story down – for a number of reasons.

The first reason: my children, Derek and Audrey and my five grandchildren – three in Holland and two in the UK. Maybe some will follow a career in film, or maybe not. Either way, it is likely that some of them will live somewhere other than Ireland. This memoir may be their only link with the film industry – and the Irish Film Industry, in particular – who knows? At any rate, this will hopefully spare Derek and Audrey having to recount my 'film lore' for their children (they will have enough to do, filling in the blanks!). Besides, like most people, I want to leave something behind me, to mark my existence on the planet!

I also wanted to pay a tribute to the people who helped me, in many ways, as I found my way in the film world. Some of them are mentioned here, some have passed on, others have retired; some are well-known names, others known only to their families, friends and colleagues. All of them had a profound influence on me.

On cinema screens, these names flash by on a long list of closing credits. The audience leaves, as the credits roll and people watching the movie at home on television go and make the tea, or flick over to another channel! But, in the film world and to a film technician, these names are important; the only evidence of our work. Many, including myself, never even made some credits! Through this memoir, I want to thank them, collectively and through my story, I hope to maintain a connection with them and with my work – and my life – in the film industry.

I would like the special effects profession to be remembered as it was; the profession that has brought me such varied experiences, such excitement and a decent living. As I've watched the advance from heavy camera equipment and cumbersome lights, aptly named 'brutes', to high-definition cameras and sophisticated lighting, the advance from our own hefty, home-made smoke machines to mini 'foggers' and especially the advance in digital effects and the onset of virtual reality, I wonder if technology will make us redundant; special effects technicians could be a dying breed!

Over the years, I have also watched the rise and fall of the famous and, from the 'cowshed', still requiring relentless efforts to keep it standing, nestling – like the big house – amidst a growing sprawl of Nissen huts, car parks and corrugated workshops, I have observed the changing fortunes of Ardmore Studios, now celebrating its golden jubilee. Marking my own forty-plus years in special effects; all these years after my first intoxicating venture into Ardmore and the world of movie-making, I count myself lucky. My dreams of adventure have been fulfilled. Computer-generated fires, rain and explosions still look fake, but before technology catches up, I would like to echo one of Hollywood's greats, who paid tribute to the work of the special-effects professionals. He said: 'The audience is treated to the results, but I have smelled the cordite, seen the hidden wires and experienced the meticulous and personal care for the safety of everybody without compromising the finished effect.'

Thank you, Steven Spielberg!

Photo: Derek Nolan

The cowshed, 2007

Stills from ads for Harp (top), filmed at Luggala, County Wicklow, in the early 1980s, and Canada Dry, shot at Malahide railway station, for both of which I supplied the special effects

GLOSSARY

AD

Assistant director. There can be more than one AD on a film unit: the First, Second, Third and so on, each with different tasks. The First AD stands by the director and the camera when filming and calls the directions to the rest of the shooting crew. ADs also distribute call-sheets and look after actors on set.

Blanks

Blank cartridges containing gunpowder and used in guns, simulating the actual fire from a gun or rifle, but without real bullets.

Blood bags

Can be clear plastic or latex (depending on the size and extent of the 'wound' to be shown) and filled with theatrical blood and sealed. The 'blood' will appear when the bag is pierced with a knife, dagger or lance, or when exploded by a charge to simulate a bullet hit.

Breakaways

Hand props (such as bottles, drinking glasses, chairs) or parts of a set (such as stairs, a window or a wall) constructed to break in a certain way upon cue, during a fight – or from gunfire.

Bullet hits

Simulating gunfire on walls, vehicles and actors. On inanimate objects, bullet holes are carved out in the wood, plaster or metal. These are then packed with small explosive charges and camouflaged. Connecting wires lead to a firing mechanism off-camera, controlled by the effects technician. On actors, a miniature metal plate protects the wearer from injury. A small groove in the plate holds a 'blood bag' filled with blood. A 'squib' (small charge) is placed on the bag and secured with special tape. The plate is then housed on a leather pad, with tape or straps encircling the actor's body.

Call-sheet

Typed sheets, showing location, date, the next day's start time, scenes to be shot, weather forecast (if shooting outdoors), notice of health-and-safety requirements, any other special requirements, and so on. The sheet is circulated to cast and crew at the end of each working day.

Cut

To stop the camera or action, or indicating the end of a scene. It is also a term used in editing: to 'cut' is to edit or shorten a scene by cutting the film.

DOP

Director of photography: the person in charge of the camera department. He or she decides, along with the director, on how a set will be lit, and filmed.

Fire

Refers to a 'practical' or working fire in a fireplace or a stove (interior). Also refers to buildings on fire, vehicles on fire and stunt people on fire, as well as bonfires and smaller fires for dressing a set – e.g. the aftermath of a riot or bombing raid. All fire is controlled, and health-and-safety fire cover is present.

Generator

Equipment used to provide electrical power for the production when filming on location.

HOD

Head of department: the person in control of the department: the effects supervisor is in charge of the effects department, the construction manager is in charge of the set-construction department, and so on.

Lifters

Refers to a mortar explosion moving or lifting an object or objects, by force. When a roof or wall has to be blown out, or a car lifted, a mortar (usually an explosive in a steel tube) may also be fitted with a piston and plunger.

Mortar pots/ Mortar tunes

Steel containers for explosives, used in the ground or encased in sand on a platform, for instance in a fireworks display.

Pan

To 'pan': a term used to describe the way in which the camera moves (pans) as it follows an actor or vehicle walking or driving past.

PM

Production manager – usually responsible for sourcing and hiring a crew, controlling the budget, paying wages. Person in charge of production administration.

Prep

Work-time (a day, or weeks, or sometimes months) preceding filming, including set construction, set dressing, wiring a set for lighting, buying props and materials, and making up effects equipment.

Pyrotechnics

Controlled materials (used in creating special effects for film) that can be ignited, burned or exploded on cue by the special-effects crew. These materials include propane fire equipment, bullet hits, and all types of explosives. Pyrotechnic materials must only be handled by a licensed pyrotechnics supervisor.

Sound stage

A large building specifically designed for filming. A sound stage has thick, densely insulated walls to prevent sounds penetrating from outside. High, unobstructed ceilings usually have catwalks, to enable lighting technicians and effects crew to place lights, extractor vents, and so on above the sets.

Tracking vehicle (also known as a *camera car*)

An open-back truck, rigged to carry camera equipment and crew and used to film moving-vehicle shots. Can also be fitted with a rig to carry cars, carriages, motor bikes etc.

Wet-downs

The wetting of pavement (sidewalks and streets) for filming. It is usually done at night, using hoses or mobile water 'bowsers' (tankers) fitted with sprinklers. The wet streets reflect streetlights, neon signs, shadows and so on.

Wrap

'A wrap!' means that the shooting day is over. Also refers to removing all of the set dressing, props and equipment from a set or location, when shooting of the film has ended (final wrap).

FILMOGRAPHY OF GERRY JOHNSTON

PYROTECHNICS & PHYSICAL EFFECTS DIRECTOR

FILM	DIRECTOR	RELEASE DATE
The Blue Max	John Guillerman	1966
Darling Lili	Blake Edwards	1970
Von Richtofen and Brown (The Red Baron)	Roger Corman	1970
Ryan's Daughter	David Lean	1970
Underground	Arthur H. Nadel	1970
The MacKenzie Break	Lamont Johnson	1970
Quackser Fortune Has a Cousin in the Bronx	Waris Hussein	1970
Zeppelin	Etienne Périer	1971
A Fistful of Dynamite	Sergio Leone	1971
Images	Robert Altman	1972
The MacKintosh Man	John Huston	1973
Zardoz	John Boorman	1974
Black Beauty (TV)	John Reardon Charles Crichton Alan Gibson	1974
A Quiet Day in Belfast	Milad Bessada	1974
Barry Lyndon	Stanley Kubrick	1975
Mother Mafia's Living Field	Unknown	Unknown
War of Children	Unknown	Unknown
Un Taxi Mauve (The Purple Taxi)	Yves Boisset	1977
The Last Remake of Beau Geste	Marty Feldman	1977

Exorcist II: The Heretic	John Boorman	1977
The Greek Tycoon	J. Lee Thompson	1978
The Flame Is Love (TV)	Michael O'Herlihy	1979
The First Great Train Robbery	Michael Crichton	1979
North Sea Hijack	Andrew V. McLaglen	1979
Strumpet City (TV)	Tony Barry	1980
Cry of the Innocent (TV)	Michael O'Herlihy	1980
The Outsider	Tony Luracshi	1980
The Big Red One	Samuel Fuller	1980
Sea Wolves (The Last Charge of the Calcutta Lighthorse)	Andrew V. McLaglen	1980
The Manions of America (TV)	Charles S. Dubin	
	Joseph Sargent	1981
Excalibur	John Boorman	1981
Roses from Dublin	Lazare Iglesis	1981
The Year of the French (TV)	Michael Garvey	1982
Ballroom of Romance	Pat O'Connor	1982
Angel (Danny Boy)	Neil Jordan	1982
Remington Steele (TV)	Don Weiss	1983
The Irish RM (TV)	Roy Ward Baker	
	Robert Chetwyn	
	Pater Sykes	1983
Educating Rita	Lewis Gilbert	1983
The Country Girls (TV)	Desmond Davis	1984
Children in Crossfire (TV)	George Shaefer	1984
The Last Days of Pompeii (TV)	Peter R. Hunt	1984
James Joyce's Women	Michael Pearce	1985
Allan Quartermain and the Lost City of Gold	Gary Nelson	1986
Flaming Borders	Sahib Haddad	1986
The Fantasist	Robin Hardy	1986
Rawhead Rex	George Pavlou	1986
Soweto (Cry Freedom) (TV)	Richard Attenborough	1987
The Dawning	Robert Knights	1988
The Courier	Joe Lee	1988
A Man Called Sarge	Stuart Gillard	1990
My Left Foot	Jim Sheridan	1989
The Field	Jim Sheridan	1990

Living Doll	Peter Litten	
	George Dugdale	
	Peter MacKenzie-Litten	1990
Troubles	Unknown	Unknown
The Playboys	Gillies McKinnon	1992
The Railway Station Man	Michael Whyte	1992
The Snapper	Stephen Frears	1993
Into the West	Mike Newell	1992
Fatal Inheritance	Gabrielle Beaumont	1993
In the Name of the Father	Jim Sheridan	1993
Widows Peak	John Irvin	1994
The Family (TV)	Michael Winterbottom	1994
A Man of No Importance	Suri Krishnamma	1994
Words Upon the Window Pane	Mary McGuckian	1994
Frankie Starlight	Michael Lindsay-Hogg	1995
An Awfully Big Adventure	Mike Newell	1995
Moondance	Dagmar Hirtz	1995
Braveheart	Mel Gibson	1995
Michael Collins	Neil Jordan	1996
Trojan Eddie	Gillies McKinnon	1996
Spacetruckers	Stuart Gordon	1997
The Butcher Boy	Neil Jordan	1997
This Is the Sea	Mary McGuckian	1997
Drinking Crude	Owen McPolin	1997
Dancing at Lughnasa	Pat O'Connor	1998
The Tale of Sweeney Todd (TV)	John Schlesinger	1998
Saving Private Ryan	Steven Spielberg	1998
The Most Fertile Man in Ireland	Dudi Appleton	1999
Rebel Heart (TV)	John Strickland	2001
My Green Freedom	Unknown	Unknown
Reign of Fire	Rob Bowman	2002
The Abduction Club	Stefan Schwartz	2002
Laws of Attraction	Peter Howitt	2004
The Blackwater Lightship (TV)	John Erman	2004
Man About Dog	Paddy Breathnach	2004
Johnny Was	Mark Hammond	2006
Strength and Honour	Mark Mahon	2007

Also provided effects services to numerous TV commercials, theatre presentations, promos and events.

PRODUCER CREDITS
Drinking Crude (1997)
Keystone Killers (short, 2008)

ACKNOWLEDGEMENTS

When I began writing about my adventures in the world of movie-making, I did not expect that another 'adventure' awaited, in real life – a quadruple heart bypass, in May 2007!

Probably the most traumatic event in my life, it has instigated a number of lifestyle changes, chiefly a renewed awareness that life is precious and that every moment is a gift. I almost didn't make it through post-surgery, and I am thankful, therefore, to God for another chance – and to be here to complete my story and to be back at work!

I am eternally grateful to my son, Derek, who kept vigil by my hospital bed, keeping family and friends informed, until I was out of danger, and for his presence and words of encouragement to me during that time.

I am thankful to my medical team and to my family and friends, for their gifts, prayers, phone calls and visits – all vital contributions to my recovery.

Thanks also to my family for their encouragement with this project: Derek, for his critique and for his help and enthusiasm in the early days of my career, to Audrey, for her love and understanding, and to Chloe, Ciarán, Tara, Saoirse and Carraig , and my extended family, Nicola and Pierre, for being in my life.

To my life and business partner, my late wife, Georgina, for her love, her help and fond memories. To all the relatives, friends and neighbours for their support during the difficult years of Georgina's illness. To the staff of RehabCare, at Park House, the district nurses, and the staff at Our Lady's Hospice, for their care of Georgina.

To my brother Cormac and sister Barbara, and my brother Terry, who has kept me 'on track' throughout my career. To my parents, the late Eddie and Lillie Johnston, and my late uncle Frank, his wife Etta and all the girls, for a home-away-from-home when I was setting out in the world at seventeen.

To all my colleagues and associates in the film industry, especially my dear friends Sean Corcoran, Peter Dawson, Michael McNieve and John Higgins, as well as the many producers, directors, art directors and production managers who gave me the opportunity to do what I love, and, of course, my fellow special-effects wizards, with whom I have had the pleasure of working, both in Ireland and around the world.

Special thanks to Esme, for helping me with this book, and for her hard work, dedication, infinite patience and talent; to Derek Nolan and Yvonne for their technical expertise, hospitality and valued friendship; and to Eileen Bennett, for the initial editing and 'vote of confidence' in this project. Finally, to Seán, Peter, Orlaith and Sinéad at Liberties Press; working with them has been a new and pleasurable experience.

Gerry Johnston
April 2008